# AKERS'
# Simple Library Cataloging

## 6th edition

*Completely revised and rewritten*

*by*

## ARTHUR CURLEY

*and*

## JANA VARLEJS

The Scarecrow Press, Inc.
Metuchen, N.J.      1977

All catalog cards in this volume, whether printed or typed, are reproduced at 75 per cent of actual size.

Library of Congress Cataloging in Publication Data

Akers, Susan Grey, 1889-
    Akers' simple library cataloging.

        Bibliography: p.
        Includes index.
        1.  Cataloging.  I.  Curley, Arthur.  II.  Varlejs,
Jana.  III.  Title.  IV.  Title: Simple library cataloging.
Z693.A52  1976                025.3                76-26897
ISBN 0-8108-0978-8

# CONTENTS

iii

# INTRODUCTION

What is simple library cataloging? Is it watered
down, compromisingly abridged, haphazard? Not at all.
Just as a "simple" explanation--simple in the sense that it
is clear, precise, and in terms understood by an intended
audience--can render a complex matter comprehensible, so
simple library cataloging can be a system of organization
that is clear, precise, and suited to the needs of a specific
institution and its users.

Obviously, a small library with only three, four, or
even a dozen staff members would not wish to adopt the staff
organization chart of a very large institution with numerous
department heads, division coordinators, and deputy assistant
directors. Not only is such an organization pattern unnecessary in a small institution; its imposition would create chaos.
Similarly, most systems of cataloging and classification were
designed with the needs of large libraries in mind. Like the
organization chart, they need to be adapted and simplified to
be of maximum value to the smaller library. The objective
of simplification is certainly not compromise with the quality
of cataloging; rather, it is the improvement of library service through more efficient cataloging and processing procedures.

The small library may serve fewer users than its
larger counterparts, but the informational needs of any of its
patrons, taken individually, may be just as considerable as
the needs of those who belong to a larger community or institution. Precisely because its resources are limited, the
small library must strive for excellence in providing access
to the materials it does possess. In fact, its very smallness
may permit some forms of excellence which would be unat-
tainable in most larger institutions. Just as the small library can give greater personal attention to its clientele, so
it can give greater attention to the precision and accuracy
with which its materials collections are organized. The man-
ageable number of collections (of plays and short stories, for

1

example) and of multi-volume sets in such institutions often makes possible close analysis of contents and other special reader services; even more so, since the small library can usually forego the extensive bibliographic description required by complex cataloging codes to identify uniqueness of edition. And, of course, the small specialized library may be as strong as many a large library in its own areas of concentration and contain materials in a greater variety of formats, yet need the advantages of simplified cataloging procedures since its staff is too small to include an extensive technical services section.

Consistency in cataloging practice, involving adaptation to changes in classification and subject-heading authority files, is often much more feasible in the small library than in the large, where even minor changes in a new edition of the Dewey Decimal Classification, for example, can affect so many thousands of volumes cataloged by the rules of earlier editions as to render retrospective adjustment virtually impossible. Moreover, since "simple" library cataloging reduces the degree of subdivision both in classification numbers and in subject headings, it reduces even further the extent to which changes in national cataloging practices threaten consistency in the collections and card catalogs of small libraries which do so simplify. When simplification is judiciously applied, then frequently--in the words of Mies van der Rohe--"less is more."

In developing a catalog for a particular library one needs to consider the community or institution which is to be served. Is it growing or shrinking? What is the present size of the library? Its probable future size? Is it likely to become part of a larger cooperative system in the near future? In deciding upon what materials to acquire, what records to keep, what methods to use, are there any special requirements that might affect them? For instance, in a school or college library, what courses are offered? Does a library have to submit reports to a central agency, such as a state library, the city or county superintendent of schools? Does a library receiving funds from a special source have to keep an inventory of the disbursement of those funds in a prescribed way? What information is required for reports to these external agencies?

The use to be made of the materials and the best ways of serving the library's clientele are the first considerations in deciding upon the type of cataloging. Costs and time,

however, must also be considered. It is not worthwhile to
develop a plan which will require a larger staff and involve
higher costs than are available or likely to become so, or
which will absorb so much of the present staff's time that
other library services are neglected. Adopt the simplest
plan for control of material which will meet the needs of the
library's clientele now and in the foreseeable future. Materials should be prepared and put out for use as soon as possible
after they are received. For example, a book, pamphlet, or
map which would be of significant use in a course if it is
made available this week may be of little or no value if it
becomes available only after a delay of weeks or months.
Simplification or streamlining of cataloging procedures is essential in small or understaffed libraries. On the other hand,
a system which simplifies to the extent that it does not distinguish clearly between materials, or one that creates work
which will have to be done over as the library grows, is not
a good system. Time and money saved in organizing materials in such a way that reference work is obstructed and
users frustrated are not really an economy. A good system
for one library may not be a good system for another library,
because of different conditions. But the importance of cooperation among libraries and the value of many centralized services are strong arguments for reasonable consistency in cataloging and classification practices. Also, our patrons must
sometimes use other libraries--particularly young patrons as
they advance through school--and their ability to do so ef-
fectively is enhanced if the libraries are organized according
to common rational patterns.

A catalog is a concise index to the varied materials
in a library. It answers such questions as: What books
have you by John Updike? Do you have a recording of Beethoven's ninth symphony? Have you material on the Navajo
Indians? The catalog can also answer questions about the
individual author or book; for instance: What is the most
recent book in the library by Kurt Vonnegut? Does Alistair
Cooke's America include illustrations? Who published The
Last Whole Earth Catalog? Besides showing what authors'
works are represented in the library, whether or not the library has material on a given subject or contains a particular book, whether or not a certain book has illustrations,
and so forth, the catalog may bring out portions of books;
for example, it may tell the patron that High Tor is to be
found in Barrett H. Clark's Nine Modern American Plays,
and that material on Halloween is included in J. Walker Mc-
Spadden's The Book of Holidays. The catalog also tells where
in the library a book is located.

The catalog in most libraries consists of cards containing the information required to answer questions such as the ones in the examples above. (Book catalogs are another way of presenting the same information in a different format, but the cataloging principles are the same and the procedures followed, at least in the initial stages of preparing the catalog, are the same.) Each book owned by the library is represented in the catalog by several cards, so that whether a patron looks under Galbraith, under <u>Money</u>, or under economics, he will find a card for Galbraith's book, <u>Money</u>. In other words, the book has been "entered" under three "headings": author, title, and subject:

```
Galbraith, John Kenneth
   Money:  whence it came, where it
went.  Houghton, 1975.
   324 p.
```

```
Money
Galbraith, John Kenneth
   Money:  whence it came, where it
went.  Houghton, 1975.
   324 p.
```

```
ECONOMICS
Galbraith, John Kenneth
   Money:  whence it came, where it
went.  Houghton, 1975
```

A book may also be sought under the name of a series of which it is a part, under a joint author, under an illustrator, etc., and cards (added entries) for these or other headings under which a patron might look should be included in the catalog. In addition to the cards for specific books there are reference cards referring the reader from a form of the author's name under which he may look to the form used in the catalog:

Mertz, Barbara

see

Michaels, Barbara, pseud.
Peters, Elizabeth, pseud.

There are also cards referring the reader from the term or terms under which he may search for material on a subject to the term or terms used in the catalog for that subject:

GUIDANCE

see

COUNSELING

All of these cards--author, title, subject, added entry, analytical, and reference--when interfiled in alphabetical order constitute a dictionary catalog.

In keeping with the spirit in which Susan Grey Akers first published this manual in 1927, its primary purpose continues to be: providing for the librarian of the small public, school, college, or special library the necessary directions for classifying and cataloging a collection of printed and audiovisual materials so that they may be made readily and economically accessible; serving as a beginning text for practical study of cataloging, as collateral reading in basic cataloging courses; and as a possible source for the practicing librarian who seeks a broader understanding of the principles which underlie standard classification and cataloging policies.

Occasionally, more detail is given in this book than may be needed by most small libraries, but a good librarian will want a thorough understanding of the rules so as to be able to interpret printed cards and to have a firm basis for decisions about choosing outside cataloging services or simplifying in-house cataloging. Also, the librarian who understands the basic principles of how material is entered in a catalog will be better able to help patrons use the library's catalog. Even decisions about the style of the catalog cards are of some importance. While the primary concern must be to produce a record of the library's collection that is as accurate and as intelligible to the library user as possible, it is also worth considering how much is gained by the staff when the rules for preparing the cards are well thought out, clear and comprehensive enough to preclude any waste of time on the part of librarian or typist.

In attempting to adapt the complex body of established cataloging rules for effective use by small libraries, simplification has of course been a goal, but enabling the small library to achieve excellence in providing access to its resources has been the overriding objective of this manual.

CHAPTER 1

## CLASSIFICATION

In the words of John Cotton Dana, "to classify books is to place them in groups, each group including, as nearly as may be, all the books treating a given subject, for instance, geology; or all the books, on whatever subject, cast in a particular form, for instance poetry; or all the books having to do with a particular period in time, for instance, the Middle Ages.... Its purpose is ... to make ... books more available."[1]

If a miscellaneous collection of books is to be used with ease, it must be arranged in some way. Medieval libraries sometimes arranged books according to size, a not unreasonable practice given the extreme variations in dimensions of handwritten books and manuscripts. But while this may have been physically practical for shelving arrangements, it must have been exhausting for the scholar who needed to consult numerous volumes on the same topic but of varying sizes. Books could be sorted and put on the shelves in alphabetical order according to their authors. Of course, this would be fine for the reader who wished to see all the novels by Thomas Hardy, but pity the plight of the student of English history, whose materials would be scattered to the far corners of the alphabet. Although a collection arranged alphabetically would be many times more useful than one without any arrangement, the collection arrangement which is the most desirable is a classified one. Libraries are consulted more for material on a given subject than for any other purpose. Readers like to have the books on the same subject together, as they much prefer examining the books to searching a list or a catalog.

As well as bringing together different materials on the same subject, classification can also serve to show relationships between subjects. Geometry, algebra, and calculus are all related as members of the mathematics family, which in turn is related to astronomy, physics, geology, and the other

7

sciences. The obsession of early philosophers with trees of knowledge and other such constructs suggests the extent to which classification of knowledge is a prerequisite for broader understanding. The establishment of interdisciplinary studies programs at colleges and even some elementary schools in recent years signifies continued and increased recognition of the interrelatedness of branches of learning. Classification helps the library borrower to locate a book more readily, but it also helps the library present the written record of human endeavor in a logical interrelated pattern that has itself evolved with the growth of human knowledge.

Book classification systems invariably employ a number or other symbol to represent each subject. This has the advantage of permitting a considerable amount of information to be represented in a tiny space on a catalog card and on the spine of the book, providing a quick means of identifying that a particular book corresponds to a particular catalog entry, and presenting a sequential arrangement (numerical or alphabetical) which is universally understood.

DEWEY DECIMAL CLASSIFICATION

In order to classify books by subject, some scheme or system of classification must be adopted. The system most widely used in the United States, especially in public and school libraries, is Melvil Dewey's Decimal Classification (DDC). It has also been adopted by many libraries in other countries. The American Library Association's The Booklist, Bowker's American Book Publishing Record (BPR), The H. W. Wilson Company's Standard Catalog series, and many other library publications which provide cataloging information use this classification system. Even though the Library of Congress (LC) uses its own classification scheme, the appropriate Dewey Decimal number is included on most LC printed catalog cards. The DDC is published in two forms, the unabridged[2] and the abridged;[3] both versions are revised and issued in new editions periodically. The abridged edition is intended for the use of small general libraries of all kinds, but particularly for public and school libraries. In this manual, the discussion of the DDC and the examples, unless so noted, refer to the tenth abridged edition.

The system is called a decimal system because it divides all human knowledge into ten classes, with each class subdivided into ten divisions, each subdivision into ten further ones, and so on beyond the decimal point, the numbers being considered as decimals, not consecutive numbers. One of the great advantages of this system is that it permits infinite expansion after the decimal point whenever a subject gains such complexity as to require further subdivision. Moreover, while any classification system would enable books on the same subject to be kept together, the sequential harmony of decimal numerals also permits relative proximity of books on related topics.

The ten main classes of the system are:

| | | | |
|---|---|---|---|
| 000 | Generalities | 500 | Sciences |
| 100 | Philosophy | 600 | Technology |
| 200 | Religion | 700 | The arts |
| 300 | Social sciences | 800 | Literature |
| 400 | Language | 900 | History, geography |

One hundred three-digit numbers are the notation used to designate each class, e.g., 500-599 for the sciences. The first division of each class is used for general works on that class, e.g., 500-509 for general works on the sciences; the subsequent divisions for the main divisions of the subject, e.g., 510-519 for mathematics, 520-529 for astronomy and allied sciences, 530-539 for physics, etc. In turn, each subdivision is divided into ten sections, e.g., 511 for works on mathematical generalities, 512 for works on algebra, 513 for works on arithmetic, 514 for works on topology, and so on. The system can be further subdivided by adding a decimal point after any set of three digits from 000 to 999. Adding as many digits as are required, e.g., 513.26 (in the unabridged edition) for works on fractions; 523, descriptive astronomy; 523.7, the sun; 523.78 (in the unabridged edition), eclipses. The abridged edition of the Dewey Decimal Classification shortens or reduces the numbers (and occasionally changes them), hence neither 513.26 nor 523.78 are in the 10th abridged edition. Similar omissions will be found throughout the abridged edition.

A general library of 10,000 or 15,000 volumes would probably find the degree of subdivision provided by the abridged version adequate. In a typical library of such size, a book on eclipses could readily be found in a quick search through its collection of astronomy books. But a larger library with dozens of books on astronomy would find the search for titles on eclipses a somewhat time-consuming and frustrating exercise. In general, a public or school library of 20,000 volumes or more--or one which expects to grow to that extent--will need the degree of categorical subdivision provided by the unabridged version of the DDC. The following example shows how much more detailed the unabridged edition can be:

Abridged DDC:

| | |
|---|---|
| .7 | Sun |
| | Including charts, photographs |
| | Class heliographs, coronagraphs, heliostats in 522; sun tables in 525 |
| .702 2 | Illustrations and models |
| | Class charts and photographs in 523.7 |
| [.79] | Charts and photographs |
| | Number discontinued; class in 523.7 |

Unabridged DDC:

| | |
|---|---|
| .7 | Sun |
| .702 | Miscellany |
| .702 1 | Tabulated and related materials |
| .702 12 | Formulas, specifications, statistics |
| | Class tables in 525.38 |
| .702 2 | Illustrations and models |
| | Class charts and photographs in 523.79 |
| .702 8 | Techniques, apparatus, equipment, materials |
| | Class heliographs, coronagraphs, heliostats in 522.5, spectroscopy in 523.77 |
| .71 | Constants and dimensions |
| | Size, mass, gravitation, location, parallax |
| .72 | Optical, thermal, electromagnetic, radioactive phenomena |
| .73 | Apparent motion and rotation |
| .74 | Photosphere, sunspots, faculae |
| .75 | Prominences, chromosphere, flares, corona |
| .76 | Internal constitution |
| .77 | Spectroscopy |
| .78 | Eclipses |
| .79 | Charts and photographs |

If a miscellaneous collection of books is to be classified according to the decimal system, the books will be grouped by their subject matter, with general books on all or many subjects (e. g. , encyclopedias) in one group, books about philosophy in a second, books about religion in a third, and so on.  Books in each general subject group will be subdivided into groups representing more specific aspects of that subject.  The divisions of the social sciences (300-399) illustrate the principle of subdivision by more specific subject:

| | | | |
|---|---|---|---|
| 300 | The social sciences | 350 | Public administration |
| 310 | Statistics | 360 | Social pathology & services |
| 320 | Political Science | | |
| 330 | Economics | 370 | Education |
| 340 | Law | 380 | Commerce |
| | | 390 | Customs & folklore |

Additional subdivisions continue the progression from the general to the specific.  Economics, for example, is further divided as follows:

| | | | |
|---|---|---|---|
| 330 | Economics | 335 | Socialism & related systems |
| 331 | Labor economics | | |
| 332 | Financial economics | 336 | Public finance |
| 333 | Land economics | 337 | [open] |
| 334 | Cooperatives | 338 | Production |
| | | 339 | Macroeconomics |

An illustration of one more level of breakdown is given for Labor economics (331):

331. 1  Labor force and market
331. 2  Conditions of employment
331. 3  Workers of specific age groups
331. 4  Women workers
331. 5  Special categories of workers
331. 6  Categories of workers by racial, ethnic, national origin
331. 7  Labor by industry and occupation
331. 8  Labor unions (Trade unions) and labor-management bargaining
331. 9  [open]

Of course, no classification scheme is perfect.  The range of human knowledge and speculation cannot be reduced to neat pigeon-holes without conflict or overlap.  Most major

divisions of the 300's are recognizable as branches of the
social sciences, but they are hardly equal branches. One
could argue that Commerce (380) should really be a subdivision of Economics (330), or that Folklore (390) does not
really belong in the 300's at all. History is generally considered to be one of the social sciences, but in the DDC it
is a separate class (900-999), far removed from its sister
disciplines. The separate status of history is more than
justified, of course, by the volume of published material.
So, while logical foundations are important to the scholarly
integrity of a classification scheme, its practicality as a tool
of organization is not undermined by occasional lapses from
structural perfection. In fact, even if there could be devised
a system devoid of logical inconsistencies, books themselves
would continue to cut across subject lines in defiance of the
cataloger's wishful demands that they fall neatly into convenient categories.

From class to class in the DDC there are variations
in the pattern of subdivision. In literature (800-899) one
might logically expect to find division by poetry, prose,
drama and other major branches. Instead, recognizing that
library users will more often seek English poetry rather than
all poetry, or French literature rather than one literary
form in all national literatures, the DDC divides literature
first by language and nationality:

| | | | |
|---|---|---|---|
| 800 | Literature | 850 | Italian, Romanian, Rhaeto-Romanic |
| 810 | American (in English) | | |
| 820 | English & Anglo-Saxon | 860 | Spanish & Portuguese |
| 830 | Germanic languages | 870 | Italic languages, Latin |
| 840 | French, Provençal, Catalan | 880 | Hellenic languages |
| | | 890 | Literatures of other languages |

On the other hand, in the 700's (the arts), nationality is ignored and the subdivision is basically by form:

710 Civil & landscape art
720 Architecture
730 Plastic arts /Sculpture
740 Drawing, decorative & minor arts
750 Painting and paintings
... etc.

It is at the next level of subdivision that books in the
800's are grouped by literary form:

| | | | |
|---|---|---|---|
| 820 | English & Anglo-Saxon literature | 825 | English speeches |
| | | 826 | English letters |
| 821 | English poetry | 827 | English satire & humor |
| 822 | English drama | 828 | English miscellaneous writings |
| 823 | English fiction | | |
| 824 | English essays | 829 | Anglo-Saxon (Old English) |

It would be surprising, indeed, if a group so individual-istic as creative writers did not provide an occasional challenge to the neatness of the classification scheme designed by librarians to keep literary practitioners in their places. Take the Nobel Prize winner, Samuel Beckett. Although a native of Ireland and a disciple of James Joyce, he lives in Paris and writes in French. To complicate matters further, he translates his own French plays and novels into English. Clearly, this great international writer is the nemesis of perfectionist catalogers, but most libraries choose to honor the language of composition and place the works of Samuel Beckett in the literature of his choice, the 840's. T. S. Eliot, the American-born poet, never changed his language of composition, but he did choose citizenship as well as residence in England. While many American writers live abroad--in fact, the great American literary movement of the twenties was largely centered in France--and while many scholars insist that no governmental document can instantly transport a writer from one national literature to another, catalogers can be as human as writers, and Mr. Eliot is generally accorded his own national preference, the 820's.

It was certainly shortsighted on Mr. Dewey's part to have reserved so much of the 800's for the literature of Western Europe, leaving the literatures of East Indo-European and Celtic; Afro-Asiatic (Hamito-Semitic); Hamitic and Chad; Ural-Altaic, Paleo-Siberian, Dravidian; East and Southeast Asian; African; North and South American aboriginal, and all other languages to be squeezed into the 890's. The Decimal Classification Committee may someday perform major surgery on the 800's, but the enormous cost to libraries that such a major re-classification would represent is a powerful deterrent. All libraries except those specializing in Oriental or other non-Western literatures are well advised to make do with the present imperfect scheme, rather than risk the considerable expense and confusion which are likely to result from haphazard tampering with the DDC.

In classifying works of literature, as we have seen, one must first determine the nationality of the author and then the

branch of literature (poetry, for example) which the book at hand represents. However, there is one major exception to this policy which is made by nearly all public and school libraries, and that is in the case of fiction. Theoretically, American fiction is 813, English fiction is 823, German fiction is 833, and so on. But, putting practicality above theory--which is what the service-oriented cataloger should do--it is clear that most library patrons are interested in the form (fiction) first, rather than nationality. To make the reader of novels go to one national literature for Hemingway, another for Graham Greene, and still another for Franz Kafka would not be good public service. So, most libraries file all fiction together in one section, arranging the books alphabetically by author without assigning a classification number.

## STANDARD SUBDIVISIONS

Although classification is generally by subject, sub-arrangement is often desirable by the form or presentation of a subject, e. g. , a dictionary of medicine, a periodical of history, a work on how to teach mathematics. These various forms or methods of treatment of a subject are shown in "Table 1. Standard Subdivisions." Earlier editions of the DDC called them "form divisions." These major subdivisions are:

| | | | |
|---|---|---|---|
| -01 | Philosophy and theory | -06 | Organizations |
| -02 | Miscellany | -07 | Study and teaching |
| -03 | Dictionaries, encyclopedias, concordances | -08 | Collections and anthologies |
| -05 | Serial publications | -09 | Historical and geographical treatment |

The dash (-) preceding each number in this table emphasizes the fact that these standard subdivisions are never used alone but may be used with almost any number from the classification schedules, e. g. , 513, arithmetic; 513. 07, study and teaching of arithmetic. Analyzing the number for mathematics 510: $\underline{5}$ indicates that it is in the general class of the pure sciences, $\underline{1}$ that it is in the division for mathematics, $\underline{0}$ that it is general mathematics not limited to arithmetic, algebra or any one of the other sections. In "synthesizing the notation," or "building the number," duplicate zeros are cancelled; thus 510 (mathematics) and -07 (study and teaching) become 510. 7, not 510. 07. Although standard subdivisions are always preceded by a zero, if a zero is already there to

round out the number to three digits, it is unnecessary to add another zero, and thus 07 or 0.7 may mean study and teaching when added to the number for a subject.

Note that standard subdivision -07 is for books on how to study or how to teach, not for textbooks on the subject; e.g., 507 would be for a work on how to teach science, not for a textbook on science, which would go in 500. In the first instance, the content of the book is methods of teaching; in the second the content is science.

The following is an example of how the standard subdivisions are applied in the 900's:

900 General geography and history and their auxiliaries
901 Philosophy and theory of general history
902 Miscellany of general history (including chronologies)
903 Dictionaries, encyclopedias, concordances of general history
904 Collected accounts of specific events (e.g., earthquakes, volcanic eruptions, tidal waves, floods, storms, wars and battles, explosions, fires; mine, transportation, nuclear accidents; adventures)
    Note: -04 is to be used only when specifically included in the schedules.
905 Serial publications on general history
906 Organizations of general history
907 Study and teaching of general history
908 Collections of general history
909 General world history

Standard subdivisions are always preceded by a zero, but zero and a figure do not always mean a standard subdivision; e.g., under 759, .01-.06 signify periods of development, not limited geographically--e.g., 759.05 is used for painting and paintings of the period, 1800-1900. Standard subdivisions under the numbers for European history have two zeros; e.g., 941.003 would be the number for an encyclopedia of the history of Scotland; 944.005, for a serial publication on French history. This is necessary since .01-.08 are used for period divisions of history; e.g., 941.03 is the number for the Early period of independence, 1314-1424, of the history of Scotland; 944.05 for the First Empire, 1804-1815, in the history of France. Standard subdivisions should be used with great care, first making sure that the numbers have not been used for some other purpose.

Another method of differentiating between books on the same subject is possible when a book's treatment of a topic is confined to a particular geographical location. The notations to be used are given in "Table 2. Areas," and, as in the case of the standard subdivisions, are never to be used alone, and are therefore preceded by a dash, e.g., -7, North America. However, unless the schedule specifically allows these notations to be added directly, the standard subdivision -09 must be interposed between the number in the schedule and the area notation. A library having many books on a subject, several of which are on a given continent, country, or locality may expand the number for that subject by using the area notation. For instance: the number for mammals is 599, with no instruction to add area notations directly. Thus one begins by adding -09. Then, turning to the Area Table, one finds -6 Africa, and adding these one has 599.096 for mammals of Africa; or for Tanzania, 599.09678. The latter number is rather long for a small library and would only be used if the library had quite a large collection of books on mammals, many of which were on African mammals in specific locales, and it was desirable to bring them together.

In addition to the standard subdivision and area tables, the 10th abridged edition includes two new auxiliary tables: "Table 3. Subdivisions of Individual Literatures" and "Table 4. Subdivisions of Individual Languages." As in the first two tables, the notations are preceded by dashes and are not intended to be used alone. A major difference is that the notations of Tables 3 and 4 are to be used only when permission to do so is specifically given in the 800 and 400 schedules.

Sometimes it is desirable to combine notations from two tables. In the literature table, provision for using standard subdivisions is incorporated within the table. For example, an encyclopedia of French drama would be classed in 842 (French drama). To derive a more specific number, we are instructed to add to base number 84 the appropriate notation from Table 3. Under -2 for Drama in Table 3, we find that -201 to -207 may be used for standard subdivisions from Table 1. Since the standard subdivision for encyclopedias is -03, the resulting number is 842.03. In Table 4, however, we are instructed to add standard subdivisions from Table 1 to -1 to -8. Thus a book on how to teach French to Americans would be classed in 448.07 (44 is the base number, -8 is the language for foreigners, -07 is the standard subdivision for teaching).

In addition to the four tables, the DDC provides another way to expand some numbers via the direction "add to." For example, under 560.9, Historical and geographical treatment of Paleontology, we find: "Add to 560.9 the numbers following 547.9 in 574.909-574.99, e.g., marine paleontology 560.92." In earlier editions of the DDC, the corresponding instruction was "divide like" (a specific span of numbers). The principle involved has not changed, but the new and more detailed instructions are less confusing and easier to use.

Just to suggest the lengths to which the DDC system can be carried for the purpose of specifying the exact subject of a book, consider the following highly unabridged example:

> A staff member of the Northwestern University Library Cataloging Department has identified what is believed to be the longest Dewey number ever under serious consideration for assignment: a 23-digit monster for <u>Arab Attitudes Toward Israel</u> by Yehosafat Harkabi, 301.-15433012917492705694. The meaning of the number can be broken down as follows: 301--Sociology; 1543--Opinions, attitudes, beliefs on specific topics (Add 001-999); 301--Sociology; 29--Historical and geographical treatment (Add "areas"); 174--Regions where specific racial, ethnic, national groups predominate (Add from Table 5); 927--Arabs and Maltese; 0--General relations between two countries (Add "areas"); 5694--Palestine, Israel. In other words: Historical and geographical treatment of opinions on countries where Arabs predominate, and their relations with Israel. 4

## REDUCTION OF NUMBERS

In a classification system using Arabic numerals for the symbols of the classes and the decimal principle for subdivision of those classes, numbers grow in length as the classification is expanded to make a place for divisions of a subject. The library which does not need these subdivisions simply uses the broad number, omitting any figures at the end which it does not need. For example, the number for the period of United States history when Franklin Delano Roosevelt was president is 973.917, but the small library with a limited number of books on U.S. history may use only

973. 9, Twentieth century, 1901- , or 973. 91, Early twentieth century, 1901-1953.

Whenever a cataloger considers shortening a classification number, two important factors must be kept in mind. The first question is how many titles on the subject the library is likely to own within some reasonably projected time span. Currently the library may have only three books about American history during FDR's administration, but a few years from now it might have ten different titles and would find it a nuisance to have those ten scattered throughout several shelves of books dealing with half a century's worth of American history. The second question has to do with the cataloger's ability to shorten a number in a manner consistent with the internal logic of the classification scheme adopted by the library and compatible with general policy decisions governing the degree of breakdown needed in the various classes. For example, the cataloger may have a book for which LC suggests the number 327'. 12'0951, with the apostrophes indicating logical points at which the number may be cut (see card 1). If the library is a small one and uses the 10th

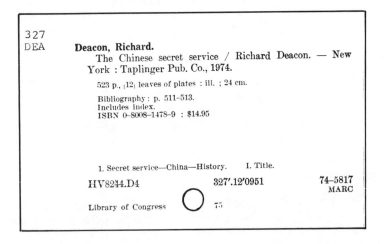

| 327 | |
|---|---|
| DEA | **Deacon, Richard.**<br>    The Chinese secret service / Richard Deacon. — New<br>York : Taplinger Pub. Co., 1974.<br><br>    523 p., ₁12₁ leaves of plates : ill. ; 24 cm.<br><br>    Bibliography : p. 511–513.<br>    Includes index.<br>    ISBN 0–8008–1478–9 : $14.95 |

1. Secret service—China—History.    I. Title.

HV8244.D4                                327'.12'0951                                74–5817
                                                                                           MARC

Library of Congress                          75

Card 1.    Printed LC card with suggested DDC number shortened by cataloger

abridged DDC, the cataloger will find that the schedule does not include 327. 12, the number for espionage and subversion in the unabridged DDC, and therefore would be correct in using 327, which stands for international relations, including espionage, in the abridged DDC.

Another example: the full number for a book on social conditions in New York City suggested by LC is 309. 1'747'104 (see card 2). Since the abridged DDC allows for additions of area notations to 309. 1 up to the state level but not to the city level, the library could use 309. 1 (no area notation), 309. 17 (North America), 309. 173 (U. S. ), 309. 174 (Northeast U. S. ), or 309. 1747 (New York State), depending on what decision it had made on the degree of breakdown needed within 309. 1. Ordinarily, the breaks shown by the apostrophes should be preferred. Always, care should be taken that the reduced number is logical as well as consistent with the library's policy. The decision should be recorded in the cataloger's copy of the DDC. For example, if the annotated DDC indicates the following:

309        Social situation and conditions

         Class social pathology and its alleviation in 362

.1        Historical and geographical treatment

         Add "Areas" notation 1–9 from Table 2 to base number 309.1
         Use to show country; state if in U.S.

the cataloger would class the book in 309. 1747 to specify that the book is about New York State (see card 2 on page 20).

When reducing a number provided by a cataloging aid or a centralized service, it is extremely important that the cataloger always check the shortened number with the annotated schedule in order to maintain consistency in the library's practice and to ascertain the suitability of the derived number. This is especially important for users of the 10th abridged edition, because numbers derived from the 18th unabridged DDC do not in all cases correspond with those given in the abridged edition (further discussion of this problem follows on page 29).

In addition to the above precautions, keep in mind that a number should never be shorter than three digits and should not end in a zero beyond the decimal point. Make the number as specific as possible, i. e. , use 510, 520, 511, etc. , rather

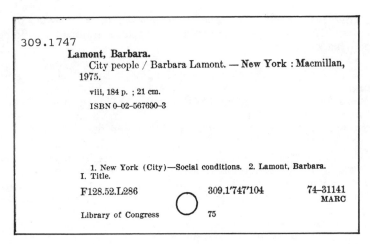

309.1747
    **Lamont, Barbara.**
       City people / Barbara Lamont. — New York : Macmillan,
1975.

       viii, 184 p. ; 21 cm.

       ISBN 0-02-567690-3

       1. New York (City)—Social conditions.  2. Lamont, Barbara.
     I. Title.

       F128.52.L286               309.1'747'104        74–31141
                                                   MARC

       Library of Congress         75

Card 2.   Printed LC card with suggested DDC number shortened by cataloger

than putting everything in 500, and make sure that the shortened number makes sense. Record all decisions for reduc-
tion in the schedules.

## THE RELATIVE INDEX

     One of the important features of the Dewey Decimal
classification system is its relative index. D. J. Haykin[5] defined a relative index as one "which will show under each entry the different senses in which the term is used and the
diverse aspects of the subject with their appropriate places
in the classification system."

     In order to select a class number for The Saturday
Night Special, a book urging control of small cheap handguns,
the classifier might begin by looking in the index under
"handguns." Finding that there is no such heading in the index, the classifier would think of other possible headings to
search and would discover the following entries:

          Firearms
            art metalwork               739.7
            *other aspects see* Guns

| Guns | | |
|---|---|---|
| artillery | | |
| art metalwork | 739.7 | |
| mil. eng. | 623.4 | |
| control | 363.3 | |
| law | 344.5 | |
| pub. admin. | | |
| central govts. | 351.7 | |
| hunting & shooting sports | 799 | |
| *s.a.* Small arms | | |

(s. a. means
see also)

| Pistols | |
|---|---|
| hunting & shooting | 799.2 |
| *other aspects see* Small arms | |

Revolvers *see* Pistols

| Small | |
|---|---|
| arms | |
| art metalwork | 739.7 |
| manufacturing | 683 |
| mil. eng. | 623.4 |

The most promising numbers suggested in the index are 363. 3, 344. 5, and 351. 7. Turning to these numbers in the schedules and examining each in terms of its context, the classifier will find yet another possible number, i. e. , 364. 4, Prevention of crime and delinquency, to which the user is referred in a note under 363. 3. The point that must be made here is that one should never assign a number from the index without going to the schedules. A tentative choice of a class number may be confirmed or altered by an examination of its relationship to other numbers in that category, or instructions or annotations in the schedules may modify the number or lead to a further search. Note that the numbers printed in boldface type (hunting and shooting sports, 799, in the example above) are always broad numbers which are broken down in the schedules. It is a good practice to begin with the schedules, skimming the three Summaries at the beginning of the schedules if necessary, and then to check the index to be sure that all possible aspects of a subject have been considered. Returning to the example of The Saturday Night Special, if the classifier's first thought is to put this under crime prevention in 364, the more specific number-- 363. 3--might be bypassed, unless the classifier remembers to read back up the 360's schedule or checks the index.

CLASSIFICATION AIDS

At this point in the discussion, the reader has no doubt come to the conclusion that classification must be one of the most time-consuming and therefore costly of library chores. Fortunately, this need no longer be the case, for an increasing variety of cooperative cataloging services and reference aids are available. Small libraries can have their books processed by a larger library or by a regional processing center, can buy their books pre-processed from a jobber, or can order catalog cards from the Library of Congress or other sources, as discussed in chapter 12.

Even when cataloging is done by the library, there are a number of tools available which can ease and speed the cataloger's work. The cataloging job can be initiated at the time that a title is ordered. For example, if a library uses The Booklist as a major selection aid, the typist who prepares the order slips can add the classification number and subject headings suggested by The Booklist to the duplicate slip which is retained by the library as a record of the order, so that cataloging can be speeded when the item arrives. When material is selected for purchase from another reviewing source, it may be checked against American Book Publishing Record (BPR) or the Weekly Record for suggested class numbers and other data at the time of ordering or when the material is received. When the library uses a retrospective selection aid such as H. W. Wilson's Standard Catalogs, Bro-Dart's The Elementary School Library Collection, or one of the other classified sources listed in Appendix C, the cataloging data can be noted at the time the order is placed, as suggested in connection with The Booklist, above; or the checked copy of the selection aid can be used by the cataloger when the material comes in.

An increasingly helpful aid is the Cataloging in Publication (CIP) program, which began in 1971. Over 1,000 publishers submit material in galley form or provide publication data (over 21,000 titles annually)[6] to the Library of Congress, whose catalogers determine the classification numbers and catalog entries for the book. Thus when the book is published, this data appears on the verso of the title page and can be used for the preparation of catalog cards when the book arrives in the library.

Whether a library buys catalog cards or uses the various aids mentioned above, the classification number should be checked with the library's official, annotated copy of the DDC to insure consistency. This is especially necessary if a library uses the abridged edition, for many aids give unabridged DDC numbers. Moreover, different aids may show complete agreement or considerable variation as to the number for a given title. To return to the example of The Saturday Night Special, the number assigned to it by Book Review Digest is 623.4, while LC and The Booklist chose 363.33, and Wilson's Public Library Catalog has it under 363.3. Since 623.4 represents Ordnance, under Military and Nautical engineering, the Book Review Digest cataloger apparently interpreted the author's intent differently. The local cataloger must examine the book and judge which number is better, keeping in mind local needs and policies.

The various aids will be found very useful as a check on one's classification and may suggest more desirable classification numbers when the specific topic is not included in the index to the tables. If one is continually in agreement with the aids, presumably one knows how to classify. In case of doubt always consult the aids. But having consulted the aids, be sure to consider the particular library's collection and see that the number suggested is in accordance with its practice and is the best place for the given book in that library.

An aid may change its policy, as The Booklist has done in regard to the use of 810 and 820. At one time all literary works of American or English authors were put together, and 821 (English poetry) was used for both American and English poetry. The sixth edition of the Public Library Catalog has Irving Adler's 1974 revised edition of Thinking Machines under 519.4, while the 1959-1963 Catalog had the earlier edition in 510.78. The change reflects the revision of the DDC, and should therefore not come as a surprise to the cataloger. If a library is to adopt such a change in policy, all of the books and records involved should have the classification numbers changed, while bibliographies such as the Standard Catalogs may ignore their earlier practice and simply be consistent in present and future issues. It is a saving in time for the library to make the change when the aid first makes it. Otherwise the library using it in its cataloging must assign different class numbers to all books issued after a change is made by the aid, and if the library purchases printed cards it must then revise them.

GENERAL RULES FOR CLASSIFYING

Once the cataloger is thoroughly familiar with the classification system, has examined the auxiliary tables and read the introductory matter, is aware of the various aids available, and understands the library's policies, the work can begin. The first step in determining the class number for a title is to find out what classification information is already at hand. If a card set has been obtained from a cooperative or commercial source, the number suggested should be checked against the library's annotated copy of the schedules, for it may need to be shortened or modified in some other way. If cards are not available, check the back of the title page for CIP data, and if that fails, check BPR or a similar aid, and proceed as above.

If no classification information is available, the book which is to be classified should be carefully examined to see what it is about, what the author's purpose was in writing it, what class of readers will find it most useful. To do this, read the title page, preface, all or part of the introduction, look over the table of contents (as this spreads out before the examiner the skeleton of the book), and scan parts of the book itself. Having determined to what main class the book belongs, e.g., history, turn to the table for that class--in this case, 900. An examination of the table shows that 900 is divided according to place and time. Such questions arise as: what country or section of a country is the book about? Does it cover the entire history of that country or section, or only a specific period? Of course, if it covers the entire world from creation to the present time, it goes in the general number, 909. But if the book is limited to United States history, it will go in 973. The figure 9 indicates that it is history, 7 that it is limited geographically to North America, and 3 that it is further confined to the United States. The 900 class, which includes history, geography, and biography, is a good one with which to begin the study of classification. It is readily determined whether or not a book treats of history, geography, or biography; and if it is history, the country and period of time covered are usually clearly indicated.

If the book is one of literature, the first deciding factor is the nationality of the author; the second, the literary form. Thus Masefield's poems are put with other books of English literature and in the section for poetry, 821. A book on the theories of electricity and electronics would go in the main class science, the division for physics, and the section for electricity and electronics, 537.

The figures are the symbol of the class; e.g., 620 stands for engineering and allied operations, and all general books on that subject would be so marked. If a book is on a specific kind of engineering, the third figure changes to show that fact; e.g., 621 represents applied physics, which includes mechanical, electrical, and other types of engineering. Having discovered what a book is about and its place in the classification scheme, one puts the number representing that subject in the system (the notation) in the book and on its cover, so that all books may be kept together on the shelves in the order of their classes.

Many books are on two or more subjects, or two or more aspects of the same subject. To give an illustration, a book on farming may treat of both the economics and the technology of farming; a work on wine, its commercial and domestic manufacture and public health measures regarding it. There is no single number for farming or for wine, as the DDC system is designed to categorize material according to fields of knowledge or disciplines rather than by specific topics. Thus the book on farming should be thought of as being either an economics or a technology book and classified accordingly.

Having determined the subject and the aspect of it covered, and the discipline within which it falls, the next step is to locate the classification number for it in the schedules. As indicated in the Second Summary (the 100 divisions), 630 in Technology (applied sciences) is the division for the technology of farming; 330 the division for economics. The Third Summary shows that 338 is the number for production. Turning to 338 in the schedules, one finds 338.1, Agriculture (including food supply); turning to 630, one finds 631.2, Agricultural structures; 631.3 Agricultural tools, machinery and equipment. But which of these numbers should one use if the book discusses both the price of crops and the various types of harvesters? The choice depends upon the relative emphasis given by the author to the two aspects of his subject, as explained in the following guidelines.

The rules below are adapted from W. C. B. Sayers[7] and Lake Placid Club Education Foundation's Guide.[8] The classifier should also refer, as needed, to the various sections in the introduction to the DDC.

1. Subject versus form: Class a book first according to its subject, and then by the form in which the subject is presented, except in generalia and in literature, where form is the distinguishing element. For example, Grove's Dictionary of Music and Musicians would be given the number 780.3; 78 shows that it is about music, 0 that it is not limited to one or more particular aspects of music, and 3 that it is in the form of a dictionary. Masefield's poems would be given the number 821; 8 showing that it is literature, 2 that it is by an English writer, and 1 that it is poetry. The literary form here determines its symbol, not the subject matter.

2. Subject emphasis: In determining the subject, consider the main emphasis or purpose of a book. For example, in the introduction to John K. Cooley's Baal, Christ, and Mohammed: Religion and Revolution in North Africa, the author states that he has "tried to set out some main themes in the relationship between religious faith, alien imperialism, and the native Berber revolutionary spirit." An examination of the table of contents and further reading in the introduction show that the book treats of the religion of North Africa, missions in North Africa, and analyzes the reasons for the Islamic dominance in North Africa. Hence Cooley's book would be classified in 209.61, the history of religion in North Africa; or in the very small library, simply in 209.

3. More than one subject: If a work deals with two subjects, class with the one emphasized most; e.g., class the effect of one subject on another with the subject affected. If the emphasis is equal, class with the one treated first. If the emphasis is about equal and both subjects are treated concurrently, class with the subject coming first in the schedules. If a work deals with three or more subjects, these same principles apply, except that if the emphasis is about equal but the subjects are subdivisions of one broader subject, class with the broader subject. For example, the preface to M. S. Stedman's Religion and Politics in America states that "the purpose of this book is to advance an understanding of the relationships between religion and politics on both the empirical and the theoretical level...." Stedman would be classified in 261.7, Christianity and civil government. Skilling and Richardson's Sun, Moon and Stars deals with the sun, moon, planets, stars, astronomers and observatories, with about equal space and emphasis on each. All sections are subdivisions of the broad subject, descriptive astronomy, and therefore this book would be classified in 523.

4. <u>Contrasting opinions or systems</u>: If a work treats
of two different opinions or systems, with about equal treatment of each, but advocates one, class with the one advocated; but if more attention is paid to one, class with it, regardless of advocacy. For example, a book discussing capitalism and communism would be classed in 335.4, Marxian
systems, if the bulk of it dealt with communism, even though
the author clearly preferred capitalism. But a book which
dealt equally with the two and also advocated capitalism
would go in 330.12, Free-enterprise economic systems.

5. <u>More than one aspect</u>: A work may deal both
with the theory or basic principles of a process and with its
application to a specific subject. If the theory is preliminary
to the application, and the author's purpose is to describe the
application, class with the application, but if the "application"
is only an example (with much less space given to it) and the
author's purpose is to describe the theory, class with the
theory. <u>How to Fix Your Own TV, Radio, and Record Play-
er</u> contains general information about TV, radio and record
players, so that when repairing them the worker can under-
stand and recognize the parts and their relation to one another. It also includes material on how to diagnose the
trouble and how to locate, remove, replace, or repair the
faulty part. This book would be classified in 621.38, Electronic and communication engineering, rather than in 537.5,
Electronics. Similarly, a book about the theory of electro-
dynamics would go in 537.6, but its application, as in a book
about electric trains, would go in 621.33.

6. <u>Subject not provided</u>: Do <u>not</u> make up a number
for a new subject which does not appear in the DDC. A
new edition may use that number for something else. Follow the usual procedure for classifying and stop when you
locate the most specific number that will contain the subject
of the book, even if it is only a three-digit number. Later,
if the number for that subject is worked out by the DDC
editors, you can add to the number already assigned to the
book. For example, a number for "hippies," 301.44, is
specified for the first time in the 10th edition, but there
were many books published on this subject before the new
DDC appeared. A classifier using the 9th edition who wanted
to bring together books on hippies might have been tempted
to use one of the open numbers under 301, Sociology, such
as 301.6. This would have turned out to be a poor decision,
since the 10th edition uses 301.6 for something else and
broadens 301.44 to include hippies. The classifier would

have been wise to use simply 301, to which the .44 could have been added later.

7. General versus specific: Class in the most specific number that will accommodate a book. If a subject is limited by place, form or other aspect and there is a number in the schedules for that more precise aspect, prefer the specific to the more general number. Thus James Truslow Adams' Provincial Society, 1690-1763 would be classified 973.2, the number for colonial history of the United States, not 973, the general number for United States history; Maeterlinck's The Life of the Bee, 595.7, Insects, not 592, Invertebrates. The closeness of the classification, however, also depends upon the amount of material the library has on the subject or is likely to have in the future. Hence Maeterlinck's book in small libraries using the abridged DDC would go in 595.7, whereas larger libraries using the unabridged edition would put the book in 595.799. Formerly, all books on Southeast Asia in the average public or school library were put in 959, but with the recent importance of that region to Americans, closer classification became necessary in order to bring together books on Vietnam, Cambodia, etc.

8. Evaluations: The classifier is not a critic nor a judge, but sometimes must make an evaluative decision as to which of two or more numbers will be best. For example, I Never Danced at the White House, a collection of columns by Art Buchwald, might go in 817, as he ranks as a humorist of some merit. As a general rule, however, a journalist's columns would be classified in the 070's.

Always record in the schedules all decisions on optional numbers, reductions, and other variations. Place a book where you think it will be most useful, but avoid changes in recommended DDC practice.

When ready to classify a collection of books, first sort them by general groups, then examine those in each group carefully to see precisely what they are about. This is much easier than taking books as they come and switching one's thoughts from science to religion, to drama, to electronics, and so forth. A knowledge of the rules for classifying will be found very helpful, but one learns to classify by classifying. Keep in mind the purpose of classifying, namely, "to make books more available" to the readers for whose benefit classification is used. Be as consistent as possible; if in doubt about a class for a certain book, see what other books owned by the library are in that class, or consult bibliographic aids which include classification numbers.


## CHANGES AND CHOICES

Complaints about the increasing degree of detail and complexity of successive editions of the abridged DDC prompted the editors of the tenth edition to trim and simplify to the extent that it is more accurate to call this current volume an adaptation rather than an abridgment of the 18th unabridged DDC. Not only have numbers been shortened and omitted, but some numbers beyond the decimal point are different from those given in the 18th edition. Moreover, there are also changes in numbers used in the 9th abridged, some numbers having been relocated and others dropped. All of the changes are clearly indicated in the 10th edition, in separate lists as well as in the schedules themselves. Two entirely revamped sections are 340 (Law) and 510 (Mathematics). The old schedules and concordances are given in an appendix for the use of libraries wishing to reclassify their books on these subjects.

A very helpful discussion of the changes is Lois M. Chan's "The Tenth Abridged Dewey Decimal Classification and Children's Room/School Library Collections."[9] As she points out, the 10th edition may be too abridged in some parts of the schedules, as in the 590's, where all mammals are lumped in 599. A library wishing to continue to use 599.1-599.9 to separate its books on mammals could write in the old numbers on that page, but this might lead to conflicts in the event of a different distribution of these numbers in a future edition.

As new editions come out, they should be purchased and adopted by even the smallest library, not only for the purpose of keeping up to date as new subjects appear and are incorporated, but also so that advantage may be taken of time-saving cataloging aids and centralized services, which usually reflect the latest editions of DDC.

If the library has a very small amount of material on a subject the number for which has been changed in the tables, it would be well to change it immediately; if a great deal of material, the amount of work involved may make it impossible. In the case of such an extensive change as that represented by the entirely new schedules for law and mathematics introduced in the 10th edition, it is not wise to attempt to change the classification numbers of books already cataloged.  Simply adopt the new schedules, and give copies to the public service staff of the concordances between the old and the new numbers.  While the library will have arithmetic books under both 511 and 513 for some years, the discrepancy will eventually disappear as the old books in 511 are worn out and discarded.

For new subjects, however, it is often worth changing the number, as there is likely to be less material on hand. If a new subject has been classified broadly at its first appearance, later--when the nature of it is more apparent and when the library has more on it--the subject may be divided to better advantage.  This is easily done by adding numbers after the decimal point.  The number of new subjects unprovided for in the classification system increases as the scheme grows older.  This is why it is so necessary for a library to get the new editions as they appear.

As a result of changes in the numbers from one edition of the DDC to another, sometimes there are different numbers given for the same subject in different aids and on printed cards.  When the Library of Congress adopts a new edition of the DDC, it does not (and cannot) revise the numbers previously assigned to books in subject categories for which the DDC has provided new numbers.  Therefore, a library which orders LC cards for two books on the same subject which were published several years apart could very well discover that the class number for one is not the same as the number assigned to the other.  For example, if a library ordered two books on geometry, J. E. Thompson's Geometry for the Common Man and Podendorf's Shapes: Sides, Curves and Corners, and also ordered cards for them from the Library of Congress, it would find that LC suggests 513 for Thompson but 516 for Podendorf.  The Thompson book was first cataloged by LC in 1962 when the number for geometry was 513, while Podendorf (1970) was assigned 516 in accordance with the revised DDC.  It is up to the cataloger to change the older card to conform with the new schedules.

Not only is the classifier faced with changing class numbers from edition to edition, but the current schedules also give specific authority for certain choices in numbers. For example:

913-919    Geography of and travel in specific continents, countries, localities, extraterrestrial worlds

. . .

If preferred, class in 930-960

but:

930-990    General history of specific continents, countries, localities

. . .

(It is optional to class here general geography of and travel in specific continents, countries, localities, extraterrestrial worlds; prefer 913-919)

The librarian must face these changes and choices and make the necessary decisions in order to keep the library's material consistently classified. For that reason it is particularly important to record in the schedules all decisions regarding changes and choices. Taking the example of the 900's above, if a library decides to put all the books of French geography, travel, and history in 944 rather than dividing them between 914.4 and 944, there must be a note to that effect in both places in the schedules. However, it is seldom wise to depart from preferred DDC numbers.

Probably the greatest number of options offered by the DDC is in the 920's for biographies. Many small libraries choose to treat biographies and autobiographies of individuals somewhat in the manner of fiction, marking them B or 92 and arranging them alphabetically by the name of the biographee rather than the author. Collective biographies can all be put in 920, or can be divided according to profession, e.g., 925 for scientists. Another possibility is to classify biographies of people closely identified with a specific field in the number for that subject, so that the reader who looks on the shelf for baseball would find biographies of players along with other books on the sport. A disadvantage of this method, if one wishes to identify the biographical nature of a work, is that it requires the addition of the standard subdivision -092, which can result in a rather long number, such as 796.357092 for a biography of a baseball player. However, when a book deals more with the work a person has done in a particular field than with that individual's life as a whole, it should be classed with the subject rather than relegated to the 920's. Thus a book about how Einstein developed the theory of relativity should go in 530.1092, but a book which told his life story might go in the general biography section. Again, the policies adopted by a library for biographies should reflect user preferences, should be spelled out in the cataloger's copy of the classification schedules, and should also be communicated to the public services staff.

## SHELF ARRANGEMENT OF BOOKS WITHIN A CLASS

The larger the number of books within any one class the more need there is for some symbol which can be used in arranging the books within that class. Another factor to consider besides the size of the collection is the actual need for keeping the books in exact order on the shelves. Many libraries use no symbol whatever on the spines of the books of fiction, though fiction may comprise a rather large number of books even in the small library. A book with no symbol on its spine is understood to be fiction and is to be arranged alphabetically by author on the shelf.

Other libraries use a symbol for fiction, F or Fic, and many of these add the author's surname to the spine if it is not there originally or wears off. For instance $\frac{F}{Milne}$ on the spine of Milne's Winnie the Pooh makes it easy to shelve and locate this book. The catalog cards would have the symbol F or Fic on them. Some libraries use SC (Short Story Collection) to designate books of short stories and shelve them immediately following the books of fiction. In public libraries juvenile fiction may be designated by a J or some other symbol. Similarly, a different symbol may be used to indicate a picture book for young children, because the shapes and sizes of these books make it desirable to keep them on specially built shelves. Reference books are usually marked with an R above the classification number in order to indicate that they are not shelved with other books of that number, but are kept in a section of the library devoted to reference works.

In the case of nonfiction, library practice varies. In order to provide sub-arrangement by author, some libraries use "book numbers" as well as classification numbers. Book numbers do have the advantage of making it possible to keep the books within a class--i.e., those having the same content and therefore the same classification number--in exact order with a minimum of difficulty. When added to the class number (usually directly below it as a second line of the call

number), the book number can also provide for each volume
a distinctive symbol (or call number) which can be used for
circulation control, record and inventory purposes, as well
as for shelf location. However, the amount of work involved
in determining and applying the number, plus the confusion
which it sometimes causes patrons, reduces the advantages
for small libraries. Public and school libraries of 75,000
volumes or fewer can usually manage to do without book numbers, and even many larger libraries use them only for certain sections of their collections.

A book number basically is a combination of letters
and figures taken from an alphabetic order table, such as the
Cutter-Sanborn table. [10] In fact, this system became so widely used in the early part of the century that the term "cutter
number" is often used to describe a great variety of book
number symbols. The basic elements of the revised Cutter
book number system consist of an initial letter followed by
numerals to represent a name. This provides an alphabetic
arrangement by means of an author symbol which is usually
much shorter than the author's name. The figures are also
treated as decimals, so as to make possible the insertion of
a new name between any two combinations already used. For
example, consulting the Cutter-Sanborn Table, one would assign book numbers as follows:

Miles -    M645
Millikan - M654
Mills -    M657

If just two numerals are used, the above book numbers would
be M64 for Miles and M65 for Millikan, but M657 for Mills
in order to distinguish between it and the Millikan book if
the titles being cataloged have the same classification number.
However, if the book by Millikan is classified in 530 and the
one by Mills in 591.5, M65 may be used for both, since the
classification numbers differ.

Books of individual biography in the collection should
be arranged by the name of the subject of the biography (the
biographee, not the biographer), so that all of the biographies of one person will come together on the shelf. Therefore, many book numbers may begin with the same initial letter or letters. To illustrate: Agassiz, A262; Allen, A425;
Arliss, A724; or, shortening them to two figures: A26, A42,
A72. Thus they may be distinguished with three symbols.
By adding the initial letter of the biographer's name, one may

readily differentiate several biographies of the same person and arrange them in alphabetical order by author: e.g., Goss's biography of Johann Sebastian Bach would have the book number B11G and Wheeler and Deucher's B11W; Dan Beard's autobiography, B36, and Clemens and Sibley's biography of Beard, B36C. Note that the autobiography has no letter added after the number B36 and would therefore stand before the biographies on the shelf.

Many libraries have found the first letter or the first three letters of the author's surname a satisfactory substitute for Cutter numbers and use author letters for both fiction and nonfiction. Thus Stevenson's <u>Treasure Island</u> might be marked $\frac{F}{S}$ or $\frac{F}{STE}$ on the spine, the same symbol being used on the catalog cards to show the location of the book.

In the class of individual biography there are likely to be some cases of persons with the same surname or surnames beginning with the same letter or letters. To illustrate, Franklin D. Roosevelt's biographies might be marked ROO; if the library also has biographies of Eleanor Roosevelt and Theodore Roosevelt, one way to differentiate among them is to add a comma and the initial of the first name. But it is highly questionable whether such minute differentiation is necessary in most small libraries. Another illustration may be drawn from the Adamses: Henry Adams' <u>Letters (1892-1918)</u>; Mrs. Henry Adams' <u>Letters, 1865-1883;</u> and J. C. Miller's <u>Sam Adams, Pioneer in Propaganda.</u> They could all be assigned the class symbol B for biography or 92 with A, A1, and A2 as book numbers. If the Cutter-Sanborn tables are used, the books present no problem if three figures are used; the books would be marked A213, A215 and A217 respectively, below the class number. There are not likely to be many such cases in the small general library. Cutter-Sanborn numbers may be used for individual biography even though just the initial letter is used in other classes.

If book numbers are not used, individual biographies should have the biographee's name underscored on the spine of the book for convenience in shelving. It should be added where it does not appear; for example, Eaton's <u>Leader by Destiny</u> should have "Washington" written on the spine and be shelved under Washington's name, rather than Eaton's. Also, in the case of literary and art criticism, it is the subject of the book instead of the author whose name should determine shelf arrangement.

The name by which the book is to be shelved should also be added if necessary and underscored on the spine in the case of books with editors, translators, joint authors, pseudonyms, or whenever there may be doubt as to the choice of name. If fiction is published anonymously but the author is known and the book is entered in the catalog under the name, it should be added to the spine. If a book which is published under a pseudonym is cataloged and consequently shelved under the real name, the name under which it is to be shelved should be underscored or added to the cover and spine.

## References

1. J. C. Dana, A Library Primer (Boston: Library Bureau, 1920), p. 98.

2. Melvil Dewey, Dewey Decimal Classification and Relative Index. 18th ed. (Lake Placid Club, N.Y.: Forest Press, 1971), 3 v.

3. Melvil Dewey, Abridged Dewey Decimal Classification and Relative Index. 10th ed. (Lake Placid Club, N.Y.: Forest Press, 1971).

4. American Libraries, 6:588, November, 1975.

5. D. J. Haykin, Subject Headings: A Practical Guide (Boston: Gregg Press, 1972), p. 2.

6. Booklist, 72:333, November 1, 1975.

7. W. C. B. Sayers, An Introduction to Library Classification. 9th rev. ed. (London: Grafton, 1954), pp. 179-180.

8. Lake Placid Educational Foundation, Guide to Use of Dewey Decimal Classification; Based on the Practice of the Decimal Classification Office at the Library of Congress (Lake Placid Club, N.Y.: Forest Press, 1962).

9. Library Journal, 98:2620-2625, September 15, 1973.

10. C. A. Cutter, Alphabetic Order Table, Altered and Fitted with Three Figures by Kate Sanborn (Springfield, Mass.: H. R. Huntting Co.).

CHAPTER 2


SUBJECT HEADINGS


While a book can have only one classification number and be shelved in only one place, it is quite possible that a specific book contains important material about several topics, or information about some subject which is too specialized to merit its own classification number. To compensate for this limitation of the classification scheme, library catalogs contains entries under subject--sometimes several for a single title.

This chapter deals with the problem of determining the subject of a book, and the topic or topics under which it should be listed in the catalog. It is usually found that more library users look for material on some subject than for a specific author or title. Entering material in the catalog under subjects involves a knowledge of the terms people use, and selection of as specific a term as the material warrants.

For geographic headings, e.g., Madagascar versus Malagasy Republic, which term do the newspapers use? the radio and TV programs? the magazines? Differences in the vocabularies of people in different sections of the country are important in certain fields. With reference to geographic subdivisions, e.g., BIRDS--U.S., consider these questions: does the library have anything on birds in countries other than the United States? Is it likely to have? When the reader asks for a book on birds, though he does not say so, does he not mean birds in the United States? Then use the general subject heading, BIRDS. Use simple, modern subject headings; avoid cumbersome phrases and unnecessary subdivisions.

Some libraries find that subject entries for certain types of fiction serve a real purpose and improve service, especially for children. If mystery stories, to take a ubiquitous example, are entered in the catalog under the heading MYSTERY AND DETECTIVE STORIES as well as under author and title, time will be saved for both readers and library staff, although the time saved by the staff in serving the public may possibly be counterbalanced by the time spent in assigning headings and making the extra cards. Most libraries will find the analytical indexes in standard bibliographic guides adequate substitutes for fiction subject headings in the library's own catalog. The H. W. Wilson Company's Standard Catalogs include subject headings for fiction, and Irwin's A Guide to Historical Fiction is only one of a number of available indexes to special categories of fiction.

For example, the young reader who wants a story about the American Revolution can be guided to Forbes' Johnny Tremain by consulting the index to the Junior High School Library Catalog. Similarly, someone who wants fiction about the Puerto Rican experience in America can be directed to Mohr's Nilda. Turning to the main entry for Nilda in the Junior High School Library Catalog, we see that it gives not only the citation and an annotation, but also suggested subject headings under which the book can be entered in the card catalog: PUERTO RICANS IN NEW YORK (CITY) --FICTION, and FAMILY--FICTION.

If the library buys LC cards or other prepared cataloging, the cards for children's and young adult fiction will quite often include subject headings. However, if the library does its own cataloging, it is more economical to restrict subject headings for fiction as much as possible and to rely on the Standard Catalogs and other bibliographic aids. In any case, subject cards should be made only if a book, whether fiction or nonfiction, gives definite information on a particular subject.

## DETERMINING THE SUBJECT

To determine the subject of a book for which cataloging information cannot be found elsewhere requires a careful examination of its contents. For this reason the subject headings should be determined and assigned at the same time as the classification number; otherwise examining the book and determining what it is about has to be done twice. The two topics are separated in this manual because both are difficult and it is better to take them up separately until each is clearly understood.

Read the title page, look over the table of contents

carefully, scan the preface or introduction, and dip into the book itself in several places.  This scrutiny will show what the book is about and what the author's purpose was in writing it.  Such an examination may bring out the fact that the book treats of one subject, of several distinct phases of a subject, or of two or more subjects.  No matter how many subjects a book covers, it can be given only one classification number and can stand on the shelves in only one place; but it may be entered in the catalog under as many subject headings as are necessary.  If the book treats of one subject it requires only one subject entry, e. g. , Alistair Cooke's America would be entered in the catalog only under the general heading UNITED STATES--HISTORY.

On the other hand, Toynbee's Half the World; the History and Culture of China and Japan needs to be entered under two subjects, CHINA--CIVILIZATION and JAPAN--CIVILIZATION.  Similarly, Edwin H. Colbert's Wandering Lands and Animals should be represented in the catalog by two subject cards, one under FOSSILS and one under CONTINENTAL DRIFT.  Another type of book has one general topic but includes a number of specific topics, as for example, Patricia Lauber's This Restless Earth.  The general subject is geology, and a card will be made for the catalog with that word as a heading (see card 3).  But the book will be much more

```
551        GEOLOGY
LAU        Lauber, Patricia
             This restless earth.  Ill. by
           John Polgreen.  Random House, 1970.
             129 p.  ill.

             Replaces the author's:  All
           about the planet earth, 1962.
```

Card 3.  Subject entry for a book

useful in the children's library if it is also entered in the catalog under the special topics with which it deals, e. g. , pages 21-42 are on earthquakes, pages 45-67 on volcanoes, pages 76-81 on mountains, pages 82-96 on oceans.  Subject analytical cards may be made for each of these topics, or as many of them as the library is likely to have calls for.  This depends upon the other material available on the subject and the special interests of the library's users. A subject analytical entry is a subject card for a part of a book, with the specific pages in which the subject is covered cited as part of the heading (see card 4).

```
551          EARTHQUAKES, p. 21-42:
LAU          Lauber, Patricia
             This restless earth.  Ill. by
             John Polgreen.  Random House, 1970.
             129 p.  ill.

             Replaces the author's:  All
             about the planet earth, 1962.
```

Card 4.   Analytical subject entry for part of a book

Thus the book is examined, its subject determined, and one or more subject cards are made for the catalog. Whether these cards are general subject entries or subject analytical entries for a particular portion of the book depends upon whether two or more subjects are discussed together throughout the book or each subject is discussed separately.

SELECTING SUBJECT HEADINGS

When deciding upon the heading for a subject entry, choose that heading which most truly represents the contents of the book or a certain part of the book; that is, the most specific subject or subjects possible. For example, if a book is about trees--how to identify them or their uses of ornamentation--select the specific term TREES. The subject heading BOTANY includes the subject TREES, but it obviously includes a great deal more, and this book tells of no other plant than the tree. The subject heading FORESTS AND FORESTRY would be used for a book which treats of trees as they grow in forests, how to care for and preserve forests, but not for a book which treats trees as individual varieties, trees as an ornament for lawns and streets, and the like. It would not, therefore, be a suitable heading for this book. Likewise, Fabre's The Life of the Fly would have the specific heading FLIES, and not the general one INSECTS. Of two equally correct and specific headings, such

as BIRDS and ORNITHOLOGY, the choice depends upon the
type of library, and a reference may be made, directing the
reader from the term not chosen to the heading used in the
catalog.   In a public or school library, choose the heading
BIRDS as the term commonly used by the readers.   In a
special ornithological library, use the heading ORNITHOLOGY,
for the users of such a library are quite familiar with the
scientific term.

Consider opposite terms such as tolerance and intoler-
ance.   A book on one of these subjects necessarily includes
material on the other.   Choose one, e. g. , TOLERATION,
and put all the material under it, referring from the other
term.

Select as many subject headings as are necessary to
cover the contents of the book, but do not multiply them need-
lessly.   Test each heading by asking whether or not a patron
would be glad to find the book or books listed under the given
heading if he or she were looking for material on that topic.
It would be an unusual book which would need more than three
subject headings, and one or two will cover most books.   In
the Children's Catalog, Isaac Asimov's Great Ideas in Science
has the general subject headings SCIENCE--HISTORY and
SCIENTISTS, and many subject analytical entries, e. g. ,
ARCHIMEDES, pages 20-28; GALILEO, pages 29-35; PY-
THAGORAS, pages 10-19; etc.   But it is not desirable to
analyze books already indexed in other books available in the
library.   The usefulness of such books as Cutts' Scenes and
Characters of the Middle Ages, which is not analyzed in any
of the Wilson Standard Catalogs, would be greatly increased,
however, by having subject analytical entries made for each
of the groups described, e. g. , KNIGHTS AND KNIGHTHOOD,
PILGRIMS AND PILGRIMAGES.

Another example of the kind and number of subject
headings may be illustrated by Louis Auchincloss' Pioneers
and Caretakers:   a Study of Nine American Women Novelists,
which is about American fiction and American authors.   The
Senior High School Library Catalog lists this book and suggests as subject headings:   AMERICAN FICTION--HISTORY
AND CRITICISM; AUTHORS, AMERICAN; and WOMEN AS
AUTHORS.   In addition, nine analytical entries are made for
the women discussed.   If the library owns this catalog, the
librarian will not need to make these nine analytics, since
the reader can refer to the printed index to find references
on individual authors.   The three subject cards, however,

are necessary.  When the suggested headings are checked
with a standard printed list of subject headings such as
Sears, AMERICAN FICTION is found in its alphabetical place;
below it the heading AMERICAN LITERATURE; the form subheading HISTORY AND CRITICISM is included in the list of
subdivisions to be used in the fields of literature and music.
The form subheads may also be used under the headings for
the different types of literature, so for this book the heading
AMERICAN FICTION--HISTORY AND CRITICISM may be used.
The heading AUTHORS, AMERICAN is also found in the
Sears list, and below it:

x American authors (which means: do not use, refer from)

So a second subject card should be made with the heading
AUTHORS, AMERICAN, and a reference card should be made,
reading:

---

AMERICAN AUTHORS

see

AUTHORS, AMERICAN

---

Card 5.   See reference card

---

Why use the terms AMERICAN FICTION, AMERICAN LITERA-
TURE, etc., but AUTHORS, AMERICAN?   The aids and the
lists agree that it is important to bring all material in the
catalog together under AUTHORS, AMERICAN; AUTHORS,
ENGLISH; while with the terms literature, poetry, fiction,
etc., it is more useful to put the national adjective first and
bring together everything on the literature of one country, as
AMERICAN DRAMA, AMERICAN FICTION, AMERICAN LIT-
ERATURE.   Among these headings in the catalog will be the
reference from AMERICAN AUTHORS.

Besides subject entries for books and parts of books,
subject cards may be made to call attention to an entire group
of books.   One method is to prepare one subject card for all
the books on a general subject, by simply referring the reader to the books on the shelves by classification number, and
to the shelf list to find the books which may be temporarily

out of the library. This practice is particularly useful in very small libraries where the patrons frequently choose their books directly from the shelves and use the catalog primarily to see whether there are any books on a subject and where they are. Also, the librarian's time is saved and space is saved in the catalog.

---

551.2    VOLCANOES

      Books about volcanoes will be found on the shelves under 551.2.

      For a complete author list of the books in the library on volcanoes, consult the shelf list under 551.2.

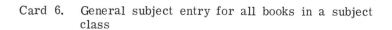

---

Card 6.    General subject entry for all books in a subject class

---

      If the library has books with chapters on a subject, e.g. volcanoes, not indexed in the Wilson Standard Catalogs, or if the library does not have these aids, subject analytical cards for the catalog should be made for this material. Chapter 8 gives details on how to make these cards. If there is a general subject entry in the catalog already, it should be amended to include a third paragraph: "For parts of books on volcanoes, see the cards following this one."

      Subdivisions. Some subjects need to be subdivided to be exact. Most subjects can be divided by either phase, form, geographical area, or period of time. For instance, the subject heading BIRDS would be used for a general book on that subject. But if a book is limited to the protection of birds or to migration, the general heading BIRDS can be limited by adding a phase subdivision, e.g., BIRDS--PROTECTION, or BIRDS--MIGRATION. If, however, the book is not a book about birds but a list of books about birds, the form subdivision BIBLIOGRAPHY should be added and the heading becomes BIRDS--BIBLIOGRAPHY. Or the book may be on birds of a specific place, and the heading may be limited by a geographical area subdivision, e. g. , BIRDS--BRAZIL.

For some subjects, notably history, next in importance to the geographical area is the period of time covered. For a general history in which there is no geographical limitation, the period of time covered is the significant factor. For a book such as William H. McNeill's A World History, which covers all countries and all periods up to the present, the subject headings would be CIVILIZATION--HISTORY, and WORLD HISTORY. But a history which, though including all lands, ends at the beginning of the Middle Ages would have the subject heading HISTORY, ANCIENT. A general history of the United States, however, would have the subject heading U. S. --HISTORY. A time subhead may be added, e. g. U. S. --HISTORY--REVOLUTION, or U. S. --HISTORY--1898-1919. The use of subheads depends upon whether or not the book is limited to one phase, period of time, etc. , and the amount of material on that subject which the library has or expects to have.

If the collection contains only a few books treating United States history, they may as well all have the same subject heading, namely, U. S. --HISTORY. A slightly larger library may have a dozen or so books and expect to add more. If it has six general works covering the history of the United States from the Revolution to the present time, three books dealing exclusively with the Revolution, four on the Civil War period, five on the history of the period 1898 to 1919, etc. , it would be well to group them in the catalog under headings such as U. S. --HISTORY; U. S. --HISTORY--REVOLUTION; U. S. --HISTORY--CIVIL WAR; U. S. --HISTORY --1898-1919.

A subject heading, as noted before, is the word or words used to describe the content of the book; thus Peterson's How to Know the Birds will have the subject heading BIRDS. Novels do not usually have a definite subject and are read for their style, characterization, etc. , rather than for information. This is also true of poems and plays. They have author and title entries in the catalog but seldom subject entries. The heading POETRY is not used for a book of poems, but for a work on the appreciation and philosophy of poetry, and POETICS is used for works on the art and tech-

nique of poetry, so that a book like Robert Hillyer's In Pur-
suit of Poetry requires two subject headings, POETICS and
POETRY. If the library has much material on poetry, it
may subdivide the heading; i.e., POETRY--HISTORY AND
CRITICISM. The literary works of an individual are represented in the catalog only under the writer's name and under
the title if distinctive. Whoever wishes to read T. S. Eliot's
The Waste Land will look under Eliot or under Waste Land.
Eliot's collected poems will be found only under his name,
not under POETRY. It is, however, worthwhile and practical
to bring together in the catalog collections of poems, essays,
or dramas of three or more authors. This is done by adding
a form subdivision to the heading. The heading POETRY or
AMERICAN POETRY is used for books about poetry, while
the headings POETRY--COLLECTIONS or AMERICAN POETRY
--COLLECTIONS are used for such works as Untermeyer's
Modern American Poetry. These latter headings, POETRY--
COLLECTIONS and AMERICAN POETRY--COLLECTIONS are
called form headings, as they refer to the form in which the
material is written, not to its content.

```
AMERICAN POETRY--COLLECTIONS

    Books of poetry by individual
American poets will be found on the
shelves under 811.  Collections of
poetry by several American poets
will be found under 811.08

    For a complete list of books in
the library of poetry by individual
American poets, consult the shelf list
under 811; for collections, 811.08.
```

Card 7.  General subject entry for all books in one or more
         classes

Form cards similar to card 7 might take the place of
the form heading POETRY--COLLECTIONS and AMERICAN
POETRY--COLLECTIONS and direct the reader to the books

on the shelves. If this practice is adopted, similar cards
would be made for ENGLISH POETRY--COLLECTIONS;
AMERICAN DRAMA--COLLECTIONS; ENGLISH DRAMA--
COLLECTIONS, etc.

To sum up this matter of the choice of subject headings: use the term (or terms) which most clearly describes
the contents of a book and is most likely to be familiar to
the users of the library, remembering that readers use different libraries if not simultaneously at least over a period
of time. When choosing between synonymous headings, prefer the one that is most familiar to the people who use the
library, is most used in other catalogs, has the fewest mean-
ings other than the one intended, or brings the subject into
conjunction with related subjects. But keep subject headings
simple and do not subdivide extensively unless the library
has considerable material on each subdivision.

LISTS OF SUBJECT HEADINGS

Next in importance to choosing the right subject heading for a given book is to use the same wording for all the
subject headings for books or parts of books on the same
subject, so that they may be brought together in the catalog.
To do this it is essential to have a carefully worked out list
of headings from which to choose and to check it to show
which headings have been used.

The list most widely adopted by small public and
school libraries is Sears List of Subject Headings. A list
used for many years in elementary and junior high school
libraries as well as children's departments in public libraries
was Rue and LaPlante's Subject Headings for Children's Materials.[2] This is now considerably out of date, but is worth
consulting as an example of a list designed to meet the needs
of a specific user group and as a source of suggestions for
additional cross reference headings for children's collections.
The list used by most larger libraries is the LC list of subject headings.[3] LC cards give headings from this list, but
other cards which use Sears subject headings are available
for purchase (see chapter 12). In general, libraries with
fewer than 50,000 volumes prefer the Sears list, while larger
libraries or special libraries with subject concentration need
the greater comprehensiveness of the LC list. Although
there are some major differences in use of terms (ORNITHOL-
OGY versus BIRDS, for example), it is the degree of specificity

Beauticians
  *See* Beauty operators
Beautification of cities and towns
  *See* Urban beautification
Beautification of the landscape
  *See* Landscape protection
Beautiful, The
  *See* Aesthetics
      Art—Philosophy
Beauty
  *See* Aesthetics
      Art—Philosophy
      Beauty, Personal
**Beauty, Personal**  *(RA778)*
  sa Beauty contests
     Beauty culture
     Beauty shops
     Body-marking
     Charm
     Cosmetics
     Costume
     Hair
     Hand
     Skin
     Teeth
     Toilet
  *x* Beauty
     Complexion
     Grooming for women
     Grooming, Personal
     Personal beauty
  *xx* Beauty culture
     Beauty shops
     Cosmetics
     Face
     Hygiene
     Toilet
     Woman—Health and hygiene
  — Early works to 1800
  — Juvenile literature
**Beauty, Personal, in literature**
**Beauty contests**
  *xx* Beauty, Personal

**Beauty culture**  *(TT950-979)*
  sa Beauty operators
     Beauty, Personal
     Beauty shops
     Cosmetics
     Hairdressing
  *x* Cosmetology
  *xx* Beauty, Personal
     Beauty shops
     Cosmetics
  — Equipment and supplies
          *See* Beauty shops—Equipment and
              supplies
  — Examinations, questions, etc.
  — Juvenile literature
  — Law and legislation
          *See* Beauty shops—Law and
              legislation
  — Study and teaching  *(Direct)*
  — Vocational guidance
**Beauty operators**  *(Direct)*
  sa Collective labor agreements—
        Hairdressing
     Wages—Beauty operators
  *x* Beauticians
     Cosmetologists
     Hairdressers
  *xx* Beauty culture
     Beauty shops
**Beauty shops**
  sa Beauty culture
     Beauty operators
     Beauty, Personal
     Cosmetics
  *xx* Beauty culture
     Beauty, Personal
  — Accounting
  — Designs and plans
  — Equipment and supplies
     *x* Beauty culture—Equipment and
        supplies
  — Law and legislation  *(Direct)*
     *x* Beauty culture—Law and legislation
  — Management

---

## Sears

Beautification of the landscape. *See* **Landscape
      protection**
Beauty. *See* **Esthetics**
**Beauty, Personal**
  *See also* **Cosmetics; Costume; Hair**
  *x* Complexion; Good grooming; Grooming,
      Personal; Grooming for women; Per-
      sonal appearance; Personal grooming;
      Toilet
  *xx* **Beauty shops; Hygiene**
**Beauty shops**
  *See also* **Beauty, Personal; Cosmetics**

and cross-referencing which chiefly distinguishes the two lists, as demonstrated by the parallel excerpts on the opposite page.

If the library is served by a regional cataloging and/ or processing center, it must perforce adopt the same list of subject headings as is used by the center, for the savings afforded by cooperation will be negated if many of the headings have to be changed to conform to the local list. Fortunately, much of the disadvantage of LC headings for small libraries has been alleviated by LC's adoption of a list of Subject Headings for Children's Literature. [4] This is, in effect, a list of exceptions to the master LC list, and brings headings into much closer alignment with Sears usage. The ALA Committee on Cataloging Children's Materials has recommended the adoption of the LC list in the interests of standardization, and the latest edition of Sears has incorporated many of the LC children's literature headings. Therefore, school libraries and public library children's departments should not automatically dismiss the idea of using LC headings, but should examine the options carefully.

How to use lists of subject headings. Determine what the book is about; then look in the list of subject headings adopted by the library for a suitable heading which expresses the content of the book. On examining the Sears List, an excerpt from which is reproduced below, note that the headings are listed in alphabetical order and that some are in boldface type. Those in boldface, e. g. BUYING, are to be used as subject headings.

Note that just below the heading BUYING is a paragraph beginning "Use for..." This type of explanatory note is given below some of the headings to explain for what kind of material they are to be used. Following this note the words see also introduce one or more suggested headings that may be better for the book in hand than the first subject heading looked up. If that is the case, turn to such headings as CONSUMER EDUCATION and SHOPPING in their alphabetical places in the list. But if BUYING is the better term, use it. Note that the next line begins with x. This means that the term or terms following the x should not be used as headings, and that a see reference should be made from the term or terms not used to the one that is chosen for the heading. Thus a see reference should be made from PURCHASING to BUYING.

Business failures. *See* **Bankruptcy**
**Business forecasting**
  *x* Forecasting, Business
Business law. *See* **Commercial law**
**Business letters**
  *See also* **English language—Business English**
  *x* Business correspondence; Commercial correspondence; Correspondence
  *xx* **English language—Business English; Letter writing**
**Business libraries**
  *x* Libraries, Business
  *xx* **Libraries; Libraries, Special**
Business machines. *See* **Office equipment and supplies**
Business schools. *See* **Business education**
**Busing (School integration)** (May subdiv. geog. state or city)
  *x* Racial balance in schools; School busing; School integration
  *xx* **Segregation in education**
**Butter**
  *See also* **Margarine**
  *xx* **Dairy products; Dairying; Milk**
Butter, Artificial. *See* **Margarine**
**Butterflies**
  *See also* **Caterpillars; Moths**
  *x* Cocoons; Lepidoptera
  *xx* **Caterpillars; Insects; Moths**
**Buttons**
  *xx* **Clothing and dress**
Buyers' guides. *See* **Consumer education; Shopping**
**Buying**
  Use for works on buying by government agencies and commercial and industrial enterprises. Works on buying by the consumer are entered under **Consumer education; Shopping.** See notes under these headings
  *See also* **Consumer education; Instalment plan; Shopping**
  *x* Purchasing
  *xx* **Consumer education; Industrial management; Shopping**

Below x Purchasing is a line beginning with an xx. This is to suggest related terms, which if also used as subject headings in the catalog should have references made from them to BUYING, so that attention may be called to all related subjects. Such a reference from one heading that is used to another that is used is called a see also reference. Sunset's Garden and Patio Building would have subject entries in the catalog under GREENHOUSES; LANDSCAPE GARDEN-ING; and PATIOS. There would be see also references from related headings; for instance, LANDSCAPE ARCHITECTURE, see also LANDSCAPE GARDENING, if there were other books in the catalog under LANDSCAPE ARCHITECTURE.

Proper names are generally not included in subject heading lists. Names of persons and of organizations are the subject headings for material about the person or organization. The form of the name to be used for the subject heading is determined from the rules in chapters 3 and 4. For instance, Hesketh Pearson's Dizzy, the Life and Personality of Benjamin Disraeli would have as its subject heading DISRAELI, BENJAMIN; and a history of Yale University would have as its subject heading YALE UNIVERSITY. While this type of heading is not found in printed lists, Sears does include JESUS CHRIST because of the unique subdivisions required, and SHAKESPEARE in order to provide a model for subdivisions which can be used for similarly prolific and important authors. Names of places are also omitted from most printed lists, with the exception of a few which are included for the purpose of serving as examples for subdivisions under geographic names.

There are several other broad classes of headings within which the cataloger is permitted to supply the specific name. When using Sears, battles, birds, fish, etc. are examples of such categories. Thus, although the term SHARKS does not appear in Sears, it--rather than FISHES--should be used as the subject heading for a book about sharks. Whatever printed list is adopted by a library, the cataloger must study the prefatory material and directions very carefully before beginning to use the list.

## SUBJECT CROSS REFERENCES

In deciding upon subject headings, as explained before, sometimes it is found that there are two or more different terms that might be used for the same subject. For example, which is better, AVIATION or AERONAUTICS? MARIONETTES or PUPPETS? COUNSELING or GUIDANCE? Unless there is some very good reason for not doing so, one should always use the heading given in the subject heading list adopted by the library. If one looks up these groups of terms in Sears,

the choices will be AERONAUTICS, COUNSELING, PUPPETS
AND PUPPET PLAYS. However, some persons who will
use the catalog will undoubtedly look under the terms AVIA-
TION, GUIDANCE, and MARIONETTES. When they find
nothing, will they think of the other terms? They may not.
Therefore, adopt one of these terms and refer from the other; e.g. use COUNSELING and refer from GUIDANCE. The
lists of subject headings not only suggest headings to be used
but list synonymous and related terms from which it is wise
to refer.

Some librarians do not consider see also references
necessary for the small library's catalog and do not make
them. Other librarians feel that they are needed especially
in the small catalog, since the collection is limited, and that
all material on related subjects should be brought to the in-
quirer's attention. The choice must take into account the
budget for technical services versus that for reference services and the sophistication of the library's clientele. The
optimum balance between user satisfaction and economy has
to determine the cataloging policies of any given library. If
a library chooses to make the minimum number of cross
references, a copy of its subject heading list should be kept
at the card catalog for consultation.

Most see references are made at the time that the subject heading to which they refer is first used, since they are
synonyms for the heading decided upon. One should avoid
making too many references for the small catalog. It is not
desirable to make see references from terms not in the vo-
cabulary of the public; for example, one would not refer
from CHASE, THE or GUNNING to HUNTING, or from HABI-
TATION, HUMAN to HOUSES, even though they are suggested
in Sears, unless the public using the library in question
might be likely to look under chase or gunning or habitations.
One need not make a card DUNGEONS see PRISONS if the
book to be entered under PRISONS has nothing in it on dungeons.

Before making see also's one should consider the following questions:

- Does the catalog have material under the term referred
  from?
- Is the term suggested for a reference one which anyone
  is likely to use?
- Is there material in the book on the topic that this refer-

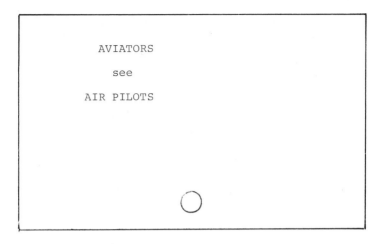

Card 8.   See reference card

Card 9.   See also reference card

ence term suggests?  For example, does the book on pantomimes have anything on the ballet?  If it has, make a reference from BALLET.

It is true that after a reference is once made from

one subject to another, there is no way of telling which of
the books actually covers that phase of the subject except by
examining the books. To revert to the example above, if
there is a card in the catalog which reads BALLET, see
also PANTOMIMES, the reader turns to PANTOMIMES and
there, among several books on the subject, finds upon examination one or more which contains something on the ballet,
and is satisfied. But if, on the other hand, he turns to the
subject PANTOMIMES and finds a few books, none of which
has the slightest reference to ballet, he may lose faith in
the catalog.

Thus a catalog may be made much more useful by the
wise and restricted use of see and see also references, since
the first subject the reader thinks of may not be exactly the
same as the term used for a heading for that subject in the
catalog. References, especially see also references, should
be made sparingly, as it is annoying to turn card after card
and find only see so and so, or see also so and so.

Another and a slightly different kind of reference is
the so-called general reference card (see card 10). In

```
          MANNERS AND CUSTOMS

              see also

          names of ethnic groups, countries,
          cities, etc. with the subdivision
          SOCIAL LIFE AND CUSTOMS, e.g.

          U.S. - SOCIAL LIFE AND CUSTOMS


                    ◯
```

Card 10.  General reference card

Sears, in the list of see also's under MANNERS AND CUS-
TOMS is found: "... also names of ethnic groups, countries,
cities, etc., with the subdivision Social life and customs, e.g.,

U. S. --SOCIAL LIFE AND CUSTOMS. " This sort of reference
is very useful in a catalog and saves much duplication, as
otherwise it would be necessary to list on a reference card
a heading for each individual country with the subdivision
SOCIAL LIFE AND CUSTOMS.

Keep down the number of cross references. Be sure
that no reference leads to a heading not in the catalog. Do
not make a see also reference from a subject on which there
is no material, but wait until there is material on that subject.
On the other hand, one may make temporary see references.
For example, in order that the reader may find the small
amount of material on the ballet that is included in the book
on pantomime, one may make a temporary card, BALLET
see PANTOMIMES. Later, if there is a card with the heading BALLET, the reference card may be changed to read
"see also. "

OTHER AIDS FOR SUBJECT HEADINGS

Appendix C contains information on where to find
lists of subject headings for special subjects. Even small
public libraries and school libraries will have material on
subjects not included in general lists nor authorized by them.
This is especially true of new subjects which are constantly
developing, such as Watergate, or aspects of older subjects
in which there is a sudden revival of interest, such as Art
Deco or Bermuda Triangle. The subject headings used in
general and special periodical indexes, bibliographies of special subjects, and the terms in general and special encyclopedias will be found very helpful in determining the wording
for such headings. First be sure that no term in the regular list meets the need, then look in the authorities mentioned for the best possible term.

Great care should be taken in the use of indexes coming out at regular intervals, e. g. The Booklist, the supplements to the Wilson Standard Catalogs, the various periodical
indexes, since these lists can best serve their purpose by
changing their headings to suit the latest development of the
subjects. If a heading in a catalog is changed, all the cards
with that heading should be changed.

To illustrate how the various aids may vary, take the
subject of Watergate. Readers' Guide in 1972 introduced the
headings WATERGATE INCIDENT, 1972 and WATERGATE

TRIAL, but the cumulative 1973/74 issue uses WATERGATE CASE.  LC uses WATERGATE AFFAIR, 1972-, as does the Public Library Catalog, but Sears 10th edition does not have any heading for this subject.  The library which uses Sears but wishes to introduce a heading for Watergate in its catalog must anticipate which form of the heading Sears is most likely to adopt in its next edition.  Since the trend has been for Sears to follow LC whenever possible, it would probably be wise to adopt LC's form of the heading.  A phone call to a nearby larger library which uses LC is a quick and economical way to find out what the LC wording is.

## CHECKING LISTS OF SUBJECT HEADINGS FOR TRACING

When a heading is decided upon for the first time, it is checked in the list of subject headings to show that it has been adopted for entry.  Note the check mark (✓) before WATERWAYS in the section from Sears reproduced below. In this way the librarian can tell which subject headings have been used without referring to the catalog.  This is a great convenience, and care should be taken that each subject heading is checked the first time it is used.  In cases where there is no suitable heading in the adopted list and a heading is selected from some other source, this heading is written in the printed list of subject headings in its alphabetical place.  The sample from Sears shows the subject heading WATERGATE AFFAIR, 1972- written in.

As subject headings used for the catalog are checked in the list, so also are subject references used in the catalog. This shows the librarian which of the references have been made.  If it is decided to discontinue a heading in the catalog, this checked list will be a guide in removing the reference to that heading.

The rule is:  Mark with a check (✓) at the left the subject heading used and the references which have been made to it; turn to each reference in its regular alphabetical place and check it and the subject heading used.  The checks on the page reproduced from Sears indicate that there are entries in the catalog under WATER SUPPLY and that a reference has been made from WATERWORKS.

✔ Water skiing
   ✔ *x* Skiing, Water
   *xx* Skiis and skiing
Water sports
   *See also* Boats and boating; Canoes and
      canoeing; Diving; Fishing; Rowing;
      Sailing; Skin diving; Surfing; Swim-
      ming; Yachts and Yachting; and
      names of other water sports
   *x* Aquatic sports
   *xx* Sports
✔ Water supply
   *See also* Aqueducts; Dams; Forest influ-
      ences; Irrigation; Reservoirs; Water
      — Pollution; Water — Purification;
      Water conservation; Wells; also
      names of cities with the subdivision
      *Water supply,* e.g. Chicago—Water
      supply; etc.
   *x* Waterworks
   *xx* Civil engineering; Municipal engineer-
      ing; Natural resources; Public
      health; Public utilities; Reservoirs;
      Sanitary engineering; Sanitation;
      Water—Pollution; Water conserva-
      tion; Water resources development;
      Wells
Water supply engineering
   *See also* Boring; Hydraulic engineering
   *xx* Engineering; Hydraulic engineering
Watering places. *See* Health resorts, spas, etc.
✔ Waterways
   Use for general works on rivers, lakes,
      canals as highways for transportation
      or commerce
   *See also* Canals; Inland navigation;
      Lakes; Rivers
   *xx* Transportation
✔ Waterworks. *See* Water supply

*[handwritten annotations in right margin:]*
✓ Watergate affair, 1972–
✓ xx Presidents – U.S.
   Election
✓ xx Corruption (in
   politics)

## ADAPTING SUBJECT HEADINGS

As discussed above, it is sometimes necessary to introduce headings for new subjects now included in the latest
edition of the list used by the library. There may be other
reasons for modifying the official list, however. For example, a library which serves children may find that the young
user often does not "think Sears"--a child who wants a book
about World War I will look under that heading, not EURO-
PEAN WAR, and the one who wants to learn about secret

codes is not likely to look under CRYPTOGRAPHY. Another problem is that many people find standard headings such as NEGROES or WOMEN AS AUTHORS racist or sexist. Fortunately, Sears now provides an appendix of alternate Black subject headings (see card 11), and LC is beginning to revise some of the terminology which has caused complaints.

```
301.45
BAL        Baldwin, James
              Notes of a native son.   Dial,
           1963.
              158 p.




              1. Blacks   2. U.S.--Race relations
           3. Europe--Race relations
```

Card 11.   Subject heading assigned from Sears alternate list
           of Black headings

Nevertheless, library literature abounds with criticism of the many biased or merely esoteric headings which remain in effect. [5] Because the small library frequently depends on centralized or commercial cataloging, it faces a serious problem when it discovers that certain subject headings are a disservice rather than an aid to library users. If cards are to be changed, additional staff time--and consequently, funds--must be spent. These costs must be weighed against the negative impression created by offensive headings or lack of access to materials caused by unfamiliar terms. A library may find that while it cannot afford to give personal assistance to every catalog user, it can manage to make at least those adjustments in subject headings which will best serve its particular clientele.

An excellent source of suggestions for alternate headings is Hennepin County Public Library's Cataloging Bulletin. [6] Using this on a regular basis to modify the library's official list occasionally, or at least to add extra see references, should not be prohibitively expensive and may prove to be a good investment in better access to materials and improved public relations. Card 12, below, is an example of a printed card modified for local use by changing the LC subject headings to Sears headings. If a patron were to look under the term HEALTH, which is not used by Sears, a cross reference from HEALTH CARE to MEDICAL CARE would lead the searcher to Lee's book.

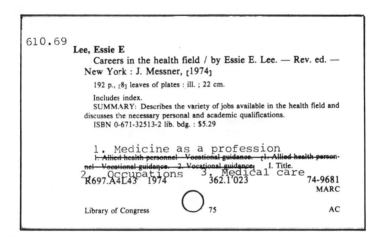

Card 12. Printed LC card; Sears subject headings substituted for LC headings

SUBJECT AUTHORITY FILE

Instead of checking a printed list of subject headings, the special library for which no single printed list is adequate may have a subject authority file on cards. This type of file has one card for each subject heading used in the catalog, and on this card is a record of all references made to that subject. When a subject heading is not taken from an adopted printed list of headings, the source is given on the card. There is also a card corresponding to each reference card in the catalog. Cards 13-16 are sample subject authority cards.

The scope or explanatory note such as that given below

some headings in Sears, e.g. under BUYING (see p. 48) in
the paragraph beginning "Use for works ... ", may be entered
on the subject authority card. The paragraph beginning See
also does not need to be given on the authority card, as its
use is in deciding whether to use this heading or one of those
suggested. When the question comes up again as to whether
to use a certain heading, the original source may be consulted. Likewise, only the see and see also references which
are made for the catalog are listed on the authority card.
In other words, in choosing a heading, a printed list is used
for its scope notes, see also's, and its suggested references
to that subject. The authority file is used to show which
headings have been used and which references have been made
to them. If all suggested references were put on the authority card it would be necessary to check those which had been
made.

```
Buying

           Refer from
     x Purchasing
     xx Consumer education




                        ◯
```

Card 13.    Subject authority card

The reference cards in the subject authority file are
made exactly as those for the catalog, except that the subject headings are not in full capitals. Subject headings in
the public card catalog need to be distinguished in some way
from other headings for the convenience of users. In most
catalogs, full capitals are used for this purpose. As the
subject authority file is only for the use of the librarian,
the terms are given with only the first letter of each heading

or subheading capitalized. Cards 15 and 16 are sample reference cards for the subject authority file.

```
Watergate affair, 1972-        (LC, 8th ed.)

              Refer from
       xx Corruption (in politics)
       xx Political crimes and offenses
```

Card 14.   Subject authority card showing source of heading

```
              Purchasing

                 see

           Buying
```

Card 15.   See reference card for subject authority file

The major advantages of a subject authority file on
cards are that it is always up to date, it gives space in the

proper alphabetical place for new subjects and for headings chosen from other sources, and that it saves having to transfer information from one printed list to another when a new edition comes out.  In view of the work entailed in the preparation of an authority file on cards, these advantages apply primarily to the special library whose area of concentration would require the addition of many specialized headings not included in printed lists of subject headings.  For most other libraries, use of a printed list such as Sears or LC as an authority file is the method to be preferred.

```
        Corruption (in politics)

        see also

      Political crimes and offenses
      Watergate affair, 1972-




                    ◯
```

Card 16.   See also reference card for subject authority file

Even when a library relies on a centralized or commercial source for most of its cataloging, it is necessary to know when a heading is being used for the first time in that library's catalog, so that see and see also references can be considered.  This does not require the time-consuming process of checking the headings on all cards received against the printed list or other authority file.  Instead, it can be accomplished in connection with filing the cards in the catalog. Since both filer and reviser must check the catalog card which comes before, and the one which comes after each new card to be filed, a subject entry can be put aside for checking whenever it constitutes a heading which is not duplicated on the card before or after.

## References

1.  Sears List of Subject Headings. 10th ed. , edited by
    Barbara M. Westby (New York: H. W. Wilson Co. ,
    1972).

2.  Eloise Rue and Effie LaPlante, Subject Headings for
    Children's Materials (Chicago: American Library
    Association, 1952).

3.  U.S. Library of Congress, Library of Congress Subject
    Headings. 8th ed. (Washington, D. C. : Library of
    Congress, Subject Cataloging Division, 1975), 2v.

4.  Included in Library of Congress Subject Headings, but
    also available separately: Subject Headings for Chil-
    dren's Literature. 2d ed. ; reprinted from Library of
    Congress Subject Headings, 8th ed. (Washington, D. C. :
    Library of Congress, Cataloging Distribution Service
    Division, 1975).

5.  Sanford Berman, Prejudices and Antipathies; a Tract on
    the LC Heads Concerning People (Metuchen, N. J. :
    Scarecrow Press, 1971).

6.  Hennepin County Public Library, Cataloging Bulletin
    (Edina, MN: Hennepin County Public Library, Tech-
    nical Services Division, bimonthly).

# CHAPTER 3

## PERSONAL NAME ENTRIES

This chapter is concerned with the names of persons as authors or subjects and the choice of the different forms for the headings in the catalog. The catalog presents a comprehensive display of the works of an author and the different editions of those works which are in the particular library. The form of the author's name used as the heading is very important, as it determines its location in the catalog. As the majority of books are written by persons (as opposed to corporations or committees, that is), one's first concern is with how to enter a personal author in a catalog. And in order that all of the material by or about one person may be brought together, the first step in cataloging is to decide upon the name and its form. This is done, when the form is not immediately apparent, by looking in printed catalogs and lists to see how the person's works are usually entered and consequently how they are known.

Even in cataloging the smallest collection, it will soon be discovered that all authors do not have simple names, such as George Bernard Shaw; and even if they have, they may publish one book as Bernard Shaw, another as George Bernard Shaw, and a third as G. Bernard Shaw. In that case, the obvious thing to do in order that all entries for books by or about the same person may come together in the catalog is to find out how the person's name most frequently appears on the title pages of his works, and then to use that form. If other forms of the name are rather well known, a reference can be made from them, i. e. , a card or cards giving other forms can direct the reader to the form of the name used.

Many libraries--large, scholarly libraries, such as university libraries and the Library of Congress, as well as the smaller public and school libraries--have adopted the policy of using the form of the name usually found on the title page of the author's works. Such cataloging aids as the H. W. Wilson Standard Catalogs have done likewise.

Usage, as shown in biographical dictionaries, encyclopedias, publishers' catalogs, is important and should be considered when deciding upon the form of a name. Printed aids, as, for instance, the Standard Catalogs, may change the form of name used merely by changing it in the next published issue. But if a library decides to change the form of a name already used in its catalog, either a reference must be made from the form formerly used to the form to be used, or all the entries for that name must be changed. Women authors marry and may use their husbands' names for later works, while some authors use pseudonyms for some works but not for others.

For most of its books, the library will buy printed catalog cards, or it may now (or in the future) participate in a cooperative cataloging center which supplies the catalog cards along with the books, or it may subscribe for such service from a commercial firm. In these cases the library will want to use the form of name used on the printed cards. A very small number of changes to conform with local practice would be reasonable, but numerous changes would defeat the whole purpose and economy of using such valuable sources. Having considered these factors, the next question is what to do about the names for books to be cataloged locally.

An investigation of any miscellaneous group of books shows quite a variety of kinds of names, and librarians have sought to simplify the task of locating them in the catalog by formulating rules to cover the points most often met. The basic authority is the Anglo-American Cataloging Rules (AACR)[1] jointly prepared and kept up to date by the library associations of the United States, Canada, and Great Britain.


BASIC RULE

According to AACR, the title page or its substitute is the normal source used to determine how a work is to be entered in a catalog. Outside sources can be used if a work is published anonymously or if there is reason to distrust the statements in the work itself.

> Enter a person under the name by which he is commonly identified, whether it is his real name, assumed name, nickname, title of nobility, or other appellation.... The form of a name of an author, editor, translator, etc., is ordinarily determined from the way it appears in his works.... [2]

Adoption of this rule represents a significant triumph of common sense in the evolution of library cataloging practice. Prior to the mid-1960s, extensive detective work was required to determine the true legal name of an author, in total disregard for the name he or she chose to use on the title page. The main result of all this expense and delay was that the library patron seeking, for example, a novel by Pearl Buck would find none of her books in the "B" section of the fiction shelves. If that patron had the patience to consult the catalog rather than simply leave the building in frustration, just possibly a cross reference would lead to the discovery that librarians, united against the world, had established "Sydenstricker, Mrs. Pearl" as the only proper place of entry for Pearl Buck's books.

Some authors are not commonly identified in their works by one particular name. If it is desirable to establish one form of entry, the name most familiar to the reading public is the logical choice. But if there is doubt, the following order of preference is suggested: 1) under the name by which the author is generally identified in reference sources; 2) under the name most frequently given in the author's works; 3) under the latest name used. For example, one would use Windsor, Edward, Duke of--not Edward VIII, King of Great Britain.

PSEUDONYMS

If all of an author's works appear under one pseudonym, use it. For example:

> Eliot, George
>     Refer from:  Cross, Mary Ann Evans
>
> If the works of an author appear under several pseudonyms or under his real name and one or more pseudonyms, enter him under the name by which he is primarily identified in modern editions of his works and in reference sources.[3]

For example, enter under Stendhal and refer from Beyle, Marie Henri and from Bombet, Louis Alexandre César. Although Stendhal is the name which most often appears on the title page of The Red and the Black or The Charterhouse of Parma, these works have been published in numerous editions, sometimes under the writer's real name, Beyle. Also, some of his lesser known novels bear only his real name. So, if each book is cataloged and shelved in strict conformity to the information on the title page--which is the rule to be followed in nearly all cases--Stendhal's books as well as his catalog entries would appear in two different places, and the student who knew only one of the names might find only some of the books. It is best in such cases to establish one form of entry and provide an appropriate cross reference in the catalog. In fact, since many borrowers go straight to the shelves, especially for fiction, the library wishing to give the best service to its patrons will use book dummies or other shelf marking devices to refer users to the correct section for Stendhal, Twain, O. Henry, Lewis Carroll, and other major writers whose works are frequently sought.

On the other hand, the mystery writer John Creasey has written over 500 books under half a dozen or more pseudonyms. The time and cost involved should prohibit changing the lettering on the spine of each of his books so as to shelve them together. Moreover, this would not be a very helpful service to the library's patrons, who will inevitably look under the name by which the book is advertised, that is, the name on the title page. Even the usual cross references in the catalog are unnecessary in cases of this sort, although one general guide card under Creasey might point out that "this author has also used the names Ashe, Gordon; Halliday, Michael; ... " etc. Similarly, Ellery Queen is a well known joint pseudonym for Frederic Dannay and Manfred Lee. But Queen is the name under which virtually all library users will look, and reference from the real names are unnecessary. While general rules of cataloging are extremely helpful and enable the cataloger to make books quickly available instead of having to worry at length about the "right" form of entry, the rules are only guidelines, and should not be followed so slavishly that the catalog becomes filled with unnecessary, redundant, and confusing entries. Every rule of cataloging must pass this test: will it really help the library user?

LENGTHY NAMES

If the forms of name appearing in the works of an author vary in fullness, in most cases the fullest of these should be used. James Fenimore Cooper should not be reduced to James Cooper, but Joseph Hilaire Pierre Belloc will be found without difficulty if only Hilaire Belloc, the name by which he is primarily known, is used. Refer from the full name if anyone is likely to look under it, especially if the first name has been omitted. In any case, the forthcoming revision of AACR is likely to recommend entry under the most common form of a name, certainly a sensible step from the point of view of patron service.

Initials should be spelled out if necessary to distinguish two or more persons. A first forename represented by an initial should always be spelled out if the surname is a common one, e.g., for D. H. Lawrence, spell out the first names so that the entry reads Lawrence, David Herbert but refer from Lawrence, D. H., because many people will look under the initials first. If further differentiation is required, add the person's dates of birth and death:

> Adams, Charles Francis, 1807-1886
> Adams, Charles Francis, 1835-1915
> Adams, Charles Francis, 1866-1954

## COMPOUND SURNAMES

Use the form by which the person prefers to be known. If in doubt, use the form in which the name is listed in reference sources:

> Lloyd George, David
> Refer from:  George, David Lloyd

If the elements of the surname are hyphenated, even occasionally, enter under the first:

> Day-Lewis, Cecil
> Refer from:  Lewis, Cecil Day

In other cases of names known to be compound surnames the entry element is determined by normal usage in the language of the person involved:

> García Lorca, Federico
> Refer from:  Lorca, Federico García

References should be made from the other part if it is at all likely that anyone would look under it.

## SURNAMES WITH PREFIXES

The practice most common in the person's own language should determine the form of entry. Standard reference works are the best sources for examples, but the following are some of the most frequently encountered:

Dutch and Flemish: Enter under the part of the name following the prefix, except when the prefix is ver:

> Ver Boven, Daisy
> Gogh, Vincent Van

English: Enter under the prefix:

> De Quincey, Thomas
> De Voto, Bernard
> La Farge, Oliver
> Du Maurier, Daphne
> Van Buren, Martin

French: If the prefix consists of an article or of a contraction of an article and a preposition, enter under the prefix:

> Du Chaillu, Paul
> Le Rouge, Gustave

If the prefix consists of a preposition or of a preposition followed by an article, enter under the part of the name following the preposition:

> La Fontaine, Jean de
> Musset, Alfred de

German: If the prefix consists of an article or of a contraction of a preposition and an article, enter under the prefix:

> Vom Ende, Erich

If the prefix consists of a preposition or a preposition followed by an article, enter under the part of the name following the prefix:

> Goethe, Wolfgang von
> Mühll, Peter von der

Italian: In general, enter under the prefix:

Da Ponte, Lorenzo

However, in the case of medieval and early modern Italian names, de, de', degli, dei, and de li are rarely construed as prefixes:

Medici, Lorenzo de'

Portuguese: Enter under the part of the name following the prefix:

Fonseca, Martinho Augusto da

Scandinavian: Enter under the part of the name following the prefix:

Linné, Carl von

Spanish: Enter under the part of the name following the prefix, except when the prefix consists only of an article:

Cervantes Saavedra, Miguel de
Gama, Vasco da
Las Heras, Manuel Antonio

References may be made under the various prefixes explaining how names with such prefixes are entered in the catalog.

## TITLES OF NOBILITY, HONOR, ADDRESS, ETC.

The practice of adding titles of rank and honor to authors' names is a painless one if cards are purchased from the Library of Congress or some other such source. But for the small library the task of establishing correct titles can be a difficult and an unnecessary one. Admittedly, an author's claim to title may be the sole basis for any public interest in a book by or about him, in which case it may be a valid public service for the catalog to point out that this is Lady Beverley Blowser, so that readers may know at once that this is the eccentric heiress who rents out her servants for laboratory experiments and not just some common Beverley Blowser. But unless the noble person uses his "title" on the title page, or would be confused with others of like name, the small library can spare itself the trouble of de-

termining whether so-and-so is now an earl or still a lowly
baron.


FORENAME ENTRIES

Sometimes a title of nobility or similar descriptive is
necessary, as in the case of a person whose name does not
include a surname, such as King Alfred or Pope Innocent.
A person whose name does not include a surname and who is
not primarily identified by a title of nobility should be entered
under the part of his name by which he is primarily identified
in reference sources.    Include any secondary name acquired
informally, e. g. , John the Baptist.    But, add after the name
any identifying word or phrase that is commonly associated
with the name, but which cannot be regarded as an integral
part of it:

> Joseph, Nez Percé chief.
> Clovis, King of the Franks
> Gustav I Vasa, King of Sweden
> Mary, consort of George V. King of Great Britain
> Constantine I, Emperor of Rome
>     Refer from:   Constantine, Saint
> Francis of Assisi, Saint
> Augustine, Saint, Bp
> Gregory I, Pope
>     Refer from:   Gregory, Saint, Pope Gregory I
>                   Gregory the Great, Pope
> Clement VIII, Antipope
> Bessarion, Cardinal
> Newman, John Henry, Cardinal
> Dositheos, Patriarch of Jerusalem
> Gregorius, Abp of Corinth

Occasionally people who do have surnames (or their equiva-
lents) are generally referred to by their first names by both
the public and many reference sources, e. g. , Michelangelo
Buonarroti.    While LC enters him under Buonarroti, most
library users look under Michelangelo.

If LC printed cards are used, they must be adapted
or cross reference cards must be made for the catalog.

CLASSICAL NAMES

Enter under the form of name most commonly used in reference sources, e. g. :

Cicero, Marcus Tullius
Horace

CONCLUSIONS

When a cataloger is uncertain of the correct form of a name, it is best to consult a reference source such as a biographical dictionary, encyclopedia, or other standard authority. One reliable aid should suffice, provided that the aid gives the full name and does not suggest other forms. If other forms are indicated, several aids have to be consulted in order to decide which form to use.

Where one form is as well known as the other, choose one and always use it. A few authors use their real names for one type of writing and a pseudonym or pseudonyms for other types. Ray Stannard Baker wrote under his own name except when writing his essays, for which he used the pseudonym David Grayson. In some libraries his books are entered in the catalog under both his real name and his pseudonym, his essays under Grayson, his other works under Baker, with see also references connecting the two. For the small library it would seem better to put all his works under his own name and refer from Grayson, David, pseud. , but where printed cards or cooperative cataloging services are used, consistency with the policy followed by these sources should be maintained by the library.

There may be cases where the cataloger does not know whether the name is real or a pseudonym. Consider it a real name. If later it proves to be a pseudonym, add the abbreviation pseud. to the name as given in the catalog and make a reference from the real name.

Some libraries find it useful to have authors' dates of birth and death included in the heading on the catalog card:

Cather, Willa Sibert, 1876-1947
Bennett, Arnold, 1876-1931

In a number of schools the pupils are required to know the

dates of birth and death of the authors on whose works they
report. Where bibliographical tools are few, it can be convenient for both pupils and librarians to have these dates on
the catalog cards. The librarian, in looking up the forms of
the name for the heading in the catalog, may note the dates
and include them in the heading. If the dates are not readily
found, they may be omitted and added later. However, dates
are essential only for the identification of different persons
whose names are the same.

## AUTHORITY FILE FOR NAMES

Some librarians, especially in special libraries, may
find it convenient to have an authority file for the names used
in their catalogs. The librarian may decide to enter all of
Elizabeth Janet Gray's books under Vining, Elizabeth Gray.
A card would then be made using the adopted form as heading. It would be followed by the title of one of the books
to identify the author, by a list of the authorities consulted
in deciding on that form, and by a note indicating a reference
from the other form of the name. After an author's name
has been established, all that is necessary when a book is
added is to look in the authority file for names, note the
form adopted, be sure it is the same person, and use that
form for the new title.

The items and form for the cards in this file may be
described as follows: 1) The heading on the name authority
card is the one adopted for the catalog. 2) The title is that
of the first book by that author cataloged for that library and
serves to identify him. 3) The date is the copyright date
(if no copyright date, the imprint or some other date) of that
book, as found on the back of the title page, preceded by the
word "copyright" and given on the card as [c1952]. 4) The
abbreviations are for the bibliographical and biographical aids
in which the librarian looked. 5) An n to the left of the abbreviation for the name of an aid means that the author's
name was found in that aid; a t means that the title was found.
6) If the author's dates of birth and death are included in
the heading, a d may be added to indicate that the date or
dates were found. 7) If the form of the name in the aid
differs from that given in the heading on this card, or if the
date differs, the variant form is put in parentheses after the
abbreviation for the aid. 8) If references are made from
other forms of the name, they are indicated on the line or
lines directly above the hole in the card, preceded by an x,
the symbol for a see reference.

```
        Vining, Elizabeth (Gray) 1902-
          Windows for the Crown Prince.
        [c1952]

    ntd C. B. I. 1943-1948 (Gray, Elizabeth
          Janet (Mrs. Morgan Vining)
    nt Bklist v.48




          x Gray, Elizabeth Janet
```

Card 17.   Name authority card for person as author

---

If the name is not that of the author of the book, but the subject or the illustrator, for example, it is given above the author's name and is indented farther to the right.   To the left of the author's name is given an abbreviation which stands for the relation of the name in the heading to the book. The form is shown in card 18, the authority card for Henry Hudson, subject of James Maurice Scott's biography.   The

```
          Hudson, Henry, d. 1611.
    subj. Scott, James Maurice, 1906-
          Hudson of Hudson's Bay.   1951.

      n Amer. ency. 1951 ed.
    ntd Std. cat. for h.s. libs. 6th ed.
    nd Webster's dict. (? - 1611)
```

Card 18.   Name authority card for person as added entry

abbreviation subj. indicates that Hudson is the subject of this book. The remainder of the card would have exactly the same form as the card for Vining. The aids would be those consulted for Hudson. There would be another authority card for the heading Scott, James Maurice, the same form as card 17.

The name authority file may have an authority card for every name used as a heading in the catalog whether as author, subject, illustrator, or in any other capacity, or only for those names requiring cross references.

If the library uses printed cards, which are discussed in chapter 12, and is able to get them for practically all of its books, it is best to use the form of the name given on the printed card; thus an authority file for names would be unnecessary. If a special library's collection, however, is of such a nature as to include many works by authors with complicated names--foreign names, for instance--and there are no printed cards for many of them, a name authority file will be found to save time. It records, once and for all, the form of name to be used, the information obtained in establishing the form of name, and the references to it which have been filed in the catalog.

If the library is small and the catalog is near the desk, a name authority file is not necessary; the catalog it-self may be the authority file. If this plan is followed, when references are made from other forms of the name than that adopted, either a special file of name references must be maintained or these references must be noted on the first main card for that author; when that card is withdrawn, the tracing of the references must be transferred to another main card, and so on.

The value of an authority file for names depends upon: 1) whether or not printed cards are used; 2) whether or not the names to be entered are so complicated that any one of a number of different forms might be used; 3) whether there are one or more references from other forms to be recorded; 4) the distance from the desk of the cataloger to the catalog.

## References

1.  Anglo-American Cataloging Rules, North American Text

(Chicago, American Library Association, 1970).

2. Ibid. , p. 73.

3. Ibid. , p. 74-75.

CHAPTER 4


CORPORATE NAME ENTRIES


There is a kind of publication for whose contents no
single individual is responsible; examples include the publications of societies, institutions, business firms, churches,
governments and their agencies, and conferences. Among
such publications are: Annual Report of the Board of Regents
of the Smithsonian Institution, Journal of the National Education Association of the United States, Collections of the State
Historical Society of Wisconsin, Handbook of the Layton Art
Gallery. Are not the Smithsonian, NEA, State Historical
Society of Wisconsin, and the Layton Art Gallery the authors
of these publications? Since this is so, the works are entered in the catalog under their authors' names in the same
way as are other works.

Just as personal names upon closer observation group
themselves into certain classes--simple surnames, compound
surnames, names with prefixes, etc. , so corporate names
may be grouped as subordinate and related bodies; geographical names; governments, government bodies and officials;
conferences, congresses, meetings, etc. ; religious bodies
and officials; radio and television stations.

In determining the proper entry for corporate bodies,
several factors must be considered. For instance, is the
work of a subordinate unit to be entered directly under the
specific unit or under the parent body? What is the proper
entry for legislative decrees of the chief executive as opposed
to legislative enactments; for a constitution of a state; for
texts of a religious observance?

Cataloging the publications of corporate bodies can be
very difficult and time-consuming. Of course, in comparison
with clearcut works of personal authorship, institutional publications will account for only a small percentage of a general
library's acquisitions. On the other hand, these are precisely
the kinds of materials for which printed cards or other cata-

loging aids are frequently found to be unavailable. In the
back rooms of small libraries--and even some not so small
ones--one can often discover numbers of annual reports,
government documents, and other elusive corporate publications which have been waiting so long for someone to figure
out what to do with them that they have become rather out
of date.

Since many of these publications arrive as unsolicited
gifts, the first question to be asked is whether the library
really has any particular need for such-and-such an item.
A "free" publication does not long remain so if several dol-
lars in staff time are spent in researching the proper way
to catalog it. The next question to be asked is whether a
publication which seems worth keeping really needs to be
cataloged. Many reports of institutions and government agencies are better suited to the pamphlet file. If the library
has a business section, annual reports filed alphabetically in
pamphlet boxes or displayed like periodicals may be of even
greater use than if they are fully cataloged. If either topic
or format suggests a short life-span, then such alternatives
to full cataloging should certainly be considered. For publications of corporate authorship which must be cataloged
locally, guidelines adapted from AACR are offered in this
chapter. However, a library with a collection devoted to a
special subject such as law or religion is more likely to en-
counter large numbers of corporate publications than is the
small general library, and therefore even the smallest special library will find these guidelines insufficient and will
need to use the complete AACR.

## FORMS OF ENTRY

A corporate body may be entered directly under its
name, as a subheading of the higher body of which it is a
part, as a subheading of the government of which it is an
agency, or as a subheading of the name of the place in which
it is located. Whether the entry is to be direct or indirect
depends upon how easily the name of the body provides unique
identification, and on its relationship, if any, with other
bodies. The most important consideration must be the form
under which library users will most readily find the entry.
As in the case of personal names, the form by which the
corporate body is predominantly known should be given pri-
ority.

Direct entry. A corporate body with a distinct identity, which is unlikely to be confused with any other body with a similar name, is entered directly under its own name:

> Bodleian Library
>> Refer from: Oxford University. Bodleian Library

but:

> Rutgers University. Graduate School of Library and Information Science

1. A subordinate unit of a corporate body is entered directly when it is responsible for a work rather than serving only as the information or publication agent for the parent body (again, only if the subordinate unit will not be confused with any other body):

> Title page:
>> Media programs: district and school. Prepared by the American Association of School Librarians, ALA

> Enter under:
>> American Association of School Librarians

2. A peace treaty or multilateral treaty other than a trilateral one is entered under the name by which it is known:

> Treaty of Paris, 1763
> Universal Copyright Convention

3. Religious bodies, other than local ones, are entered directly under their names:

> Catholic Church
> United Lutheran Church in America
> Church of England

4. Church councils which are ecumenical, interdenominational or Early Christian, and concordats with conventional names are entered directly under their names:

> Vatican Council, 2d, 1962-1965

5. Conferences, congresses, meetings of persons,

either as individuals or as representatives of various bodies, for the purpose of studying, discussing, or acting on a particular topic or topics, are entered under their names directly (i. e. , when there would otherwise be no corporate entity):

World Peace Congress, 1st, Paris and Prague, 1949

6. Joint committees, commissions, or other units made up of representatives of two or more corporate bodies are entered under the joint name:

Joint ILO/WHO Committee on Occupational Health
Refer from both International Labor Organization and World Health Organization

Entry under parent body. Corporate bodies which are a part of or are associated with another body are entered under their own names or under the other body's name according to the following rules:

1. If the responsibility of the subordinate unit for preparing the work is not stated prominently, or if the subordinate unit cannot be identified adequately by its name alone, enter the work under the parent body. Compare this rule with rule 1 under direct entry.

2. If two or three subordinate units are credited with responsibility for the work, enter it under the one indicated as primarily responsible; otherwise under the first one named. Make added entries for the other units if you think it helpful.

3. If authorship is divided among more than three subordinate units of the same parent body, enter under parent body.

4. Enter a subordinate body as a subheading under a higher body if:

a) Its name includes the name of the higher body:

British Museum. Trustees (Name: Trustees of the British Museum)
Harvard University. Law School (Name: Harvard Law School)

b) It is clearly a component part of something else:

New York University.  Division of Education
Columbia University.  Teachers College
Indiana University.  Audio-Visual Center

c)  Its name is so general that the name of the higher body is required for its identification:

Bell Telephone Laboratories.  Technical Information Library  (Name:  Technical Information Library)

5.  Omit units in the hierarchy of an organization which
are not needed for establishing the smaller body as a part of
the larger one:

American Library Association.  Cataloging and
Classification Section.  Bylaws Committee.
(Hierarchy:  American Library Association,
Resources and Technical Services Division,
Cataloging and Classification Section, Bylaws
Committee)

When in doubt about whether or not to include an intervening
unit, show the entire hierarchy.  There is a good possibility
that a future revision of AACR will call for full hierarchy,
at least for government documents.

6.  Enter a graduating class organization of an educational institution under the institution with a conventional-
ized subheading in the form of Class of (year):

Dartmouth College.  Class of 1880

7.  Enter a part of an American political party which
is below the national level under the name of the party followed by the name of the jurisdiction in parentheses.  Add
the specific name of the unit, omitting any superfluous words:

Democratic Party (Texas).  State Convention, Waco,
1857 (Name:  State Convention of the Democratic Party of the State of Texas)

Government entries.  The conventional name of a
country, province, state, county, municipality, or other political jurisdiction is used as the heading for its government,
unless the official name of the government is more familiar:

Massachusetts <u>not</u> Commonwealth of Massachusetts

1. Agencies: Agencies through which the basic legislative, judicial, and executive functions of government are exercised should be entered as subheadings of the heading for the government:

> U.S. Supreme Court
> Gt. Brit. Air Ministry. Lib.

Other bodies created or controlled by a government but which have distinct identities of their own should be entered directly under their own names. Cultural organizations, parks, authorities, and similar institutions fall in this category:

> National Science Foundation
> National Agricultural Library
> Veterans Administration Hospital, Durham, N.C.
> Mather Air Force Base
> Grand Teton National Park
> Houston Independent School District
> Minneapolis-St. Paul Sanitary District
> National Coal Board
> Tennessee Valley Authority
> Canadian National Railways
> Federal Reserve Bank of Richmond
> Church of England

2. Officials: The heading for a sovereign, president, other chief of state, or governor, consists of the title of his office followed by the inclusive years of his reign or incumbency and, in parentheses, by his name in brief form--all as a subheading under the name of the government. If the title varies with the incumbent (e.g., King and Queen) use a common designation of the office (e.g., Sovereign):

> Gt. Brit. Sovereign, 1936-1952 (George VI)
> U.S. President, 1946-1952 (Truman)

If, in addition to the heading for a chief of state, a heading is established for him as a person, make explanatory references under each heading:

> George VI, King of Great Britain, 1936-1952
>
>> Here are entered private communications, public speeches, and collections that include both private and official communications. For pub-

lications constituting official acts of the sovereign (e.g., messages to Parliament, proclamations, etc.,) see entries under

Gt. Brit. Sovereign, 1936-1952 (George VI)

When the heading applies to more than one incumbent, omit dates and names from the heading:

North Carolina. Governor

The heading for a head of government who is not also a chief of state consists of his title as a subheading under the government; dates and names are not included:

Gt. Brit. Prime Minister
Detroit. Mayor

The heading for any other government official is that of the ministry or agency which he represents:

U.S. General Accounting Office
Refer from: U.S. Comptroller General

3. Legislative bodies: If a legislature has more than one chamber, enter each as a subheading under the legislature:

U.S. Congress. Senate
Refer from: U.S. Senate

Enter committees and other subordinate units as subheadings under the legislature or of a particular chamber, as appropriate:

U.S. Congress. Joint Committee on the Library
U.S. Congress. House. Select Committee on Government Organization

Add the number and year for successive legislatures which are numbered consecutively, when the heading is for the body or chamber as a whole:

U.S. 89th Congress, 2d session 1966

4. Courts: Enter a court as a subheading under country, state, or other jurisdiction. Add the appropriate regional jurisdiction in parentheses when necessary:

> North Carolina. Supreme Court
> Vermont. Court of Chancery
> U.S. District Court (North Carolina, Eastern
> District)
> (Name: United States District Court for the
> Eastern District of North Carolina)

5. Armed forces: Enter each service as a direct subheading under the name of the government. Enter a component branch as a subheading under the service, unless its name begins with the name of the service or with an adjective derived from that name:

> U.S. Army. General Staff
> U.S. Marine Corps
> U.S. Navy. 7th Fleet
> U.S. Naval Air Transport Service
> U.S. Marine Corps. 2d Division (Name: 2d
> Marine Division)
> Canada. Army. Royal Canadian Army Medical
> Corps
> U.S. Army. Fifth Army
> U.S. Army. II Corps
> U.S. Army. 2d Engineer Combat Battalion
> New York (State) Militia
> New York (State) National Guard
> New York (State) Militia 9th Regiment Artillery
> (Name: 9th Regiment, New York State Artil-
> lery)
> U.S. Army. 83d New York Volunteers
> U.S. Army. 9th Regiment Infantry, New York
> Volunteers

6. Embassies, legations, etc.: Enter a continuing office representing the government of one country in another as a subheading under the name of the country represented. If the heading is for an embassy or legation, add, within parentheses, the name of the country to which it is accredited; if it is for a consulate or other local office, add the name of the city in which it is located:

> U.S. Legation (Bulgaria)
> Gt. Brit. Consulate, Cairo
> Australia. High Commissioner in London
> U.S. Mission to the United Nations

7. Laws: Enter legislative enactments and executive

decrees under the name of the jurisdiction, followed by the subheading Laws, statutes, etc. (for a country, state or province), or the subheading Ordinances, local laws, etc. (for a county or municipal jurisdiction):

> Title page:
>> The school law of Illinois... Prepared by T. A. Reynolds, Assistant Superintendent. Issued by John A. Wieland, Superintendent of Public Instruction. Amended by the Fifty-ninth General Assembly
>
> Enter under:
>> Illinois. Laws, statutes, etc.

Make an added entry for the Department of Instruction.

Enter administrative regulations under the promulgating agency, with an added entry under the jurisdictional heading for Laws, statutes, etc. :

> Title page:
>> Regulations under the Destructive insect and pest act as they apply to the importation of plants and plant products. Department of Agriculture, Ottawa.

Enter under the heading for the department with an added entry under the heading:

>> Canada. Laws, statutes, etc.
>> Destructive insect and pest act.

Enter constitutions and charters under the political jurisdiction, followed by the subheading Constitution or Charter:

> Title page:
>> Pocket edition of the Constitution of the United States

Enter under U.S. Constitution, and make a see also reference from U.S. Laws, statutes, etc.

Enter court rules under the jurisdiction, followed by the subheading Court rules and the name of the court governed by the rules:

Title Page:
Rules of the Supreme Court of Canada
Enter under:
Canada.  Court Rules.  Supreme Court
See also reference from: Canada.  Supreme Court

8.  Treaties: Most treaties are entered directly under their names, as discussed under the section on direct entry. A bilateral or trilateral treaty is entered according to the following order of preference: under the home country if it is a signatory; under the party on one side of a bilateral treaty if it is the only party on that side and there are two or more parties on the other; under the party whose catalog heading is the first in alphabetical order.  Add the subheading Treaties, etc. after the name of the country.  If the treaty is bilateral and there is only one party on the other side, also add the name of that party.  The date of signing always forms the last part of the heading.  Added entries are made under the other parties to the treaty.

Title page:
Loan agreement between the United States of America and the European Coal and Steel Community, signed April 23, 1954.
Enter under:
U.S.  Treaties, etc.  European Coal and Steel Community, Apr. 23, 1954.

Place name entries.  The names of some local institutions begin with, or even consist only of, a common word or phrase (such as "public library"), and therefore must be entered under the place name of the appropriate jurisdiction. The following corporate bodies fall within this category:

agricultural experiment stations
airports
botanical and zoological gardens
educational institutions
galleries
hospitals
libraries
museums

For example:

London.  University not University of London

Pittsburgh. Carnegie Library <u>not</u> Carnegie Library of Pittsburgh
Fort Lauderdale. Memorial Hospital <u>not</u> Memorial Hospital
New Hampshire. Agricultural Experiment Station <u>not</u> Agricultural Experiment Station

The whole question of whether to enter local corporate bodies directly or under place continues to be debated. Some libraries prefer to enter all of the institutions listed above under place, whether their names are distinctive or not, reasoning that this consistency is less confusing for catalog users and that a corporate name, no matter how unique, may not be remembered, while the name of the city will. For example, a patron looking for information about the new modern art museum in Washington, D. C. might forget the name Hirshhorn (the correct heading per AACR), but not that Washington is its location.

<u>Entries for religious bodies</u>. Although the rules for entering religious bodies are generally consistent with those for other types of corporate entities, there are some special provisions, and it is helpful to consider the most frequently used ones as a group. Religious bodies, other than local ones, are entered directly under their names, in accordance with the general rules.

1. Liturgical works: Enter an officially sanctioned or traditionally accepted text of a religious observance under the specific denominational church to which the work pertains, followed by the subheading <u>Liturgy and ritual</u>:

Title page:
Common service book of the Lutheran Church, authorized by the United Lutheran Church in America
Enter under:
United Lutheran Church in America. Liturgy and ritual

2. Church councils: While ecumenical, interdenominational, and Early Christian councils should be entered directly under their names as explained on page 77, a general or regional council of a corporate denominational body should be entered as a subheading under the corporate body:

Methodist Church (United States) General Conference

> Society of Friends. Philadelphia Yearly Meeting
> Catholic Church. Province of Baltimore. Provincial Council, 10th, 1869

3. Dioceses: Enter these and other subordinate units as subheadings under the parent body:

> Protestant Episcopal Church in the U.S.A. Diocese of Southern Virginia
> Catholic Church. Archdiocese of Santiago de Cuba

but:

> Greek Archdiocese of North and South America (an autonomous entity)

4. Ecclesiastical officials: The heading for a bishop, patriarch, etc., in his official capacity, consists of his title as a subheading under the diocese, order, etc., followed by the inclusive years of his incumbency and, in parentheses, by his name in brief form:

> Winchester, Eng. (Diocese) Bishop, 1367-1404 (William of Wykeham)
> Dominicans. Master General, 1486 (Barnabas Sassone)
> Catholic Church. Pope, 1958-63 (John XXIII)

5. Religious orders and societies: Enter under the name by which best known:

> Franciscans
>     Refer from: Order of St. Francis
> Jesuits
>     Refer from: Society of Jesus

6. Local churches: A local church, monastery, convent, mosque, temple, etc. is normally entered under the name of the place in which it is located:

> Baltimore. Third English Lutheran Church
> London. St. Paul's Cathedral

If a church is not associated with a local place, or if its name begins with the location, it is entered directly under its name, with the name of the county or district added whenever the name does not appear to be unique:

Tenafly Presbyterian Church
San Gabriel Mission
Tintern Abbey
Westover Church, Charles City County, Va.

If the headings for two or more churches are so similar that they are likely to be confused, the denomination or a more precise location may be added:

New York (City) St. James Church (Catholic)
New York (City) St. James Episcopal Church,
    Bronx
New York (City) St. James Episcopal Church,
    Manhattan

## CHOICE OF FORMS OF NAME

As in the case of personal authors, corporate names do not always appear in the same form on title pages. Similarly, two bodies may have identical names, and need to be distinguished in some way.

Variant forms: If different forms of the corporate name are found, choose the name as it appears at the head of the title. Also, choose the briefest form that provides adequate identification for cataloging purposes.

Huntington Library and Art Gallery
    Refer from: Henry E. Huntington Library and
      Art Gallery

In the locality or even in the region, references from the full name may be unnecessary; e.g., in California or on the West Coast, no reference may be necessary from Henry E. Huntington Library and Art Gallery. However, if changes have occurred in the official name of a corporate body, establish headings under each name for cataloging publications appearing under this name. Make appropriate cross references between the headings under which publications of the body appear in the catalog. An explanatory reference should be filed under each of the names, for example:

Pennsylvania State University

The name of the Farmers' High School was changed in 1862 to Agricultural College of Pennsylvania; in 1874 to Pennsylvania State

College; in 1953 to Pennsylvania State University.

Works by this body are entered under the name used at the time of publication.

Initial letters:  If the body has used a brief form consisting of the initial letters of its name, use this form only if it has been written in capital and lower case letters:

>Unesco
>>Refer from:   United Nations Educational, Scientific and Cultural Organization

>but

>American Federation of Labor and Congress of Industrial Organizations
>Refer from:   A. F. L. -C. I. O.

Conventional name:  When a corporate body is frequently identified by a conventional form of name in reference sources, prefer the conventional to the official name.   Also, when the name of a body of ancient origin or one that is international in character has become firmly established under an English form, enter it under this form, regardless of the forms which may appear on its publications.   Instances of conventional names of this type are especially prevalent among religious bodies, fraternal and knightly orders, and diplomatic conferences.

>Catholic Church
>Benedictines
>>Refer from:   Order of St.  Benedict
>European Economic Community
>Free Masons
>Westminster Abbey
>Yalta Conference

Additions and modifications.   Place names, dates, and other descriptors may be added in order that corporate names may be properly identified.   An atlas or gazetteer is the best source for determining the correct form of a geographical name.

1.   Add the name of the place in which the body is located if the same name has been used by another body in a different location:

Union College, Lincoln, Neb.
Union College, Schenectady, NY

2. Prefer the name of an institution to the name of the place in which a body is located when it provides better identification:

Quadrangle Club, University of Chicago

3. Add the name of the country, state, province, etc., in parentheses, instead of the local name if the name has been used by different bodies that have a character that is national, state, provincial, etc.:

Labour Party (Gt. Britain)
Labour Party (New Zealand)

4. If a local place name that is part of a corporate name is insufficient to differentiate two or more bodies, add in parentheses the name of the state, province, or country:

Washington County Historical Society (Ark.)
Washington County Historical Society (Md.)

5. If the name of a given place might be confused with another of the same name, add the name of the larger geographic entity in which it is located, such as country, constituent state, island group, etc.; state or province may be used with U.S. or Canadian local place names:

Victoria, Australia
Palma, Majorca
St. Aubin, Jersey
Winnipeg, Manitoba

6. Omit the term indicating type of governmental administration unless it is required to distinguish the place from another place of the same name:

Meath  not  County Meath

but:

District of Columbia

7. Distinguish political or governmental jurisdictions with the same name by adding in parentheses the type of jurisdiction or other appropriate designation:

New York (City)
New York (State)
Berlin (West)
Russia (U. S. S. R. )
    Refer from:  Union of Soviet Socialist Republics

8.  Omit initial articles unless required for reasons of clarity or grammar:

Library Association

but:

The Club, London

9.  Omit terms such as incorporated or limited, unless they are needed to make clear that the name is that of a corporate body:

Bell Telephone Laboratories

but:

Films Incorporated

10.  When the corporate name begins with initials, place them in parentheses after the surname:

Schirmer (G. ), inc.
Smiley (A. K. ) Public Library

11.  A conference, symposium, or other meeting should be identified by number, place, and date--in that order:

Pi Iota Gamma Society, Constitutional Convention,
    3d, Atlantic City, 1974

12.  If the name of a corporate body leaves any doubt as to its identification, add in parentheses a word or phrase to clarify the meaning of the heading:

Bounty (Ship)
WNCN-FM (Radio Station) New York, N.Y.
Friedrich Witte (Firm)

REFERENCES

As with personal names, references should be made

from the form of a corporate name under which a patron
might look but which is not used in the catalog, to the form
which is used.  For example,

> Persia
>> see Iran
>
> Quakers
>> see Society of Friends
>
> American Red Cross
>> see American National Red Cross

When a body is entered under a place or under another body of which it is a part, references should be made
whenever a patron can be expected to search under the direct name:

> State Teachers College, Bridgewater, Mass.
>> see Massachusetts.  State Teachers College,
>> Bridgewater

Similarly, if the patron is likely to look under place
or parent body for a name that is entered directly, a reference should be made:

> American Library Association.  American Associa-
> tion of School Librarians
>> see American Association of School Librarians
>
> U.S. Tennessee Valley Authority
>> see Tennessee Valley Authority

If a step or several steps have been omitted from a
hierarchy, a reference from the full form to the shorter
form should be made:

> American Library Association.  Resources and
> Technical Services Division.  Cataloging and
> Classification Section
>> see American Library Association.  Cataloging
>> and Classification Section

In determining the headings to be used for the publication of an organization one consults aids as well as the cataloging rules.  An authority card may be made if it is considered desirable to have a permanent record of the form
adopted and the aids consulted (see card 19).

Carnegie Corporation of New York

Established 1911

n Americana, 1965
n World Almanac, 1967 (Carnegie Cor-
      poration of N.Y.)

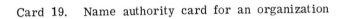

Card 19.   Name authority card for an organization

# CHAPTER 5

## UNIFORM TITLE ENTRIES


Some works to be entered in a library catalog will have neither a personal nor a corporate author because it is impossible to identify the author. In these cases, the title becomes the most important means of identifying the work. Usually it is simply transcribed as given on the title page, but there are some instances where special rules for title entry must be followed. Even when the author is known, certain other types of works also need to be entered according to these rules.


## UNIFORM TITLES

When a work has appeared through the centuries in a great variety of editions, versions and translations, a uniform title enables the cataloger to bring together in the catalog all entries for a given work, be it a poem, epic, romance, tale, play, chronicle, or religious scripture, regardless of the varying titles under which the various editions have been published. The following types of works are listed in the AACR as being generally identified by uniform titles:

> Sacred scriptures
> Creeds and confessions
> Liturgical works
> Anonymous works without titles
> Early anonymous chronicles and literary works
> Early collections entered under title
> Early anonymous compilations of ancient laws and
>      customs
> Peace treaties and international conventions

Music and laws are also usually given uniform titles in order that differing editions might be brought together under the same heading in the catalog.

General rule. When different editions, versions, translations, etc., of a work appear under various titles, one title should be selected as the uniform title under which all will be cataloged. References should be made to the uniform title from the different titles or variants of the title under which a work has been published or cited in reference sources:

> Song of the Nibelungs
> see Nibelungenlied

Works written before 1501. Use the title in the original language by which it has come to be identified in reference sources and in most modern editions:

> Beowulf
> Chanson de Roland

However, prefer a well established English title for a classical Greek work:

> Aristophanes
> The Birds
>
> Homer
> The Iliad
>
> Plato
> The Republic

Anonymous classics. For an early anonymous work originally written in a language using an alphabet other than the Roman alphabet, use the English title. The following list, based on various codes and aids, gives some headings commonly used:

| | | |
|---|---|---|
| Arabian nights | Cuchulain | Nibelungenlied |
| Arthur, King | Grail | Njals saga |
| Beowulf | Kalevala | Reynard the Fox |
| Chanson de Roland | Mabinogion | Robin Hood |
| Cid Campeador | Mother Goose | Seven sages |

Separately published parts: When a part (or parts) of a work to which a uniform title has been assigned is published separately, it may be cataloged under the title of the part, but a reference should be made from the uniform title of the main work:

Arabian nights
    For separately published stories from this work
    see
Ali Baba
Sinbad the Sailor

## SACRED SCRIPTURES

Special rules are given in the AACR for cataloging biblical literature, and a special library of religious literature, no matter how small, needs to consult those rules. The following is intended only as a guide for a small general library.

Parts of the Bible. Use the uniform title, followed by Old or New Testament (O. T. or N. T. ), followed by the specific book or commonly used group name. For a complete Bible, note the version as a subheading, and the language, if other than English:

Bible. N. T. Luke
Bible. O. T. Ezra
Bible. N. T. Epistles.
Bible. O. T. Pentateuch.
Bible. Authorized.
Bible. Latin. Vulgate.

If the library feels that it has enough material to warrant it, references from the titles of individual books, variant names of books, and group names may be made.

Other sacred scripture. The sacred literature of any other religion is entered in a similar way under a uniform heading:

Talmud
Koran
Vedas

## AUTHORITY CARDS

Name authority cards may be made for anonymous classics and sacred books. They are similar in form to those for personal names, but omit the titles and dates used for identification of personal authors. In the smaller, general libraries name authority cards are not necessary for individual books, periodicals, almanacs, encyclopedias, etc., entered under title.

```
        Chanson de Roland.

    n Children's cat.  11th ed.
    n Americana, 1965 ed.  (Roland Song, The)


                      x Roland
                      x Song of Roland
```

Card 20.  Name authority card for anonymous classic

# CHAPTER 6

## CHOICE OF MAIN ENTRY

The previous chapters have discussed the various rules guiding the forms of author, subject and title headings under which a book is entered in the catalog. The next chapter covers the rules for describing a particular edition of a work so that it can be distinguished from other editions of the same work. Since only one card needs to be made which will include all the information necessary to describe and locate a book, this chapter gives the rules for deciding which of the possible headings for a given book should go at the top of that basic card. The heading chosen is called the main entry, and the card that begins with the main entry heading and includes all the bibliographic data about the work, together with the tracings (the list of subject and added entries under which it is also entered in the catalog), is a main entry card. The main entry also determines how a work is cited in bibliographies, union catalogs, etc., and is traditionally considered as constituting the formal identification of it. When duplicated, the main entry card constitutes a unit card to which other headings can be added in order to complete the set of cards for the work. When a library does not have duplicating facilities, cards for subject and added entries are typed in abbreviated form.

## BASIC RULE

Enter under author or principal author whenever possible; otherwise, under title. AACR states that:

> By 'author' is meant the person or corporate body chiefly responsible for the creation of the intellectual or artistic content of a work. Thus composers, artists, photographers, etc., are the 'authors' of the works they create; chess players are the 'authors' of their recorded games; etc. The term 'author' also embraces an editor or compiler who

has primary responsibility for the content of a
work, e.g. the compiler of a bibliography. 1

## CHOICE OF AUTHOR

When there are several persons or bodies who have
contributed to the content of a work, the following rules apply:

Joint authors, editors, compilers, etc. When the
wording or typography indicates that one person or corporate
body is primarily responsible, enter under that name. Make
added entries for the other names if there are not more than
two, and always make an added entry for the first name
listed on the title page, even when that is not the name of
the principal author.

> Title page:
> Animal motivation; experimental studies on the
> albino rat, by C. J. Warden, with the collabor-
> ation of T. N. Jenkins, L. H. Warner, E. L.
> Hamilton and H. W. Nissen
> Enter under Warden; make no added author entries.

When the principal author is not indicated, but there are no
more than three names, enter under the first and make added
entries under the other two:

> Title page:
> Health for effective living; a basic health educa-
> tion text for college students, by Edward B.
> Johns, Wilfred C. Sutton, Lloyd E. Webster
> Enter under Johns, with added entries for Sutton
> and Webster.

> Title page:
> The correspondence between Benjamin Harrison
> and James G. Blaine, 1882-1893 ...
> Enter under Harrison, with an added entry for Blaine

If a work is in several volumes and the names of the authors
are given in a different order in each, enter under the first
name listed in the first volume:

> Title page, book 1:
> Child-life arithmetics... Three book series,
> by Clifford Woody, Frederick S. Breed, James
> R. Overman

Title page, book 2:
    ... by Frederick S. Breed, James R. Over-
    man, Clifford Woody
Title page, book 3:
    ... by James R. Overman, Clifford Woody,
    Frederick S. Breed
Enter under Woody, with added entries for Breed
    and Overman.

When a new edition changes the order in which the authors
are listed, retain the first edition main entry unless the new
edition is radically different:

Title page:
    Outline of sociology, by John Lewis Gillin and
    Frank W. Blackmar, 3d ed.
    ("A somewhat thorough rewriting." In earlier
        editions Blackmar's name appeared first
        on the title page)
Enter under Gillin, with added entry for Blackmar.

Corporate versus personal author. A work may be
issued by a corporate body, but with authorship or editor-
ship attributed to one or more persons.

1. Enter such a work under the corporate body if it
is the expression of the corporate thought or activity of the
body. Such works include official reports and records,
statements, studies, and other communications dealing with
the policies, operations, or management of the body made by
officers or other employees of the body. However, works
prepared by officers or employees which are the result of
scholarly investigation or scientific research are entered under personal author, unless written by more than three persons, none of whom is represented as the chief author.

Title page:
    Public water supplies of Colorado, 1959-60, by
    Dean O. Gregg, Eric L. Meyer, Margaret M.
    Targy, and Edward A. Moulder, U.S. Geolog-
    ical Survey. Prepared by the U.S. Geological
    Survey...
Enter under:
    U.S. Geological Survey

Another illustration is Weeds of California, by W. W.
Robbins, Margaret K. Bellue, Walter S. Ball. For sale by

Printing Division (Documents Section) Sacramento. " Printed
at the top of the page bearing the foreword is "State of California, Department of Agriculture," and on the spine of the
book, "1951. " Should this book be entered in the catalog
under Robbins, the first author on the title page, or under:
California. State Department of Agriculture, with an added
entry under Robbins? The title page states that Robbins is
Professor of Botany and Botanist in the Experiment Station,
University of California, and this information is confirmed in
his biographical sketch in Who's Who in America, 1952-1953.
CBI lists under his name Weed Control; a Textbook and
Manual, a 1952 publication of McGraw-Hill. Mr. Robbins is
clearly an author in his own right. In addition to the rules
stated above, AACR also says that if a work does not seem
to fall clearly within either the corporate or personal authorship categories, the rule is to enter it under the heading
which would be used if no corporate body were involved, with
an added entry under the body unless it functions solely as
publisher. Thus Weeds of California should be entered under
Robbins, with an added entry under: California. State Department of Agriculture. The California Blue Book, 1950, lists
the State Department of Agriculture as one of the executive
departments of the state, and the form given here follows the
rule for using the conventional name of a country, state,
municipality, etc. , as the heading for its government, and
entering a subordinate governmental body as a direct subheading under the name of the government.

2. Enter under the corporate body a work (other than
a formal history) describing the body, its functions, procedures, facilities, resources, etc. , or an inventory, catalog, directory of personnel or members:

>Title page:
>The Metropolitan Museum of Art. A guide to
>an exhibition of Islamic miniature painting and
>book illumination, by M. S. Dimand.
>Enter under:
>New York (City). Metropolitan Museum of Art
>Added entry:
>Dimand, M S

but:

>Title page:
>The Library of Congress subject headings; a
>practical guide, by David Judson Haykin, Chief,

Subject Cataloging Division
Enter under:
>Haykin, David Judson (as this is a general
>guide, not just for the Library of Congress)

Added entry:
>U.S. Library of Congress

3. An official communication, such as a message to
a legislature, issued by a chief of state or head of government should be entered under the corporate heading for the
office which he holds:

>Title page:
>>No retreat from tomorrow; President Lyndon B.
>>Johnson's 1967 message to the 90th Congress.
>Enter under:
>>U.S. President, 1963-1969 (Lyndon B. John-
>>son)

However, other speeches and writings of a head of government are entered as works of personal authorship:

>Title page:
>>The vantage point; perspectives of the Presi-
>>dency, 1963-1969. Lyndon Baines Johnson
>Enter under:
>>Johnson, Lyndon Baines, Pres. U.S., 1908-
>>1973.

Collections. Poems, stories, essays, etc., by different authors are frequently brought together by a compiler
and published as a collection. When there is a collective
title which applies to the whole book, enter under the compiler, and make author-title added entries for the works com-
piled if there are no more than three (or unless you wish to
enter all):

>Title page:
>>... Regency poets; Byron, Shelley, Keats.
>>Compiled by C. R. Bull
>Enter under Bull, with added entries under Byron,
>Shelley, Keats and under title.

If no collective title is given, enter under whatever heading
would be used for the first work listed on the title page.
Make an added entry for the compiler or editor and author-
title entries for the other works if there are no more than

three (or unless you feel that entries for all would be worth the time involved):

> Title page:
>> The vision of Sir Launfal, by James Russell Lowell; the courtship of Miles Standish, by Henry Wadsworth Longfellow; Snowbound, by John Greenleaf Whittier; edited with an introduction and notes by Charles Robert Gaston
>
> Enter under Lowell, with added entries for Longfellow, Whittier, and Gaston

Adapter or original author. Enter under the adapter when the literary style or form of the original has been changed, i.e., when it has been rewritten for children, dramatized, made into a novel or verse:

> Title page:
>> Sinclair Lewis' Dodsworth, dramatized by Sidney Howard
>
> Enter under Howard, with an author-title added entry for Lewis

> Title page:
>> The boys' King Arthur, Sir Thomas Malory's History of King Arthur and his knights of the Round Table; edited for boys by Sidney Lanier.
>
> Enter under Malory, with added entry for Lanier (it is edited, with an introduction, but not rewritten)

> Title page:
>> The book of King Arthur and his noble knights; stories from Sir Thomas Malory's Morte D'Arthur by Mary Macleod
>
> Enter under Macleod, with an added entry under Malory.

The Macleod work is similar to the one edited by Sidney Lanier, but Macleod has selected certain stories from Malory and reworded them to suit young readers. It is not Malory's language and is therefore entered under the adapter's name. Lamb's Tales from Shakespeare is cataloged in the same way: the main entry under Lamb as adapter, with an added entry under Shakespeare. Anonymous classics which are retold are treated the same way, so that James Baldwin's Story of Roland is entered under Baldwin, but has an added

entry under the uniform title "Chanson de Roland." Likewise, Eleanor Hull's Boys' Cuchulain; heroic legends of Ireland may be entered under Hull as in the Children's Catalog,
but with an added entry under Cuchulain.

Another type of book which is sometimes puzzling is
that consisting of selections from an individual work of an
author. Hill's translation of a selection of The Canterbury
Tales is an example. In some titles, the term "selected"
is used in the sense that the selections included are taken
from all the works of an author rather than from a single
work. In either case, the treatment is the same. The main
entry is made under the author's name, and the editor's or
translator's name is given an added entry.


TITLE ENTRIES

When authorship is diffuse, indeterminate, or unknown,
a work is entered under title.

Anonymous works. Anonymous works are those whose
authors are not known or, at least, are not given in the book.
There may be: 1) no indication of authorship; 2) a descriptive or generic word or phrase preceded by an article, e.g.,
by "the soldier"; 3) the title of another of the author's works,
e.g., "by the author of ... "; or 4) initials, which may or
may not be those of the author's name. In these cases, enter under title. If authorship has been attributed to several
persons, make added entries for those names, as well as for
any initials, phrases or other clues:

> Title page:
> The secret expedition; a farce (in two acts) as
> it has been represented upon the political thea-
> tre of Europe.
> Enter under title

> Title page:
> A memorial to Congress against an increase
> of duties on importations, by citizens of Bos-
> ton and vicinity.
> Enter under title

> Title page:
> Indiscretions of Dr. Carstairs, by A. DeO.
> Enter under title, with added entries under initials

Diffuse authorship. If there are more than three persons or bodies named as being responsible for a work, but
none is singled out as being primarily responsible, enter under title, but make an added entry for the first named person
on the title page:

> Title page:
> The United Nations and economic and social
> cooperation, by Robert E. Asher, Walter M.
> Kotschnig, William Adams Brown, Jr., and
> associates.
> Enter under title, with added entry for Asher

However, if an editor is named on the title page, while the
publisher is not named in the title, and the editor appears to
be primarily responsible for the work, enter under editor rather than title:

> Title page:
> Directory of American scholars, a biographical
> directory, edited by the Jacques Cattell Press.
> 4th ed. ... 1963
> Enter under title

but

> Title page:
> Directory of American scholars, a biographical
> directory, edited by Jacques Cattell ... 1942
> Enter under editor

Most audiovisual materials are entered under title, not
only because the responsibility for their creation can seldom
be attributed to a few people, but also because most kinds
of nonprint materials are customarily identified and cited by
title. The specific rules are discussed in chapter 10.

Serials. While most serials are entered under title,
rules of entry for these not only constitute a special case,
but are currently also under reconsideration. The rules as
of this date will be set forth in chapter 9, but mention is
made here of this so that the reader will not be misled into
thinking that all main entry decisions have been summarized
in this chapter.

Reference

1. Anglo-American Cataloging Rules, North American Text (Chicago, American Library Association, 1970), p. 9.

CHAPTER 7

## MAIN ENTRY/UNIT CARDS

Up to this point we have been concerned with the contents of the book and how books of similar content may be grouped together; the form of personal names and names of organizations, with reference to the choice of proper headings for catalog entries; and how to present books which have neither a personal nor a corporate author. This chapter discusses the description of the book which is to be put on the main entry or unit catalog card. This description should include such information as is necessary to distinguish the book from all other books, even different editions of the same work, and should include its scope, contents, and bibliographic relationships. This data should be presented as simply and concisely as possible and in the same form and order for all books. The basis for this description is the title page of the book and what can be gained from an examination of the book itself. Stated more simply, the purpose of cataloging is to identify the book and to distinguish it from all other books and even other editions of the same work.

A decision about the extent of descriptive cataloging is not merely a matter of following established rules for such cataloging, but is a major administrative decision affecting costs and quality of library service. On the one hand, much information about the physical characteristics of a volume (essential in a rare book library) serves little purpose in the small school or public library. On the other hand, a small library with limited reference resources is very dependent on the catalog as a reference tool. A library lacking the complete Cumulative Book Index (CBI) as well as comprehensive indexes to plays, short stories, poems, etc. in collections will depend upon the catalog for information about "contents" of books to a far greater extent than will the larger library with an extensive collection of indexes and bibliographies. Also, where the shelves are open to the readers, many readers will spend little time at the catalog looking at the cards. However, even in the smallest library, the catalog

106

may be called upon to answer some questions about a book
which is out in circulation; and in looking for material on a
subject the reader will sometimes examine all the cards before going to the shelves, considering the author, publisher,
date and length of the books.


## CATALOG CARD COMPONENTS

The information to be given on the card for a book
includes the classification number, author's name, title, publisher, date, total number of pages, information about illustrations, notes if needed, and the tracing for subject headings and added entries.

The first step in cataloging a book is to examine the
title page, from which the librarian gets most of the information for the catalog entry.  Besides the author and the title,
the title page may give the author's degrees and other data,
yet this information on the catalog card would not be of sufficient value to warrant the space it would take.  The title
page may also give a statement about the edition--as second
edition or revised edition--and may specify how the book is
illustrated.  Then there is the imprint, that is, place of
publication, publisher, and date of publication, given at the
bottom of the title page.  The librarian should examine not
only the title page for the items mentioned but also the pages
preceding the title page and the cover to see if the book belongs to a series, e.g., "The Rivers of America"; the back
of the title page (verso) for the copyright date; the colophon,
if there is one, and the prefatory matter for further information regarding the edition; the table of contents for the list
of works if the book includes a number of separate works,
e.g., plays; and the book itself: 1) for the collation--that
is, the number of pages or volumes and illustrations, and
2) for bibliographies, appendices containing material of special value and other special features which should be brought
out in the notes.

In some books, part of the title of the book, the author's name, or the place of publication or publisher's name
spreads over two pages, facing each other.  This is called
a "double title page" or a "double-spread title page."  The
necessary information is taken from both pages, and no mention of this type of title page is needed in the catalog entry.
Another kind of book it may be well to mention here is the
book with more than one title page.  In some instances there

is an added title page for the series to which the book belongs, a special title page for a second volume, or a facsimile of the title page of an earlier edition. Catalog the book from the title page for the volume rather than the series, for the set rather than the volume; catalog from the printed title page if there is also an engraved one. If such information would be useful in the particular library, include a note about the other title page or pages.

If a necessary item of description is missing from the publication itself and must be supplied from an external source, it is enclosed in brackets. If a work is published without a title page, or without one which applies to the whole work, it is cataloged from some other part of the work (cover title, caption title, etc.), and the source of the information is indicated.

However, the great majority of books acquired by the small general library will pose no special problems for the cataloger. To take an example, here is the title page of a book [opposite]. On the back of the title page is found:

ISBN: 0-385-08410-2
Library of Congress Catalog Card Number 73-81989
Copyright © 1970, by Ralph Geoffrey Newman
All Rights Reserved
Printed in the United States of America

Examination of the book shows that it has 117 pages and has a portrait of Lincoln as a frontispiece, and can therefore be said to be illustrated. After the cataloger has examined the book, the next step is to assign the classification number and the subject headings in the manner described in chapters 1 and 2. The call number, in this case B for biography with letters or a book number beneath to indicate that the biographee is Lincoln, should be written in pencil in the upper center of the page following the title page about an inch from the top. Here it will be easy to locate, and if the book is rebound it will not be cut off in the trimming nor hidden by the sewing.

The cataloger then proceeds to the "descriptive" part of the cataloging process, that is, determining the main entry and added entries (other than the subject headings) and their form, and noting the information about the book which

# ABRAHAM LINCOLN

## His Story
## in His Own Words

———— ◆ ————

*EDITED AND WITH NOTES
BY RALPH GEOFFREY NEWMAN*

> *"Abraham Lincoln
> his hand and pen
> he will be good but
> God knows when."*

DOUBLEDAY & COMPANY, INC.

GARDEN CITY, NEW YORK

1975

will be entered on the catalog card.   The completed card
might look like this:

```
B
LIN        Lincoln, Abraham, Pres., U.S., 1809-1865
              Abraham Lincoln; his story in his
           own words.   Edited, with notes by Ralph
           Geoffrey Newman.   Doubleday, 1975, c1970
              117 p.   ill.




              1.   Lincoln, Abraham, Pres. U.S.,
           1809-1865.   I.   Newman, Ralph Geoffrey,
           ed.
```

Card 21.   Main entry card

Had the library purchased a card set from the Library of
Congress, the main entry card would look like this:

```
        Lincoln, Abraham, Pres. U.,S., 1809-1865.
           Abraham Lincoln, his story in his own words / edited
        and with notes by Ralph Geoffrey Newman. — Garden
        City, N. Y. : Doubleday, 1975, c1970.
           117 p. : port. ; 22 cm.
           An amalgamation of 2 autobiographical sketches written in 1859
        and 1860, supplemented by autobiographical excerpts from Lincoln's
        letters and speeches.
           Includes index.
           ISBN 0-385-08410-2 : $6.95

           1. Lincoln, Abraham, Pres. U. S., 1809-1865.   I. Newman, Ralph
        Geoffrey, 1911-    ed.

        E457.L734  1975            973.7'092'4  [B]        73-81989
                                                            MARC
        Library of Congress          75
```

Card 22.   Library of Congress printed card for book repre-
           sented by card 21.

In the first card the essential elements are present in the same order as on the LC card, but in abbreviated form and slightly different style.  The LC card follows rules designed to conform to International Standard Bibliographic Description (ISBD) practice, which requires that elements of the description (i. e. , that portion of the card which begins with the title and ends with the ISBN and price) be grouped by areas and be separated by specific types of punctuation. The reason for this is to organize and standardize the data so that it can be readily interpreted by both people and computers across the world, and to allow enough information to be presented to suit the needs of large research libraries.

It should not be necessary for a small library to make its homemade cataloging reflect the LC format in all its details, but it is desirable that the basic information be given in the same sequence and that all entries in a given library's catalog be as uniform as possible in style, i. e. , in spelling, capitalization, punctuation, abbreviations, use of numerals, etc.  Of course, if a library uses centralized cataloging for an appreciable part of its collection, the homemade cards should be consistent with the cards obtained from outside. Since most commercial services that supply simplified cards to small libraries now base their cataloging on that provided by the Library of Congress, the components of the cards and their order do largely conform to LC practice, but there is unfortunately no single standard that determines the degree of detail provided or the spacing, indention, and punctuation used (see chapter 12 for examples of printed cards).  Therefore, the style of the sample cards given in this manual must be seen as simply one more variation on the basic pattern. As suggested above, the particular guidelines and style chosen by the user of this manual must be determined by the policy which has been adopted by the individual library.


ORGANIZATION OF INFORMATION

The skeleton cards 23 and 24 below and card 25 (see p. 113) illustrate the form used for sample cards in this manual and show the relative locations of the various parts of an entry.  Indention and spacing is intended to emphasize the different groups of information and to give prominence to certain words, such as the author's name, or whatever forms the main entry heading.

The revised chapter 6 of the AACR[1] breaks down the

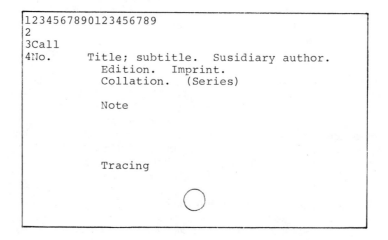

```
1234567890123456789
2
3Call
4No.      Author
5            Title; subtitle.  Susidiary author.
6          Edition.  Imprint.
7            Collation.  (Series)
8
9            Note
             Note ----------------------------
         -----------------

             Tracing--------------------------
         ----------
```

Card 23.   Skeleton card for simplified cataloging, author
           main entry

```
1234567890123456789
2
3Call
4No.       Title; subtitle.  Susidiary author.
            Edition.  Imprint.
            Collation.  (Series)

            Note



            Tracing
```

Card 24.   Skeleton card for simplified cataloging, title main
           entry

descriptive information into the following areas:  1) Title and
statement of authorship area, including title proper; parallel
titles; other titles and other title information; statement of

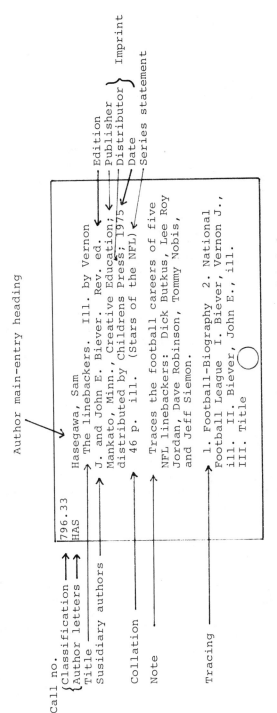

Card 25. Card with components labeled

authorship and subsidiary authorship, e. g. , editors, translators; 2) edition area, including edition statement and authorship statement relating to the edition; 3) imprint area, including publisher and date; 4) collation area, including number of volumes, pagination, illustrations, etc. ; 5) series
area; 6) notes; and 7) ISBN area for the International Standard Book Number and price.  An outline showing the ISBN
format as set forth in AACR's revised chapter 6 is given below in order to clarify the terminology and punctuation (compare with card 22).  Each part of the entry is separated from
the next one by a period-space-dash-space.

> Title proper = parallel title : other title / state-
> ment of authorship. -- Edition statement / state-
> ment of authorship relating to the edition. -- Place
> of publication : publisher, date (place of printing :
> printer)
>
> number of volumes and/or number of pages :
> illustration statement ; size & accompanying ma-
> terials. -- (Series ; numbering within the series :
> subseries ; numbering within the subseries ISSN)
>
> Notes.
> ISBN.

This method of organizing the description results in an entry
which contains all the information needed to identify the work
without reference to the heading, since the name of the author
is repeated, as in card 26.

  Source of information for description.  The information for the various descriptive parts of the catalog entry
should be derived from the following sources, which are given
in preferential order:

| Area | Primary source of information |
|---|---|
| Title and statement of authorship | Title page, or if there is no title page, the source from within the publication that is used as its substitute |
| Edition statement and statement of authorship relating to the edition | Title page, preliminaries, and colophon |

| | |
|---|---|
| Imprint | Title page, preliminaries, and colophon |
| Series statement | Series title page, title page, half title, cover, anywhere else in the publication |
| ISBN | Anywhere in the publication or in data supplied by the publisher and accompanying the book |

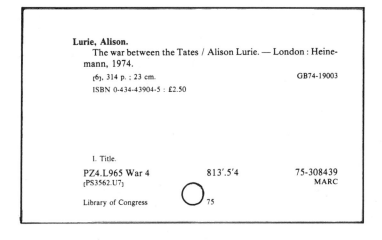

**Lurie, Alison.**
    The war between the Tates / Alison Lurie. — London : Heinemann, 1974.
    ₍6₎, 314 p. ; 23 cm.                                    GB74-19003
    ISBN 0-434-43904-5 : £2.50

I. Title.
PZ4.L965 War 4                        813'.5'4                75-308439
₍PS3562.U7₎                                                        MARC

Library of Congress            75

Card 26.   LC card, ISBD format, repeating name of author in authorship statement

---

The term "preliminaries" encompasses half title, verso of the title page, added title page, cover, and spine. If information has to be supplied from a place other than what is authorized in the table above, it is enclosed in brackets.   The collation and notes are phrased by the cataloger using standard bibliographical terminology and quotations from the work itself or outside sources, as necessary.

The discussion of the parts of the catalog card which follows below reflects the ISBD rules, but also suggests how these rules may be simplified by small libraries.

Call number.  The call number is the classification symbol plus--if used--the book number of letters of the author's surname (or of the title in case of title main entry). This code symbol, which is necessary to direct the reader to the shelves, is given on the catalog cards, on the spine of the book, and on the book card.

Main entry heading.  If the main entry is a personal author, the first line on the card is the author's surname, followed by a comma, space, the forenames, comma, space, dates of birth and death when necessary.  In most instances, the name will suffice.  If only initials appear on the title page and the forenames cannot be found, eight spaces are left after each initial so that the name may be filled in if found later.  The name of an organization as author, i.e., a corporate author, is given in the same position as that of personal author.  There are periods at the end of the main heading and each subheading, which are separated by two spaces, as in card 27.  When the main entry is a title, it

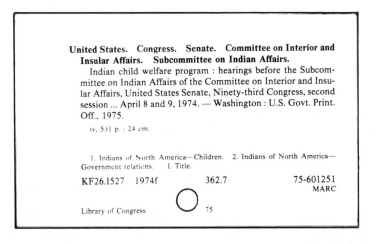

United States.  Congress.  Senate.  Committee on Interior and Insular Affairs.  Subcommittee on Indian Affairs.
    Indian child welfare program : hearings before the Subcommittee on Indian Affairs of the Committee on Interior and Insular Affairs, United States Senate, Ninety-third Congress, second session ... April 8 and 9, 1974. — Washington : U.S. Govt. Print. Off., 1975.
    iv, 531 p. : 24 cm.

    1. Indians of North America—Children.  2. Indians of North America—Government relations.  I. Title.

KF26.I527   1974f        362.7         75-601251
                                         MARC

Library of Congress          75

Card 27.   Main entry under corporate author

appears on the same line as an author main entry, but the hanging indentation is used, as in card 28.

Title.  The next part of the card begins with a transcription of the title as it appears on the title page, although

---

**Fairy tales from many lands** / illustrated by Arthur Rackham. — New York : Viking Press, 1974.

121 p. : ill. (some col.) ; 25 cm. — (A studio book)

First published in 1916 under title: The Allies' fairy book.
SUMMARY: Thirteen fairy tales from a variety of countries including Japan, Yugoslavia, Portugal, and Belgium.
ISBN 0–670–30562–6 : $6.95

1. Fairy tales. ₍1. Fairy tales₎    I. Rackham, Arthur, 1867–1939, ill.

PZ8.F16867  1974          398.2              75–304883
                                             MARC

Library of Congress        75 ₍4₎              A C

---

Card 28.   Main entry under title

---

the capitalization and punctuation may be adjusted.   Long titles may be abridged if it is possible to do so without omitting essential information.   The first words of the title are always included, even when the first word of the title repeats the author's name:

> Marlowe's Plays
> Eileen Ford's A more beautiful you in 21 days

Whenever author, publisher, etc., form an integral part of the title, the names should be included in the transcription of the title:

> The complete works of Charles Dickens
> Larousse's French-English dictionary

Additions may be made to the title if an explanation seems needed and if the word or phrase used has been found in the work itself:

> Longfellow.   [selections]

When there is an alternative title, it is always given.   Parallel and original titles may also be given after the title proper, but this will seldom be necessary in a small library.   Subtitles which are not overly long are transcribed as part of the title proper, but very long subtitles separable from the title may be omitted. In the case of collections without a collective title, list the individual titles in the order in which they are given on the title page; include any linking words used on the title page.

Author statement. Under the revised AACR chapter 6, the title statement is followed by a full statement of authorship, including subsidiary authors, i.e., joint authors, editors, translators, illustrators, writers of prefaces, etc. This is preferred, even when there is only one author, whose name has already been given in the main entry heading. For a small library, it is not necessary to add the statement "by (author's name)" following the title, even though an exact transcription of the title page would require it, if the author's name has already formed the main heading on the catalog card. However, inclusion of the author statement provides additional needed information in cases of joint or multiple authorship, since the name of only one of the authors is provided in the heading. If more than three authors are listed, the author statement includes the first name, followed by the sign of omission (. . .) and [et al.].

```
    Urban Growth Patterns Research Group
      Demographic profiles of the United
      States.  [By] Everett S. Lee . . .
      [et al.]  Oak Ridge, Tenn., Oak Ridge
      National Laboratory, 1971-
        1v.

      CONTENTS:  v. 1. The Nation, regions,
    divisions, and States.

      1. U.S.-Population-Statistics   I. Lee,
    Everett Spurgeon   II. Title
```

Card 29.   Card for publication with multiple authorship

When there are subsidiary authors, they are recorded in the order in which they appear on the title page, together with the word or short phrase defining the function of each. Where the explanatory word or phrase is not derived from the title page, it is bracketed.

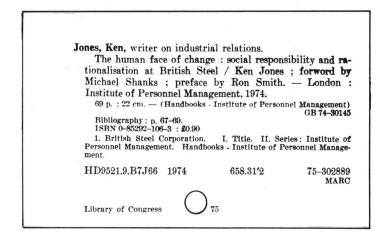

**Jones, Ken,** writer on industrial relations.
    The human face of change : social responsibility and rationalisation at British Steel / Ken Jones ; forword by Michael Shanks ; preface by Ron Smith. — London : Institute of Personnel Management, 1974.
       69 p. ; 22 cm. — (Handbooks - Institute of Personnel Management)
                                             GB 74–30145
       Bibliography : p. 67–69.
       ISBN 0–85292–106–3 : £0.90
       1. British Steel Corporation.    I. Title.  II. Series: Institute of Personnel Management.  Handbooks - Institute of Personnel Management.

HD9521.9.B7J66  1974           658.31'2          75–302889
                                                    MARC

Library of Congress          75

**Card 30.** Card showing functions of subsidiary authors in authorship statement

An author statement can also relate the name used in the heading to another name on the title page, as in card 31.

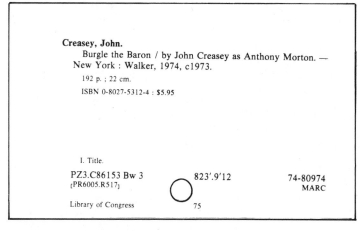

**Creasey, John.**
    Burgle the Baron / by John Creasey as Anthony Morton. — New York : Walker, 1974, c1973.
      192 p. ; 22 cm.
      ISBN 0-8027-5312-4 : $5.95

   I. Title.

PZ3.C86153 Bw 3          823'.9'12          74-80974
[PR6005.R517]                                    MARC

Library of Congress          75

**Card 31.** Authorship statement giving pseudonym

Illustration statement.   While the collation is the part
of the descriptive catalog entry which points out the presence
of illustrations, the fact that a particular artist provided the
illustrations for a specific work may be an important factor
in distinguishing one edition from another, or may be of interest for other reasons, as in children's collections (see
card 28).   When the name of the artist is given on the title
page, in the preliminaries or in the colophon, the name is
included in the entry as part of the authorship statement or
edition statement, as applicable.   When the name is taken
from a place other than the title page, it is bracketed.

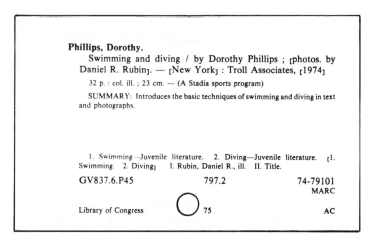

**Phillips, Dorothy.**
　　Swimming and diving / by Dorothy Phillips ; ₍photos. by
Daniel R. Rubin₎. — ₍New York₎ : Troll Associates, ₍1974₎
　　　32 p. : col. ill. ; 23 cm. — (A Stadia sports program)
　　　SUMMARY: Introduces the basic techniques of swimming and diving in text
and photographs.


　　1. Swimming —Juvenile literature.　2. Diving—Juvenile literature.　₍1.
Swimming.　2. Diving₎　I. Rubin, Daniel R., ill.　II. Title.

GV837.6.P45　　　　　　　　　797.2　　　　　　　　74-79101
　　　　　　　　　　　　　　　　　　　　　　　　　　　　MARC

Library of Congress　　　　　○　75　　　　　　　　　　AC

Card 32.   Illustrator given in authorship statement, bracketed

---

Edition.   Although the revised chapter 6 of AACR requires that the number of the edition be given even in the
case of a first edition, in simplified cataloging the absence
of an edition number on the catalog card implies that the
work is a first edition.   An impression or printing statement
is included only in the case of items having particular bibliographic importance.   The cataloger should be aware of the
lack of uniformity among publishers in the use of the terms
edition, impression, and printing, and should study the information on the title page and other preliminaries carefully.

When it is known that a work has been published in
various editions which have been revised, translated or illustrated by different people, the information about the reviser,

translator, etc., follows the edition statement, rather than being a part of the author statement:

---

Emmet, Lewis Emanuel, d. 1938.
    Emmet's notes on perusing titles and on practical convey-
ancing. — 16th ed. / by J. T. Farrand : consultant editor
J. Gilchrist Smith. — London : Oyez Publishing, 1974.

    clxl, 1316 p. : 25 cm.                     GB 74–21904

    On spine: Emmet on title.
    Bibliography: p. ₍clxl₎
    Includes index.
    ISBN 0–85120–208–X : £19.50

    1. Conveyancing — Great Britain. 2. Land titles — Great Britain.
I. Farrand, J. T. II. Smith, James Gilchrist. III. Title: Notes on
perusing titles and on practical conveyancing.

KD979.E45  1974           346'.41'0438            75–305378
                                                 MARC

Library of Congress         75

---

**Card 33.** Revision authorship shown in edition statement

---

    Imprint. The imprint of a work consists of the place of publication, the name of the publisher, and the date of publication, which are recorded on the catalog entry in that order. The imprint serves to identify and to characterize the work and sometimes to indicate where it is available. Different editions are most commonly distinguished by the differences in their imprints. The date is especially important, and can be an indication of the current usefulness of a book to the patron searching the card catalog. Imprint data derived from a source other than the title page, preliminaries, or colophon are enclosed in brackets.

    a. Choice of imprint. When it appears that a work was published in several places by one or several publishers, usually the first named place and publisher are used in the entry. However, when a place or publisher other than the first named are treated typographically or in some other way in such a manner as to indicate their primary responsibility, use these and omit the first named. If a city in the United States with an American publisher is named in a secondary position in a work containing a foreign imprint, it is included in addition to the foreign imprint:

London; New York, Longmans, Green
Paris, Gauthier-Villars; Chicago, University of
Chicago Press

If neither the place of publication nor the publisher is named
in the work, but the place of printing and the printer are,
the latter is used in the imprint.

b. Place of publication. The place of publication is
the place in which the office of the publisher is located. In
the case of well known publishers, cataloging may be simplified by omitting the place. Appendix A provides a partial
list of such publishers. If the place of publication is unknown,
the location of an institution or society publishing the work
may be given. If neither the place of publication nor printing
is known, indicate this by entering [s. l.] for sine loco.

The place of publication is followed by its country,
state, or similar designation (in abbreviated form) when the
place is obscure or might be confused with another of the
same name. If a city name is abbreviated on the title page,
transcribe it as given, but give the complete name in brackets to clarify it when needed:

Rio [de Janeiro]
Mpls [i.e., Minneapolis]

c. Publisher. The publisher statement should be
abridged as much as possible without risking confusion. Unnecessary parts may be omitted and abbreviations may be
used (see Appendix A). Names known to be forenames may
be given as initials or omitted in the case of well known publishers. However, the following should not be omitted:

--Words or phrases indicating that the name in the imprint
is not that of the publisher:

Distributed by New York Graphic Society
Printed by the G. Banta Pub. Co.
Planographed by Edwards Bros.

--Name of one of several bodies where the responsibility
is divided, as in the case where one body has done editorial supervision and another the publishing or distribution

--Phrases indicating the official status of a government

printer, or the official authorization of a private printer

--The statement that a work is privately printed, if a publisher or press is named in the imprint.

When the publisher is also the author of a work, the name may be abbreviated in the publishing statement, as long as the full name has been given in the title or author statement:

> Health today issued by the world Health Organization. Geneva, WHO, 1970

If the name of the publisher is unknown, enter [s. n.] for sine nomine.

d. Date. Various kinds of dates may appear on the title page and verso--the date of the latest printing, the copyright date, the date of the first impression of the given book, etc. The important point is to be able to identify the particular edition of the book at hand, which might vary from other editions of the same title.

The basic rule is to give the year of publication of the first impression of the edition. The date may be taken from the title page, preliminaries, or colophon; if it comes from another source, it is enclosed in brackets. When the date is taken from a preface, epilogue or introduction, that fact is indicated, e. g., [pref. 1910]. The date on the title page is always given, but qualified when it does not correspond with the date of publication:

> 1969, 1971 printing (some differences exist between them)

> 1975 i. e. 1957 (typographical error on title page, correct date discovered in preliminaries)

When the date of publication of the first impression of an edition is not known, or is different from the copyright date, give the copyright date--by itself if no other date is available, or together with the title page date:

> c1974

> 1974, c1973

If there are several copyright dates, the latest is used, unless it is only a renewal date or applies to a part of the work only. If the work is in more than one volume and the imprint dates of the individual volumes differ, the inclusive dates are given, e.g., 1971-1975.

If no dates can be found on the title page, preliminaries, or colophon, the cataloger supplies an approximate date as follows:

| | |
|---|---|
| [1892 or 1893] | one of two years certain |
| [1892?] | probable date |
| [ca. 1892] | approximate date |
| [between 1906 and 1912] | not earlier nor later |
| [189-] | decade certain |
| [189-?] | decade uncertain |
| [18--] | century certain |
| [18--?] | century uncertain |

However, the small library should not be overly concerned with establishing the date of the first impression of an edition or researching an approximate date, but should simply use the dates as they are given in the book. In the rare instances of undated material which are encountered in the small library, it is seldom a problem to approximate the decade, at least.

Collation. This term is used for the physical description of a work and includes the number of pages of a one-volume work, or the number of volumes and pages, information about the illustrations, size, accompanying materials if any, and series note, in that order. The small library does not need to follow all the collation rules prescribed by ISBD for the benefit of large research libraries. For example, the dimensions of a book can be omitted; illustrations need not be enumerated or described as to type or color; unnumbered pages can be recorded as "unpaged" rather than counted, and where a work consists of more than one volume, pagination may be ignored. The library should decide how much detail is reasonable and then follow that policy consistently.

1. Pagination: The number of volumes and the number of pages are established through an examination of the book or set. In giving the number of pages, the last numbered page of each section is recorded. A section is either a separately numbered group or an unnumbered group which is long enough (20% of the total) to warrant special attention.

In simplified cataloging, however, notation of the number of introductory pages is frequently omitted, with the cataloger simply turning to the last numbered page in the book and using that number in the collation.

If a work is in two or more volumes, and the library does not have all of them, give what it has in pencil so that the changes may be made easily if other volumes are added, e.g., v. 1, 3 (see card 29, page 118 which has "1" written in). When a book does not have its pages numbered, AACR says to count them if the total is less than 100, or to estimate by 50's if over 100. If the paging is irregular or complicated, the parts may be added, e.g., 600 p. in various pagings. If the number of bibliographical volumes or parts of a work differ from the number of physical volumes, give both, e.g., 2 v. in 1.

2. Illustrations: The title page may include a statement as to the number and type of illustrations, or this information, like the paging, may be discovered only through an examination of the book. The abbreviation ill. may be used, regardless of the type of illustration, and even a single illustration puts a work in the illustrated category. Where the number of illustrations is easily determined, it may be given, and special types (maps, e.g.) may be indicated. When a work contains only illustrations or very little text, that fact is noted.

3. Size: Size is given in centimeters, with the height first: 20 x 8 cm. Width is given only when it is less than half the height or greater than the height. AACR points out that knowing the size of a book can help the user locate it on the shelves, or can be useful when requesting interlibrary loan or photocopying service. However, most small libraries will omit reference to size unless it is particularly uncommon.

Unusual formats (boxes, portfolios, or maps and illustrative material in pockets) and accompanying material such as an answer booklet or audiorecording which are intended to be used with the work should be noted in the collation. If the accompanying material has a title or author different from that of the main work, treat it as a supplement (see page 133).

4. Series: Many books belong to a series and it is sometimes important to include this information in the catalog

---

Williams, N       M       1917–
    Recommended conservation land use of the Awatere River
catchment, Marlborough, South Island, New Zealand / by
N. M. Williams and M. D. Harvey. — Christchurch : Water
and Soil Division for National Water and Soil Conservation
Organisation, 1973.

    87 p. : 41 ill. (1 col.), maps (incl. 4 col. fold. in pocket) ; 28 cm. —
(Bulletin - Land use capability survey ; 5)        NZ 74–1

    Bibliography: p. 86–87.

    1. Land—New Zealand—Awatere River watershed.    I. Harvey,
Michael David, 1947–    joint author. II. Title. III. Series: Land
use capability survey.  Bulletin ; 5.

HD1120.5.Z8A867        333.7′2′0993152      75–307308
                                              MARC
    Library of Congress        75

---

Card 34.   Note detailed collation

---

entry.   The A. L. A. Glossary[2] defines a series as "A number of separate works, usually related to one another in subject or otherwise, issued in succession, normally by the
same publisher and in uniform style, with a collective title."
There are three kinds of series: author, subject, and publisher's.   A Dance to the Music of Time by Anthony Powell,
of which At Lady Molly's and Temporary Kings are two of
the twelve volumes, is an example of an author series;
"American Guide Series" and "Rivers of America" are examples of subject series; "Everyman's Library" is an example of a publisher's series.   Of these, the last is generally
of least importance to the library user, and therefore to the
cataloger.

The name of the series is found at the top of the title
page, on the cover of the book, on one of the pages preceding the title page, or anywhere in the book.   However, if it
appears only on the dust jacket, ignore it.   A series statement gives the name of the series to which the book belongs.
If the name begins with an article, the second word as well
as the article begins with a capital letter.   It is enclosed in
parentheses and is the last item in the collation paragraph.
If it is supplied from an outside source, it is bracketed inside the parentheses.   If the series is not of sufficient importance for an added entry, it is unnecessary for the small
library to include a series statement.

The series statement may include the number of the volume if the series consists of consecutively numbered parts. If a work belongs to more than one series, the second series statement follows the first, in its own set of parentheses. The series entered first is the more specialized or smaller of the two (see card 35). However, if one is a subordinate part of the other, the series and subseries are specified in the same statement, within one set of parentheses:

(U.S. Dept. of State. Publication 1564. Executive agreement series, 94)

---

**Ali, Florence.**
   Opposing absolutes : conviction and convention in John Ford's plays / by Florence Ali. — Salzburg : Institut für Englische Sprache und Literatur, Universität Salzburg, 1974.

   i, 109 p. ; 21 cm. — (Jacobean drama studies ; 44)  (Salzburg studies in English literature)                                          Au***

   Bibliography : p. 106–109.
   S280.00

   1. Ford, John, 1586–ca. 1640—Criticism and interpretation.   I. Title.  II. Series.  III. Series : Salzburg studies in English literature.

PR2527.A46                    822'.3                    75–307299
                                                          MARC
   Library of Congress          75

---

Card 35.   Book belongs to two series

---

Notes.   Notes may be added to catalog entries when needed to explain the title or to correct any misunderstanding to which it might lead, or to give essential information or bibliographic details not included in the title or authorship statements, imprint, or collation. They should be brief, clear, factual, and non-judgmental. The safest rule is not to add a note if there is doubt as to its value.

Information which is needed to identify a work or to distinguish one edition from another, or to aid in locating it on the shelves, but which cannot be fitted into the formal parts of the entry because of length or inappropriateness, should be given in a note. Information needed for identification

includes varying titles or individual titles in a multi-volume
work, additional title pages, names of authors to whom the
work has been attributed or other clarification of authorship,
indication of the incomplete or imperfect nature of a work.
Information needed to aid location might include the following:
the work is in microform; it is bound with something else;
it has a separate index or supplement.

Provision of other information in notes is optional.
Contents notes, including indication of bibliographies and indexes fall in this category, as do notes about bibliographical
history and relationships to other works. Each library must
decide how useful this kind of note is, and adapt its cataloging accordingly. If more than one note is needed, the following order is suggested:

1. Analytical note. When a work which is published
as a part of another is given its own entry rather than being
treated as an added entry, the fact that it is to be found in
the larger work comprises the first note:

> Flaminiani,
> Ethelinda; an English novel. Done from the
> Italian of Flaminiani. London, J. Watts, 1729.
>
> In Croxall, S., comp. A select collection of novels
> and histories. 2d ed. London, 1729. v. 5, p. 79-124.

If the section can be easily handled as an added entry, it is
given as a note in the entry for the larger work:

> Smith, Alfred Emmanuel, 1873-1944.
> Addresses delivered at the meetings of the Society
> of the Friendly Sons of St. Patrick, 1922-1944 . . .
> (New York) Society of the Friendly Sons of St. Patrick
> in the City of New York, 1945.
> 129 p. col. facsim., port.
>
> "Address of Honorable James A. Foley": p. 4-19.

An added entry would be made for Foley. Of course, if you
are sure that your patrons will not be looking for Foley's
address, you would omit both the note and the added entry.

2. Original title. The title of an earlier edition may
be given in a note, as in card 36. The same book may be
published at different times under different titles. For ex-

**Schell, Rolfe F**
  Schell's guide to Eastern Mexico / by Rolfe and Lois
Schell ; photos., drawings and maps by the authors. —
Fort Myers Beach, Fla. : Island Press, ₁1975₁

  302 p. : ill. ; 20 cm.

  Previous editions published under title: Yank in Yucatán.
On cover: Schell's guide to Eastern Mexico plus Yank in Yucatán.
Includes index.
ISBN 0–87208–024–2 : $2.95

  1. Yucatan Peninsula—Description and travel.  I. Schell, Lois,
joint author. II. Title. III. Title: Guide to Eastern Mexico.

F1376.S3 1975    917.2′6′0482    73–87598
                        MARC

Library of Congress    75

**Card 36.** Title of earlier edition and cover title given in
notes

ample, Mireille Cooper's The Happy Season, published by
Pellegrini & Cuhady in New York in 1952, was published in
London in 1951. The content of the English and American
editions is the same, but the English edition has the title
Swiss Family Burnand. If the library has a copy of one
title, an entry is made under the author for that title and a
reference is made from the author and the other title so that
the reader will be sure to find the book. A note on each entry informs the reader of the changed title. If on the other
hand the library has copies of the book under each of its
titles, each title is cataloged separately, with the appropriate
note on each entry giving the information about the other
title (see cards 37 to 39).

   3. At head of title note. "At head of title" is a
phrase used to indicate a statement which cannot be identified
as being a part of the title, a series, subseries, sponsoring
agency, etc., or which does not fit into the formal entry:

     At head of title:  They came from Ireland
       (Entry:  Judson, Clara Ingram.  Michael's vic-
         tory. )

   4. Notes that clarify or amplify the information in the
formalized description. These are given in the same order,

```
Cooper, Mireille (Burnand)
  The happy season.  New York, Pelle-
grini & Cuhady, 1952
  214 p.  ill.

  First published in London in 1951
under title:  Swiss family Burnand.
```

```
Cooper, Mireille (Burnand)
  Swiss family Burnand.  London, Eyre
& Spottiswoode, 1951
  220 p.  ill.

  Published in New York in 1952 under
title:  The happy season
```

Cards 37 & 38.   Main entries for book with changed title--
both books in library

```
Cooper, Mireille (Burnand)
  Swiss family Burnand

    see her

  The happy season
```

Card 39.   Reference for book with changed title--book not in
library

beginning with notes referring to the title. If a note is needed
to explain something about the nature of the work which is important but not clear in the formal description, it comes before notes referring to the rest of the descriptive elements:

> Prose translation.
> English and German.
> Incomplete set: v. 12 wanting.

5.  Notes that explain relationships to other editions
of the same work or to other works. A work which is revised to the point of requiring a new entry is linked with its
predecessor. Works which are abridgments, sequels, supplements, indexes, adaptations, dramatizations, parodies, re-
prints, etc., are identified as such and the original work is
cited. The following are examples:

> Based on the 3d ed. of Guide to the study and use
> of reference books by A. B. Kroeger as re-
> vised by A. G. Mudge.

> Sequel to Mutiny on the Bounty

> Reprinted from the Physical review, vol. 70, nos.
> 5-6 ... September 1-15, 1916.

6.  Bound together note. This shows that two different works (each having its own title page and separate paging)
are included within one cover, whether they were originally
issued that way or bound together subsequently. Use the following phrases, as applicable:

> Issued with
> Issued with the author's
> Issued in a case with
> Bound with
> Bound with the author's

The author's name, title, and place and date of publication of
the other work or works in the volume are given after the
above phrases.

7.  Thesis note. If a work is a thesis, it is identified as such, and the name of the degree and institution are
given:

> Thesis (M.A.)--Johns Hopkins University.

8.  Contents notes.  It is often not necessary to give
contents for collections of short stories, poetry, or plays on
cards made locally if the library has copies of printed indexes to collections.

When a collection contains an author's complete works
or more than 25 items, the contents are not listed.  For a
multi-volume work, however, contents must be given.  When
you wish to make an added entry for a part of a work, that
part must be specified in a contents note, unless it is named
elsewhere in the entry.  For example:

> Title page:
> The Basic Training of Pavlo Hummel and
> Sticks and Bones; Two Plays by David Rabe
> No contents note is necessary, even if title entries
> are wanted for both plays, because they are named
> in the title statement.

> But:

> Title page:
> Six Modern American Plays.  Introduction by
> Allan G. Halline
> If you wish to have an entry for each play, you
> must list all six in a contents note.

However, there is no rule that says you must make added
entries whenever you give a contents note.

Many books contain bibliographies and similar matter
which are often worth noting on the main entry card, even
in small libraries.  A patron wishing more material on a
subject than the library has available can be directed to
books with bibliographies for suggestions of titles he might
wish to request through interlibrary loan.  Supplements or
other material not bound with a work must be listed.  Indexes, discographies, filmographies, and appendices are also
noted, depending on the cataloger's judgment of their importance.  All of the above are known as "informal" contents
notes, and precede the "formal" contents note, which lists
the plays, stories, etc., collected in the work.  The following examples show the form in which informal notes are
given:

> Bibliography: p. 331-345.
> "Chronological list of author's works": p. 242.

Includes bibliographies and index.
Appendices (p. 157-200): A. The Anglo-Japanese
    alliance. --B. The Russo-Japanese peace treaty.
    --C. The Japan-Korean agreement.

The contents proper is given after all other notes,
forming a separate paragraph headed by the words "Contents"
or "Partial contents." The items are listed in the order in
which they appear in the work. Prefatory and similar material is not included, and introductions mentioned in the authorship statement are not repeated. The following examples
show the form in which formal contents notes are given:

CONTENTS: Irving, W. Rip Van Winkle. --
Scott, Sir W. Wandering Willie's tale. --Hawthorne,
N. Young Goodman Brown. --Hawthorne, N. Dr.
Heidegger's experiment. --Poe, E. A. William Wil-
son. --Hawthorne, N. The celestial railroad.

CONTENTS: v. 1. Plain tales from the hills.
--v. 2-3. Soldiers three, and military tales. --
v. 4. In black and white. --v. 5. The phantom
'rickshaw, and other stories. --v. 6. Under the
deodars. The story of the Gadsbys. Wee Willie
Winkie. --v. 7. . . .

Supplements. Continuations, supplements, and indexes are sometimes so dependent upon the works to which
they are related that it is best to add a description of them
to the catalog entry for the main work. A continuation or
supplement which has an author and title different from those
of the original work is generally given its own separate catalog entry, with a note and added entry indicating its relation
to the original work.

To enter a dependent supplement on the card for the
original work, use long dashes to represent the repetition of
the author and title headings, following all the notes relating
to the main work. The dashes are followed by the title of
the supplement or index; the author, compiler, or other person responsible for it (if different from the original author);
the edition statement; imprint; collation; etc. (see cards 40
and 41).

When a supplement is more like a pamphlet or addendum than a separate volume, treat it as part of the collation
for the main work, or add a brief note to the entry, as below:

```
973
C45        Channing, Edward, 1856-1931.
             A history of the United States.
           Macmillan (1905-1925)
               6 v.   ill.

               CONTENTS:   v. 1. The planting of a
           nation in the new world, 1000-1660.--
           v. 2. A century of colonial history,
           1660-1760.--v. 3. The American Revolu-
           tion, 1761-1789.--v. 4. Federalists and
           Republicans, 1789-1815.--v. 5. The

                          (  )   (Continued on next
                                      card)
```

Card 40.   Main entry for work of more than one volume with
           different copyright dates and with contents

```
973
C45        Channing, Edward.   A history of the
               United States . . . (1905-1925)
               (Card 2)

                   CONTENTS-Continued
           period of transition, 1815-1848.--
           v. 6. The war for Southern independence.

973
C45        ---- ------ Supplementary volume, gen-
           eral index, comp. by Eva G. Moore.
           Macmillan (c1932)
               155 p.     (  )
```

Card 41.   Extension for card 40, showing general index
           added to card for main work

                "Tables I, II, and III omitted by error from
           report" published as suppl. (5 p.) and inserted at
           end.

Tracings. The final item on each main catalog entry
is a record, or "tracing" of all the subject entries and added
entries made for the work. This is necessary so that all the
cards may be found and taken out of the catalog if it is necessary to make a correction or addition to them, or if the
book is withdrawn from the library.

The record of the added entries, in a single paragraph,
is typed on the front of the main entry card, just above the
hole. The first line begins at the second indention. On
printed cards, the tracing appears on each card, as all cards
are made from the same copy, but on typed cards it should
be omitted on the added entry cards. If necessary, part of
the tracing can be put on the back of the card, in which case
the word "over" is typed on the front of the card, just to the
right of the hole.

The subject headings are listed first, numbered consecutively with Arabic numerals, followed by added entries,
numbered with Roman numerals. Added entries are given in
the following order: persons, corporate bodies, title proper,
other titles, analytics, series. Within each category, the
headings are listed in the order in which they appear in the
catalog entry. Each is traced to show the form in which it
is to be found in the catalog. The tracing of the title proper
is indicated by the word "title," and is not repeated. Tracings for other titles are written out fully, preceded by the
word "title."

If the series is entered as it appears in the series
statement, only the word "series" is listed in the tracing,
but if there is any variation between the series statement and
the form of the entry, the tracing must spell it out:

Statement: (S. P. E. tract no. 36)
Tracing: Series: Society for Pure English. Tract
no. 36.

See also card 34, page 126.

If author and title analytical entries are made for all
the plays, essays, or stories listed in the contents on the
main entry card, instead of tracing each one a statement to
that effect may appear below the other tracing, e.g., "Author and title analytical entries made for each play," or
"See contents for tracing."

For examples of tracings, see the cards reproduced in this chapter and in chapter 12. Note that LC cards for children's books give alternative headings for children's collections in brackets. Also note that in cards 33 and 36 (pages 121 and 129) the names Emmet and Schell are excluded from the added entries for the titles.

## EXTENSION CARDS

When there is not enough space on a card for all of the information, added cards known as extension or second cards are made. Whenever an extension card follows, "Continued on next card" is typed (or stamped with a rubber stamp) aligned with the hole in the card and immediately to the right of it. At the minimum, the call number and the first or filing word of the first card are repeated on all extension cards and the number of the card is written in the center of the card, on the line above the heading. On the author or main card, the filing word at the top of the extension cards would be the author's surname; if the name of an organization, however, the full heading would be repeated as so many organizations begin with the same word, the name of the country, and so forth. On extension cards for added entries, repeat the entire added heading, then proceed as usual.

Printed LC cards repeat rather more of the heading than has been suggested above, and give the number of the extension card in parentheses following the heading, as in cards 42 and 43. The full heading, short title, and publication date are repeated. This ensures that the extension card can be readily matched with the first card, should they become separated.

Extension cards may be tied to the first card with heavy white thread. A pencil may be slipped in so that the cards may be turned easily without being cut. Tying makes it easier to handle the cards before they are filed, and if for any reason they have to be removed from the catalog for additional information or a correction, they can be kept together.

## MICROFORMS

It is unlikely that small libraries will have many

**Hirst, Paul Heywood.**
　　Knowledge and the curriculum : a collection of philosophical papers / Paul H. Hirst. — London ; Boston : Routledge & K. Paul, 1974 ₍i.e. 1975₎

　　　xiii. 193 p. ; 23 cm. — (International library of the philosophy of education)
　　　　　　　　　　　　　　　　　　　　　　　　　　　　GB•••

　　　Label mounted verso t.p.: Owing to printing delays this book was published in 1975.
　　　Includes bibliographical references and index.
　　　CONTENTS: Philosophy and curriculum planning.—The nature and structure of curriculum objectives.—Liberal education and the nature of knowledge. —Realms of meaning and forms of knowledge.—Language and thought.—The

　　　　　　　　　　　(Continued on next card)
　　　　　　　　　　　　　　　　　　　74-79359
　　　　　　　　　　　　　　　　　　　　MARC
　　　　　　　○
　　　　　　　　75

Card 42.　First card of two-card main entry

**Hirst, Paul Heywood.** — Knowledge and the curriculum . . . 1974 ₍i.e. 1975₎　(Card 2)
　　　　　　　　CONTENTS—Continued.

　　forms of knowledge re-visited.—What is teaching?—The logical and psychological aspects of teaching a subject.—Curriculum integration.—Literature and the fine arts as a unique form of knowledge.—The two-cultures, science and moral education.—Morals, religion and the maintained school.
　　　ISBN 0-7100-7929-X.　ISBN 0-7100-7930-3 pbk.

　　　1. Curriculum planning.　I. Title.　II. Series.
　　LB1555.H65　1975　　　　375'.001　　　74-79359
　　　　　　　　　　　　○　　　　　　　　MARC
　　Library of Congress　　　75

Card 43.　Extension for card 42

items other than periodicals on microfilm, microfiche, or micro-opaque. Should the need arise to catalog a monograph in this format, the main thing to remember is that the work from which the reproduction was made determines the data given in the formal part of the catalog entry, with physical description of the reproduction relegated to a note. Enough information about the format must be given to indicate the type of equipment needed for using the material:

---

Shirley, James, 1596-1666.
  The gentleman of Venice: a tragi-comedie presented at the private house in Salisbury Court by Her Majesties servants.  London, H. Moseley, 1655.
  78 p.  18 cm.

  Micro-opaque.  New York, Readex Microprint, 1953.
1 card.  23 x 15 cm.  (Three centuries of drama: English, 1642-1700)

Card 44.  Main entry for book reproduced in microform

---

## SIMPLIFIED ENTRIES FOR FICTION

Since the reader who wants fiction uses the catalog only to find whether or not a certain book is in the library or what books the library has by a certain author, cards for fiction may be simpler than for nonfiction.  For this reason most public libraries do not classify fiction nor assign a book number, and catalog it more simply than nonfiction when they type the cards.  Some school and college libraries, however, prefer to classify their fiction as literature and to catalog it exactly as they do their nonfiction.  Others do not classify fiction, but catalog all books the same way, whether fiction or nonfiction.

The simplest form of entry may contain only the author's full name, without dates, and the title.  Many librarians prefer, however, to follow the same policy regarding author's dates for fiction as for nonfiction.  Some librarians find the copyright date or the date of publication useful as the date answers the reader's query as to which of the titles is the most recent.

If more information regarding the book, e.g., the publisher, is desired on the catalog entries, it is better to catalog fiction and nonfiction alike.  But if this information is available in trade catalogs and bibliographical tools which are at hand, time may be saved by making simple catalog entries such as card 45 and by referring to these printed aids for the occasional calls for such information.

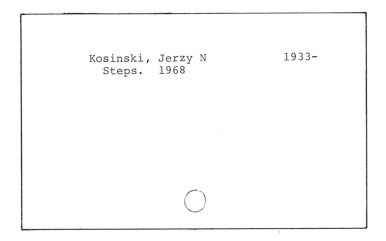

Card 45.   Simplified main entry for fiction

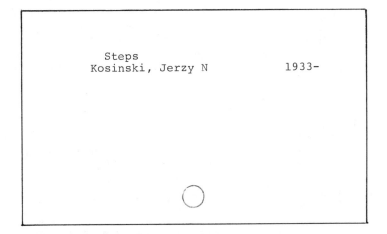

Card 46.   Title card for fiction

On the title card the information given on the author card is simply reversed, the title given on the top line, the author on the line below.   As the reader frequently remembers the title rather than the author, title entries for fiction are important.

Another type of fiction is the anonymous book, the author of which is unknown. This is the easiest of all to catalog. Obviously there can be no author card, and the only items that could go on the title card are the title and the date. The latter item may be omitted. When the author is known but the title page does not give the name, the book is cataloged as any other work of fiction, and a note states that the book is published anonymously.

If the printed cards described in chapter 12 are used for fiction, there are very few books for which the author's names and dates need to be established. If only author and title--or author, title, and dates are given for fiction, however, it may be less expensive, take less time, and be as satisfactory to type the cards for fiction in the library as it would be to order Library of Congress or other printed catalog cards.

To streamline the preparation of catalog cards for fiction even further, some libraries[3] use strips of three cards with perforated edges, as in card 47. The third card is the shelf list card, discussed in chapter 11. These cards may be obtained preprinted from several library supply houses. The advantage of using them lies in the fact that there is no wasted motion in getting cards in and out of the typewriter, and the instructions for finding the book on the shelves are helpful to the patron.

## CATALOG CARDS AND LIBRARY USERS

Despite the fact that the purpose of the catalog is to help the user locate material in the library, most librarians can cite cases where the catalog has done more to confuse than to enlighten the patron. In a letter to U*n*a*b*a*s*h*e*d Librarian, Robert Jonas cites some typical examples:

> A student asked for Harper's Magazine. I asked, 'What month?' Student: 'It doesn't say. ' I: 'Show me the catalog card, if you don't mind. ' Student: 'Here it is: "How to make cabinets [not an actual title]--Harper 1960. "' Obviously, the student didn't understand that Harper was the publisher--not a magazine.

> Client: 'How can I find 451 P?' Librarian: 'That "451 P" stands for "451 pages. "' Obviously,

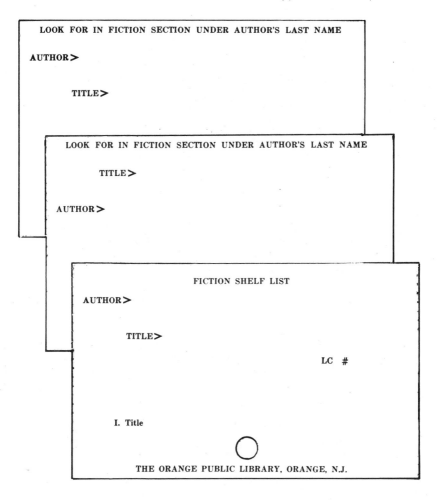

Card 47.  Strip of cards for fiction cataloging

the client didn't know that catalog cards sometimes show how many pages are in a work.  He thought '451p' was the 'Dewey Number. '

A relative of mine, who had majored in psychology, complained that he could never tell what the title of a book was, on a catalog card.  'Why don't they put the title in quotation marks--or some such thing, ' he asked me.

Now, if a catalog card could show such words
as TITLE, AUTHOR, PUBLISHER, the three 'cases'
mentioned above need not be repeated. [4]

Acting on his analysis of the problem, Jonas created
the format shown in cards 48 to 50, with the bottom portion
in the original cards in bright yellow.

Scilken's "Super Card"[5] follows the same principle,
except that the words "author," "title," etc., are typed in
their appropriate places, as shown in cards 51 to 54. He
recommends eliminating abbreviations and advocates calling
attention to the tracing, making each card serve as a cross
reference.

Until Jonas and Scilken can persuade centralized cataloging services to adopt their proposal, libraries can at least
provide conspicuous signs and guide cards which explain the
format and contents of cards and give directions for using
the catalog.

## References

1.  Anglo-American Cataloging Rules, North American Text:
    Chapter 6, Separately Published Monographs (Chicago,
    American Library Association, 1974).

2.  A. L. A. Glossary of Library Terms (Chicago, American
    Library Association, 1943), p. 124.

3.  U*n*a*b*a*s*h*e*d Librarian, 4: 10. (General Post Of-
    fice Box 2631, New York, NY 10001. )

4.  U*n*a*b*a*s*h*e*d Librarian, 15: 11.

5.  U*n*a*b*a*s*h*e*d Librarian, 12: 32.

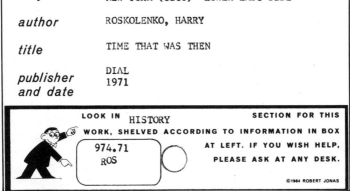

Cards 48, 49, 50. Jonas' answer to catalog card quandry

973.9 Author: Berle, Adolf Augustus.

Be          Title: Navigating the rapids, 1918-1971. Pub-
            lisher: Harcourt. Year of publication: 1973.
            859 pages.

     For other items on the subjects discussed in this book,
     look in the card catalog under the following headings:

          1.  Berle, Adolf Augustus, 1895-1971.  2. United
     States--Politics and government--20th century.  3.
     United States--Foreign relations--20th century.  4.
     United States--Economic conditions.

---

            Title: Navigating the rapids, 1918-1971.
     973.9 Author: Berle, Adolf Augustus.

     Be          Title: Navigating the rapids, 1918-1971; Pub-
                 lisher: Harcourt. Year of publication: 1973.
                 859 pages.

     For other items on the subjects discussed in this book,
     look in the card catalog under the following headings:

          1.  Berle, Adolf Augustus, 1895-1971.  2. United States--
     Politics and government--20th century.  3. United
     States--Foreign relations--20th century.  4. United
     States--Economic conditions.

Cards 51, 52, 53, 54.  Scilken's "super cards." Copyright
© 1974.  The U*N*A*B*A*S*H*E*D LIBRARIAN, The "How
I Run My Library Good" Letter, G. P. O. Box 2631, New York,
N. Y. 10001.  Reprinted with permission.

973.9   Author: Berle, Adolf Augustus.

Be          Title: Navigating the rapids, 1918-1971; Pub-
           lisher: Harcourt. Year of publication: 1973.
           859 pages.


    1. Berle, Adolf Augustus, 1895-1971.   2. United States--
Politics and government--20th century.   3. United States-
Foreign relations--20th century.   4. United States--
Economic conditions.   I. Title.

---

                THIS BOOK IS ABOUT:
             BERLE, ADOLF AUGUSTUS, 1895-1971

973.9   Author: Berle, Adolf Augustus.

Be          Title: Navigating the rapids, 1918-1971; Pub-
           lisher: Harcourt. Year of publication: 1973.
           859 pages.

  For other items on the subjects discussed in this book,
  look in the card catalog under the following headings:

    1. Berle, Adolf Augustus, 1895-1971.   2. United States-
Politics and government--20th century.   3. United
States--Foreign relations--20th century.   4. United
States--Economic conditions.

CHAPTER 8


## ADDED CATALOG ENTRIES


If every library user could be expected to know precisely which books he needed, and could also be expected to
know the exact heading under which librarians would choose
to catalog each book, there would need to be only one catalog card for each book in the library. But as every librarian
knows, library patrons frequently know only the title of a
book, or need information on some subject. So, after the
cataloger has decided on the main entry for a book, it is
necessary to consider additional entries which will enable
the card catalog to provide maximum access to the collection.

An added entry is a secondary entry; i. e. , it is any
other than the main entry. There may be added entries for
editor, translator, title, alternate title, subjects, series,
etc. An added entry card is basically a duplicate of the
main entry card, with the addition of a special heading. In
the small library, however, whether the added entry is an
exact and complete duplicate of the main entry (plus special
heading) will depend on whether the library already has in
hand a set of several duplicate cards for the book being cataloged, or whether it must prepare and type each one. In
most cases the library will have already purchased LC or
other printed cards, or it may have the facilities to make
duplicates itself from the main entry card. Some commercial sources of printed cards can even provide sets with
headings already added. But when prepared card sets are
not available for an item to be cataloged, the librarian should
consider whether all the descriptive information on the main
entry card is really needed on every other entry. The minimum information required for most added entry cards is the
heading, the call number, the author, title, publisher, and
date (with subtitle omitted). An even shorter form is per-
missible for fiction title entries, as explained on pages 138-
140. Libraries which regularly include extensive contents
notes on the main entry card may simply stamp "See main
entry for contents" on appropriate added entry cards.

## SUBSIDIARY AUTHORS

Added entries should be made for all persons or corporate bodies connected with a publication under which a catalog user is likely to search. This is especially important
when the main entry for a work is under a title or corporate
body.

Added entry cards may be made for joint authors (up
to three) for a compiler, editor, illustrator, translator, or
for the person who writes the introduction to the book of another, provided these added entries are likely to be useful.
If there are more than three joint authors or editors, an entry is made only for the first one. An added entry under
Kaufman would be useful for Hart and Kaufman's You Can't
Take It with You, because the play is frequently referred to
as Hart and Kaufman's play, and some readers will look under Hart, some under Kaufman. The book mentioned on page
102, The Boys' King Arthur, will need an added entry under
Lanier, since it is spoken of as Lanier's Boys' King Arthur.
Also, though the main entry for The Book of King Arthur and
His Noble Knights is under Macleod (see page 102), an entry
is needed under Malory for the reader who is interested in
everything in the library relating to Malory.

When the main entry is under author, an added entry
is made for an editor if he has added significant material or
if the work has been issued in many editions with different
editors, e.g. Shakespeare's plays; under a translator if the
translation is in verse or if the work has been translated
into English by many different translators; under an illustrator
if the artist's contribution is significant. If a writer like
Pope or Longfellow translates another's work, an added entry enables the student to consider not only their original
writings but their translations as well. The student interested
in The Iliad is likely to wish to see both Pope's and Latti-
more's translations, and to look in the catalog under the
translators' names, though knowing it is Homer's Iliad. Occasionally an added entry is necessary for a compiler or an
editor for the same reason. If the library is likely to have
a call for illustrations by a well-known artist, e.g. Sir John
Tenniel, an added entry under his name would make it possible to find examples of his illustrations. If the library has
a copy, and it should have, of The H. W. Wilson Company's
Children's Catalog, it may be used to locate books with illustrations by a particular artist and no added entry need be
made under illustrator. It must be remembered, however,

that reliance on this type of index presupposes the availability of a librarian who can help the patron who has failed to find the entry in the card catalog.

To make added entries of the kind mentioned, the full name in its best-known form (see chapter 3), with dates, if the library uses them, is written on the line above the author. Begin at the second indention, so that the heading of the main entry may remain in a prominent position. If this added heading occupies more than one line, succeeding lines begin at the third indention. The abbreviation, comp. , ed. , ill. , or tr. (or the full word if preferred), is given one space after the comma at the end of the heading (card 56). In the case of an added entry for a joint author or for the individual who writes the preface or introduction for another's work, no designation follows the name (card 55).

```
812        Kaufman, George
H32        Hart, Moss
              You can't take it with you, a play
           by Moss Hart and George S. Kaufman.
           New York, Farrar & Rinehart [c1937]
              207 p.  ill
```

Card 55.   Added entry for joint author

```
842.4        Wilbur, Richard, tr.
             Molière, Jean Baptiste Poquelin
                The school for wives; comedy in five
             acts, 1662.  Translated into English
             verse by Richard Wilbur.  Harcourt
             [1971]
                146 p.  ill.

                Translation of L'école des femmes
```

Card 56.   Added entry for translator

Another type of added entry is for the author and title

of a work which has been dramatized by another writer (card 57). The name of the author and the title of the original work are added above the unit card at the second and third indentions respectively.

```
         Kesey, Ken
812          One flew over the cuckoo's nest
WAS      Wasserman, Dale
             One flew over the cuckoo's nest:
         a play in two acts by Dale Wasserman
         from the novel by Ken Kesey.  New
         York, Samuel French, 1974.
             83 p.
```

Card 57.   Added entry for the author and title of a work dramatized by another writer

Added entries, except title and subject cards, are made sparingly in the small library where the collection is accessible.

TITLES

Title entries are made for all books of fiction and for most nonfiction. Consider Cyril Bentham Falls' The Second World War, a Short History and Charles L. Mee's Meeting at Potsdam. The former title is neither striking nor distinctive and may be used for many histories of the war. Undoubtedly many readers, however, will remember the latter and look for it in the catalog.

Title entries are not made for the following: works with common titles that are incomplete or meaningless without the author's name, such as "Collected works," "Autobiography," "Letters," "Memoirs," "Bulletin," "Report," "Proceedings," etc.; works with introductory words commonly used in titles, e.g., "Introduction to," "The principles of," "A story of"; works with titles that are essentially the same as the main entry heading; works consisting solely of the name of a real person, unless fictionalized; works with titles that are the same as a subject heading under which they are entered. Fenton and Fenton's Mountains illustrates the last point. The title of this book is Mountains and the subject treated is mountains, so the subject heading would be MOUNTAINS. It is unnecessary to have the same book entered in the catalog twice under the same word; but if only a title card is made it will file at the end of all the cards for material about mountains even though the author's name begins with F; hence the rule, if the first word or words of the title and the subject are the same, do not make a title card.

Title entries should be made for all works published anonymously but whose authors have been identified and used as main entries. Alternate titles, cover titles or other titles by which a work might be known should be given added entries.

As discussed above, there are two possible forms for title entries, namely the short form and the unit card form. The short form title card has the call number, title, and author. Title cards may be just like the main entry, however, with the brief title added above the heading of the unit card. This form is in accordance with the statement made above, that an added entry is a duplicate of a main entry, with the addition of a special heading. If a unit card is used, the reader need not refer to the main entry card.

---

```
940.53        Meeting at Potsdam
MEE           Mee, Charles L
```

Card 58.  Title entry, short form

---

In the preceding chapter, the author card for Cooper's The Happy Season is given as an illustration of what is done with books published under different titles. Cards 60 and 61 show the corresponding title entries.

The latter part of the title of some books is better known than the full title, e.g., The Tragedy of Macbeth. In such cases, a catch or partial title card is made, i.e., Macbeth. This card begins with the first striking word of the title, with the full title given after the author entry if the card is a unit card (see card 62). When a library has many editions of a work that requires the same added entry, it saves time and space to make one reference card.

```
940.53          Meeting at Potsdam
MEE             Mee, Charles L
                  Meeting at Potsdam.  New York,
                [1975]
                  xiv, 370 p.  ill.

                  Bibliography:  p. 354-361

                  1.  Berlin Conference, 1945.
                  2.  World War, 1939-1945--Peace
                II. Title
```

Card 59.   Title entry, unit card

```
                The happy season
                Cooper, Mireille (Burnand)
                  The happy season.  New York,
                Pellegrini & Cuhady, 1952.
                  214 p.  illus.

                  First published in London in 1951
                under title:  Swiss family Burnand.
```

Card 60.   Title entry for book with changed title--book in
           library

```
                Swiss family Burnand,   see
                Cooper, Mireille (Burnand)
                  The happy season
```

Card 61.   Reference card for book with changed title--book
           not in library

Robinson Crusoe

**Defoe, Daniel.** 1661?-1731.
    The life & strange surprising adventures of Robinson Crusoe,
of York, mariner. Edited by George A. Aitken, with illus. by J.
B. Yeats. London, J. M. Dent, 1895. ₍New York, AMS Press,
1974₎

    lxvii, 342 p. illus. 19 cm.

    Original ed. issued as v. 1 of the author's Romances and narratives.

I. Title. II. **Title:** Robinson Crusoe

PZ3.D362 Li 24         823'.5         74-13442
₍PR3403₎                                MARC
ISBN 0-404-07911-3

Library of Congress        74

**Card 62.**   Catch title entry, unit card

Hamlet
Shakespeare, William

    Editions of this work will be
found under the author's name.

**Card 63.**   Reference card for title of work available in many
editions

---

    There are other books for which both full and partial
titles should be brought out in the catalog, e.g., J. George
Frederick's A Primer of "New Deal" Economics. This work
would have an entry for the full title and for the partial title,
"New deal" economics. Another type of book which requires
both full and partial title entries is represented by card 64.
While some patrons might look under "How to ...," others
will no doubt look under Barron's. However, when the title
begins with a name which is the same as the main entry,
only a partial title entry is made. For example, the title
entry for Sylvia Porter's Money Book is Money book (see
also cards 33 and 36, pages 121 and 129).

How to prepare for the high school
        equivalency examination (GED) English
**Potell, Herbert.**                                      section
        Barron's how to prepare for the high school equivalency
    examination (GED) English section: correctness and ef-
    fectiveness of expression. Woodbury, N. Y., Barron's Edu-
    cational Series [1974]

        vii, 262 p.  28 cm.  $2.95

        1. High school equivalency examination.  2. General educational
    development tests.        I. Title.  II. Title: How to prepare for the
    high school equivalency examination (GED) English section.

    LB1627.7.P67                      373.1'2'64                    73–8161
    ISBN 0-8120-0464-7                                             MARC

    Library of Congress               74 [4]

Card 64.    Partial title entry for work entered under both full
            and partial titles

SUBJECTS

        There are usually more inquiries for material on a
subject than there are for books by a specific author or with
a particular title.  The most used cards in the catalog are
the subject cards; that is, the cards which indicate on the
top line the subject of which the book treats.  For this reason, a subject entry should be made for every book which
deals with a definite subject.  Sometimes a book covers several different topics and requires two, three, or even more
subject entries.  Subject entries are not necessary for books
containing a single poem or a single play, or for a collection
of all or part of the works of an individual author.  Chapter
2 deals with the question of ascertaining what a book is about
and what subject headings best express its contents.  There
is also the possibility of making general subject references
for entire groups of books, e.g., books on birds, airplanes,
etc., or for all books of a certain form, e.g., books of
American poetry, as shown in cards 6 and 7, pages 42 and
44.  Card 6 is repeated on page 154.  On this card, note
that the classification number is given in the same position
as on main entry cards and the subject heading in the same
position as added entry headings on the cards shown in this
chapter.  A line is skipped and a paragraph, beginning on
the second line below the heading, tells where books on the

```
551.2     VOLCANOES

              Books about volcanoes will be found
          on the shelves under 551.2.

              For a complete author list of the
          books in the library on volcanoes,
          consult the shelf list under 551.2.
```

Card 6.   General subject entry for all books in a subject
          class

given subject may be found.   Another line is skipped and the
second paragraph about the use of the shelf list is given.

A unit card with an added subject heading is given below in order to show the position of the heading.   Subdivisions
of a main heading may be separated from it by a space, dash,

```
940.53      WORLD WAR, 1939-1945--PEACE
MEE         Mee, Charles L
              Meeting at Potsdam.  New York,
            M. Evans  [1975]
              xiv, 370 p.  ill.

            Bibliography:  p. 354-361


              1. Berlin Conference, 1945  2. World
            War, 1939-1945--Peace  I. Title
```

Card 65.   Subject entry

space or other punctuation marks agreed upon locally, as a
long dash (e. g. , U. S. --HISTORY).   This heading is given in
full capitals in order to distinguish it from title or other added

entry headings. Some libraries use red ink in typing subject headings, in which case they are not capitalized.


## ANALYTICAL ENTRIES

An analytical entry is an entry for a part of a work. It may be for a complete work in itself which is published in a collection, or it may be for only a few pages inadequately described (either from the author or subject approach) by the catalog entry for the work as a whole.

Some books are made up of two or more separate works of an author, or of different authors; or they may treat of several distinct subjects or phrases of a subject. For example, the two-volume edition of De la Mare's Collected Poems contains his well-known poems for children, published under the title Peacock Pie. In this collection the library has the work, Peacock Pie, whether or not it has the separately bound edition. How can this be shown in the catalog? By making author and title analytical entries for it. Law's Science in Literature contains an essay by Madame Curie on her discovery of radium. This material on radium is as important as any that will be found in many libraries. It can be brought out by means of a subject analytical entry, i. e. , a subject entry for a part of a book. Small collections and special libraries need to have their material analyzed freely, since the analytical entry may represent the only work by the author, the only copy of the essay, play, etc. , or the only material on the subject. Frequently the analytical entry is used to call attention to an extra copy of popular material already available in another form.

It should be emphasized again that advantage should be taken of work already done. The H. W. Wilson Company's Children's Catalog, 12th edition, includes 13,272 analytical entries; their Senior High School Library Catalog, 10th edition, includes 12,661 analytical entries. Printed indexes such as Short Story Index, Play Index and others, although they may seem expensive, would be more economical in the long run than preparing analytical cards for collections of short stories and plays.

For an author analytical entry the name of the author of the play, essay, or other separate work is given on the unit card on the second line above the author of the book, the title on the line below the author of the part, followed by:

"p. 00-00:". For a title analytical entry this is reversed and the title is given on the top line, the author of the analytical entry on the next line followed by the same phrase and punctuation, namely: "p. 00-00:".

The author of the analytical entry is given on the second line of the card, the title on the third line, followed by: a comma, the paging, and a colon (in the case of a work of two or more volumes, the volume number precedes the paging, e.g., v. 2, p. 56-112:). The indentions deserve special attention. In order that the author of the main book may stand out as well as the author and title of the particular part, the author in the added heading (i.e., the analytical author) is given at the second or title indention and the title of the part analyzed at the third indention. If the name of the author of the analytical entry takes two lines, it begins on the first line and continues on the second line, third indention; and if the title of the analytical entry runs over, it comes back to the third indention.

```
                Sheridan, Richard Brinsley Butler,
                  1751-1816.
                  The school for scandal, p. 182-
808.82            265:
C67             Cohen, Helen Louise.  Milestones of
                  the drama. . . [c1940]  (Card 2)

                        CONTENTS-Continued
                The school for scandal.--Ibsen, Henrik.
                A doll's house.--Rostand, Edmond.  Cyra-
                no de Bergerac.--O'Neill, Eugene.  The
                Emperor Jones.--Further explorations.

                  1. Drama-Collections   I. Title
                Author & title analytics
```

Card 66.   Author analytical entry

If the author of the analytical entry and the author of the book are the same, an author analytical entry is unnecessary, as the person searching for the play or short story will look under the author's name, then in the contents listed on the card, for collections of plays, short stories, etc.

The two title analytical cards (numbers 67 and 68),
like the author analytical card (number 66), are unit cards
with the title and author of the respective analytics added as
headings, followed by the paging.  On card 67, the author of
the analytical entry and the author of the book are the same.
It would be absurd to give the same author twice in succession, hence the title of the analytical entry is simply added
in the regular place for an added title heading, and is followed by the paging as for all other analytical entries.  In
the second example,  card 68, since the authors are different,
the same items are given as for the author analytical entry,
but in reverse order.  If the title runs over, the second line
begins at the same indention, i. e., the third indention; and
if the author's name runs over, it continues on the next line
beginning at the third indention.  Note that when an entry requires more than one card, the card used for the analytical
entry is the one which lists the particular item being analyzed (see cards 66 and 68).

```
821          Peacock pie, v. 2, p. 95-218:
D33          De la Mare, Walter John
                Collected poems, 1901-1918.  Holt,
             [c1920]
                2v.

                CONTENTS:  v. 1. Poems, 1906. The
             listeners, 1914.  Motley, 1919.--v. 2.
             Songs of childhood, 1901.  Peacock pie,
             1913


                Title analytics
```

Card 67.   Title analytical entry--book and analytical entry by
           the same author

For a subject analytical entry the subject heading is
given as on any subject card.  The heading is followed by the
phrase regarding the paging.  If the author of the chapter or
section whose subject is being brought out in the catalog in
this way is different from the author of the book, his name

```
                The school for scandal, p. 182-
                265:
                Sheridan, Richard Brinsley Butler,
   808.82       1751-1816.
   C67      Cohen, Helen Louise.  Milestones of
                the drama. . . [c1940]   (Card 2)


                    CONTENTS-Continued
            The school for scandal.--Ibsen, Henrik.
            A doll's house.--Rostand, Edmond.   Cyra-
            no de Bergerac.--O'Neill, Eugene.   The
            Emperor Jones.--Further explorations.


                1. Drama-Collections   I. Title
            Author & title analytics
```

Card 68.   Title analytical entry--book and analytical entry by
           different authors

comes on the line below the subject, and the phrase regarding the paging follows that.   If the work is in more than one
volume and the analytical entry is for an entire volume, the
volume number is substituted for the paging (e.g., v. 2:).
If, however, the analytical entry is for only a part of a volume, both volume and paging are given (e.g., v. 2, p. 101-
137).

On subject analytical entry cards it is observed that
the title of the part analyzed is omitted because the name of
the author and the subject heading are more important than
the title and there is not space for all three at the top of the
unit card.   Dropping the author, title, etc. of a typed unit
card another line would make all other items too low on the
card.   If the title is very important, an exception may be
made by omitting the notes and contents of the unit card from
this copy of the card and substituting a note giving the title
of the analyzed part.

SERIES

A series is defined in the AACR glossary as "1.   A
number of separate works issued in succession and related to
one another by the fact that each bears a collective title gen-

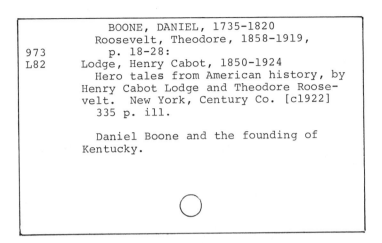

```
                 BOONE, DANIEL, 1735-1820
              Roosevelt, Theodore, 1858-1919,
  973            p. 18-28:
  L82         Lodge, Henry Cabot, 1850-1924
                 Hero tales from American history, by
              Henry Cabot Lodge and Theodore Roose-
              velt.  New York, Century Co. [c1922]
                 335 p.  ill.

              Daniel Boone and the founding of
              Kentucky.
```

Card 69.   Subject analytical entry including title of the part
           analyzed

erally appearing at the head of the title page, on the half
title, or on the cover; normally issued by the same publisher in a uniform style, frequently in a numerical sequence....
2. Each of two or more volumes of essays, lectures, articles, or other writings, similar in character and issued in
sequence, e.g., Lowell's Among my books, second series.
3. A separately numbered sequence of volumes within a
series or serial, e.g., Notes and queries, 1st series, 2d
series, etc. "[1]

A series added entry is made for each separately cataloged work which might be cited as part of the series, or
if the series might reasonably be cataloged as a collected
set.   The importance of the series determines whether or
not an added entry is made.   If the parts of a series are
numbered, the number is included in the heading.   Added entries are rarely made if all the volumes in the series are by
the same person, nor for series with titles that include the
name of the trade publisher or have nothing in common except their format.

The title of the series is given (see cards 70-71) on
the fourth line from the top at the first indention; if it runs
over, the succeeding lines begin at the second indention.   Following a comma, the words ed. by and the name of the editor

```
                 Rivers of America
975.1
C21              Canby, Henry Seidel.  The Brandy-
                 wine.  [c1941]

978.9
C77              Corle, Edwin.   The Gila.   [c1951]


975.62           Ross, Malcolm.   The Cape Fear.
R82              [c1965]
```

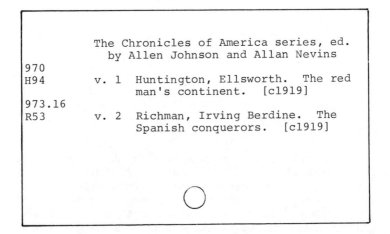

Card 70.   Added entry under series--short form

```
                 The Chronicles of America series, ed.
                   by Allen Johnson and Allan Nevins
970
H94              v. 1   Huntington, Ellsworth.  The red
                        man's continent.   [c1919]
973.16
R53              v. 2   Richman, Irving Berdine.  The
                        Spanish conquerors.   [c1919]
```

Card 71.   Added entry under series, giving volume number
           and editor of series--short form

of the series as found in the book are given.  If there is no
editor, or it seems unnecessary to give the editor's name,
the phrase is omitted.  The classification number is given on
the next line, and below that, on the same line with the book

number, are given: the author's name inverted, beginning at the second indention, with his dates omitted to conserve space; the title of the work, omitting explanatory and alternative titles; then the date. The second line of the entry for each individual work begins at the second indention. Other volumes in the series are added to the card in the same form. A line skipped, as shown on card 70, makes it easier to read the entry for any one volume. For a numbered series in which the volumes are preferably read in a certain order (see card 71), the volume numbers are given at the first indention, and the surname of the author of the individual book at the third indention.

Another way to make a series entry is to write the name of the series above the heading of the unit card. Thus a series entry is made for each book in the set, and these cards file together in the catalog alphabetically by author.

Special entry under series is necessary for important subject series, i.e., for series in which all the books deal with the same subject, e.g., "Rural Science Series," "The Chronicles of America Series." School libraries especially will find these entries useful. Even the smallest public library which owns "The Chronicles of America" would probably find a series entry useful.

```
                  The Chronicles of America series,
973.917           v. 52
B86       Brogan, Denis William
                  The era of Franklin D. Roosevelt; a
          chronicle of the New Deal and global
          war.  New Haven, Yale University
          Press [1950]
                  382 p.  ill.  (The Chronicles of
          America series, v. 52)

                  "Bibliographical note": p. 365-372.

                  1. U.S.-History, 1933-1945  2. World
          War, 1939-1945  I. Title  II. Series
```

Card 72.  Added entry under series--unit card

Another kind of series for which an added entry under the series title is useful is an author's series, e.g., "The Lord of the Rings" by J. R. R. Tolkien (see card 74).

---

|        | Golden hind series.                              |
|--------|--------------------------------------------------|
| 92<br>F92 | Frobisher, by William McFee.<br>[1934]        |
| 92<br>H39 | Hawkins, by Philip Gosse.   [c1930]           |
| 92<br>R16 | Raleigh, by Milton Waldman.<br>[c1928]        |

Card 73.   Added entry under series--biography

---

The lord of the rings, by J.R.R.
Tolkien

The fellowship of the ring

The two towers

The return of the king

Card 74.   Added entry under series--author the same

---

Card 75 shows the form to be used for a reference card from the editor of a series to the entry under the title of the series.

Some book indexes, e.g., the Cumulative Book Index, include entries under series and the libraries which have these indexes might use them for series rather than making

```
Nevins, Allan, 1890-          ed.

see

The Chronicles of America series
```

Card 75.  Reference from the name of the editor of a series

added entries.  This would mean checking the Index to see if
it includes an entry for the series before deciding not to make
one.

## EXTENSION CARDS FOR ADDED ENTRIES

Extension cards for added entries follow the same rule
for the added heading, if it is a person's name, as for main
entries; otherwise, the entire added heading and the heading
on the unit card are given as usual.  Extension cards are
omitted for added title entries and for analytical entries, unless the part given in the added heading is mentioned on an
extension card, in which case the extension card is made.
The phrase "Continued on next card" is omitted in these
cases.

## REFERENCE CARDS

On page 70 it is stated that the librarian should choose
one form of an author's name and always enter his works under that form, and that a reference should be made from any
other forms with which the public may be familiar.  This applies to all name entries in the catalog:  author, subject,
editor, compiler, etc.  These reference cards (number 76-
78) are very brief.  They should be made for all names
which might be searched for in the catalog under any other
form than the one chosen for entry.  The form of name not
used for entry is given on the fourth line from the top, at
the second indention, the word see, at the third indention on
the sixth line.  The form of name that has been adopted for
entry is given on the eighth line at the first indention.  If
the name referred from runs over, the next line begins at the
third indention; and if the name referred to runs over, the
next line begins at the second indention.

Gorham, Michael, pseud.

see

Folsom, Mary Elting, 1914-

Card 76.   Name reference card--pseudonym

Roland

see

Chanson de Roland

Card 77.   Name reference card--heading for anonymous
classic

Congress

see

U.S.   Congress

Card 78.   Name reference card--name of an organization

Cards 8 and 9 in chapter 2 are illustrations of see
and see also reference cards.   Note that both the term not
used and the term used as a subject heading are given in full
capitals, as are the subject headings on card 65.   If red ink
is used for the headings on the subject cards, it should also
be used for the subject references.   The indentions and spacing are the same as for name references.

<u>Reference</u>

1. <u>Anglo-American Cataloging Rules, North American Text</u> (Chicago, American Library Association, 1970), p. 346.

CHAPTER 9


CATALOGING SETS, SERIALS, AND INDEPENDENT
PUBLICATIONS BOUND TOGETHER


SETS

        The cataloging of sets varies as do the sets themselves.
If there is a common title for the entire set, if one volume
gives the contents for two or more volumes and the last volume contains the index to the set, then the set must be given
one classification number and be cataloged as one work.   If
the common title is distinctive the set will be known by that
title, and this fact is another argument for keeping the volumes together.   If the volumes are bound alike and have a
common title, but each volume is complete in itself, has a
distinctive title, an index, etc. , there is no reason for keeping them together.   Besides, the average reader will not select a volume from a set as readily as he will pick up an individual book.   For example, a set of the Waverley Novels,
the different volumes all bound alike--on the back of each volume:  "The Waverley Novels, Vol. XXI" (or XII, etc. )--does
not attract readers as does a binding reading "Rob Roy,"
even though "Vol. XI, " or even "Waverley Novels, Vol. XI, "
appears below "Rob Roy. "  If this volume XI is shelved with
other editions of Rob Roy, it is likely to be chosen for reading more often than if it is one of twenty-five books in the
same binding shelved together.

        To consider examples of different kinds of sets:

The Works of
John Milton
Volume I
Part I
New York
Columbia University Press
1931

All of the volumes of this set of Milton's works have identical

title pages, except for the volume number and date. Volume
I has two parts, bound separately but with the table of contents for both in Part I. The two parts are paged consecutively. The same is true of Volumes II and III. But Volumes IV to XVIII are each bound separately. Each one has
the copyright statement on the back of the title page, running
from 1931 to 1938 in the different volumes.

This set of Milton has a two-volume index with the
same binding and style of title page as the set, but it is not
included in the volume numbering of the set. The title page
is given below:

An Index
To the
Columbia Edition of the
Works of John Milton

By Frank Allen Patterson
Assisted By
French Rowe Fogle

Volume I.   A-K

New York
Columbia University Press
1940

The title page of the second volume of the index is the same
as that for Volume I, except that it has: "Volume II.   L-Z."
These index volumes will be cataloged in the same way as
the index for Channing's History of the United States, described on page 134 in accordance with the rule that works
with indistinctive or dependent titles (such as indexes or
manuals) are cataloged under the same author and/or title
as the work to which they are related. Obviously this set
of Milton's works will have to be cataloged as a set because
of the way in which the works are divided among the different volumes and because of the index. If a set is incomplete,
the dates, the number of volumes, and the number of parts
would be written in pencil, so that they may be easily changed
when another volume is added. Note that there are twenty-
one physical volumes in this set, but only eighteen from the
point of view of the division of the works; this is stated as
"18 v. in 21" (see card 79).

A type of title page which is found rather frequently

```
828
M66        Milton, John, 1608-1674
             Works.  New York, Columbia Uni-
           versity Press (c1931-38)
             18 v. in 21.  ill.

           ----An index to the Columbia edition
           of the Works of John Milton, by Frank
           Allen Patterson, assisted by French
           Rowe Fogle.  New York, Columbia Uni-
           versity Press (c1940)
             2 v.
```

Card 79.   Main entry for a set

in such works of fiction as the Waverley Novels, is the following:

The
Waverley Novels
By
Sir Walter Scott
Vol. XXXV
Redgauntlet. --I.
Edinburgh
Adam and Charles Black
1879

Other volumes of this work have the same information on
their title pages; the individual volume title and the volume
numbers are different.   On this particular title page the title
of the series is more prominent than that of the work.   Yet
Redgauntlet is one of Scott's well-known novels and will be
asked for by title.   If fiction is cataloged in the library as
nonfiction is, "The Waverley Novels" would be given as a
series note.   But if fiction is cataloged very simply with only
author, title, and date, the card for the above book would
not show that it is one of the Waverley Novels.   Regardless
of how little detail is given on the catalog cards, an added
entry under the name of the series will be found useful (see
card 74, page 162).

SEQUELS

The title page or spine of a volume will not always show its relation to a set or series. The Senior High School Library Catalog in its notes for Cooper's "Leatherstocking tales" states that The Deerslayer is the first of the tales; The Last of the Mohicans, the second; The Pathfinder, the third; and The Pioneers, the fourth. The notes also state that The Pathfinder is the sequel to The Last of the Mohicans; and that it is followed by The Pioneers, but does not list the fifth, The Prairie. The editor's note of the Everyman's Library edition of The Last of the Mohicans states "... one of the five 'Leatherstocking tales.'"

Not everyone who decides to read The Last of the Mohicans is aware that it is a part of a series. Yet the reader may well be interested in reading all the volumes in a series in which the same characters appear. The Leatherstocking Tales is a series of this type and should have a series entry. Having read and enjoyed the first work, some readers will go on to read them all.

Closely akin to the series with a common title are sequels such as R. F. Delderfield's Theirs Was the Kingdom, the second volume of a trilogy, the first volume of which is God Is an Englishman. Such books are cataloged as are any other works, with notes stating the sequence (see card 80). Such notes are very desirable, since readers are usually

```
Delderfield, Ronald Frederick
    God is an Englishman.  Simon &
Schuster, 1970.
    687 p.

    The first volume of a trilogy.
Followed by Theirs was the kingdom,
Give us this day.
```

Card 80.  Main entry for book with sequels

anxious to read sequels. Theirs Was the Kingdom would have as a note: "A sequel to God is an Englishman. Followed by Give us this day." Give Us this Day would have as a note: "A sequel to God is an Englishman, Theirs is the kingdom."

A related work with a different author and only limited dependence on another work is cataloged under its own author and title, with an added entry under the author and title--or just title--of the work to which it is related.

> Title page:
>> John Jasper's gatehouse, by Edwin Harris.   A
>> sequel to the unfinished novel, 'The mystery
>> of Edwin Drood. ' by Charles Dickens
> Enter under:
>> Harris, Edwin
>> Added entry (author-title) under Dickens

## SERIALS

A serial is defined by AACR as "A publication issued in successive parts bearing numerical or chronological designations and intended to be continued indefinitely.   Serials include periodicals, newspapers, annuals (reports, yearbooks, etc. ), the journals, memoirs, proceedings, transactions, etc. , of societies, and numbered monographic series. "

The World Almanac is such a serial.   The title page of the 1976 edition reads:

The Authority since 1868

THE  WORLD
ALMANAC
& BOOK OF FACTS
1976

Published Annually by
NEWSPAPER ENTERPRISE ASSOCIATION, INC.

The verso of the title page gives the information that the Almanac was published under the imprint of the New York World-Telegram from 1931 until 1951, and from then until 1967 under that of the New York World Telegram and Sun.

The reader consults the catalog to see if The World Almanac is in the library, and if it is, what volumes the library has.   All numbers of the Almanac are cataloged on one set of cards, and only items of importance common to all numbers are given.   A library which had cataloged the issues from 1948 on, would have added notes regarding the changes in publisher. A library which was cataloging the <u>Almanac</u> for the first time would catalog it from the title page of the most recent issue, ignoring past changes in imprint, even though it had some of the older volumes. On card 81, the

---

```
R
310
W92        The World almanac.  New York, World-
              Telegram.

           Annual
           Library has

           1948-51
           1952-67  issues published by New York
           World Telegram and Sun
           1967-     issues published by Newspaper
           Enterprise Association
```

Card 81.   Main entry for an annual; open entry (first cataloged in 1948)

---

fact that space is left following the dash after 1967 means that the library has all the volumes to date. This is called an open entry. To take another example of a serial:

WHO'S WHO
in America

38th edition
1974-1975

volume 1

Marquis Who's Who, Inc.
200 East Ohio Street
Chicago, Illinois,   60611
USA

The back of the title page lists the copyright dates of all issues of this work, ending " Copyright, 1974. " Over the years,
the title pages of the volumes have varied little in the essential data, except that the 1972-1973 edition was the first to be
issued in two volumes. This fact should be shown in a note,
but the very slight variation in the name of the publisher might

be ignored (see card 82). The volume numbers are especially helpful in cases where each volume covers more than one

```
 R
920
W62        Who's who in America.  Chicago, A.N.
             Marquis Co.

             Biennial
             Library has

           v. 33-36   1964/65-1970/71
           v. 37-     1972/3-           each v. in 2 v.
```

Card 82.   Main entry for a biennial publication; latest issue
           entered in pencil

---

calendar year.   Note that the location symbol R, meaning the
books are shelved in the reference collection, is placed on
the line above the classification number on cards 81 and 82.

Instead of repeating the library's holdings on every
subject and added entry card for a serial, the cards may be
stamped:  "For the library's holdings, see main card."

Periodicals.   Sets of bound periodicals may be cataloged just as almanacs and other serials are cataloged.   The
title pages of bound sets have most features in common with
the serials discussed on the preceding pages.   Classification
numbers may be assigned as usual, with the book number or
letters based on the title, as in card 83, and thus the periodical volumes may be shelved with books on the same subject.

The librarian of a small public, school, or even special library with sets of bound periodicals may classify and
catalog them in this way, or may not catalog them at all.
As they are conspicuous by their make-up, they are easily
located on the shelves in a one room library; and they are
used through the general or special periodical indexes rather
than through the catalog.   Many libraries keep all periodicals
together, alphabetically by title and in chronological order
under title, with the most recent unbound issues in pamphlet
boxes at the end of each sequence.

General encyclopedia sets also may or may not be cataloged. Unless the library has quite a number of encyclopedias the reader does not go to the catalog to locate them, but goes directly to the shelves. Like bound periodicals they may be easily located in a small library. Shelflist cards, however, should be made for all bound periodicals, encyclopedias, and other works, whether cataloged or not, in order that the library may have a record of such works and of what volumes of each it has.

Whether or not periodicals are cataloged, a concise listing of a library's magazine and newspaper holdings and their location is very helpful to the public. This may be simply a typed list, or in the form of a visible strip-file, which is easily updated by inserting additional strips in their alphabetical place as new material is added or a change in title or frequency occurs. The information given would be short title, frequency (perhaps), the date and/or number of the earliest volume owned, and location (e.g., Children's Room, on microfilm, etc.). If periodicals are not cataloged, the other details can be recorded on the shelf list card (see page 250) or the check-in forms used to record the receipt of periodicals can act as a substitute for shelf list cards.

If periodicals are entered in the card catalog, the entries are similar to those for annuals, etc., showing the frequency, the holdings, changes in title or author, and location. Note that the "library has" statement for Current History and Forum (card 83) gives the months as well as the years covered by the volumes. This form is used when the volumes do not coincide with calendar years. Since Current History and Forum ceased publication with volume 53, number

```
909.82
C97        Current history and Forum.  New York,
              C-H Pub. Corp.

           Monthly.  illus.
           Library has

           v. 51-53, no. 1 Sept. 1939-June 1941

                          (Continued on next card)
```

Card 83.   Main entry for a periodical, closed entry

```
909.82
C97          Current history and Forum. . .(Card 2)

             Current history combined with The
             Forum and The Century magazine, May 23,
             1940, under the title:  Current history
             and Forum; Current history and Forum
             was superseded by Current history,
             September, 1941
```

Card 84.   Extension for card 83

---

1, June 1941, this volume number and date are typed, rather
than written in pencil as the last date on card 82, thus clos-
ing the entry.   When Current History and Forum united with
Events in September 1941 to form Current History a new volume numbering began.   The library having this periodical
would add the latest volume in pencil to facilitate changing
the statement when the next volume is received, or would
leave the entry open, implying it had all the issues up to the
current one.   The notes on cards 84 and 86 explain the formation of the periodicals and allow the patron looking under the
old name to find the new title, and vice versa.   Because the
periodical Current History (card 85) had a different name and
a new volume numbering, it is cataloged as a separate periodical.


RULES FOR CATALOGING SERIALS

        While AACR suggests that serials be cataloged in the
same manner as monographs insofar as possible, modifications and changes in emphasis are required by the special
character of serials.   The fact that publication occurs over
a period of time makes bibliographic variation likely.

        A serial publication in several volumes with varying
bibliographical details is cataloged from the latest volume,
in contrast to a monograph in several volumes, which is cataloged from the first volume.   The title page, if there is one,
serves as the basic source of descriptive information.   If
there is no title page, the information on title and imprint
are obtained from the following, in the order listed, and preferably from the same source:  cover, caption, masthead,
editorial pages, or elsewhere.

```
909.82
C976        Current history.   Philadelphia,
               Events Pub. Co.

            Monthly
            Library has
            v. 1-19   Sept. 1941-Dec. 1950

            v. 46-    Jan. 1964-
                         (continued on next card)
```

Card 85.   Main entry for a periodical, open entry

```
909.82
C976        Current history. . . (Card 2)

               Formed by the union of Current
            history and Forum with Events.
```

Card 86.   Extension for card 85

Most serials are entered under title, but those which have a personal author are entered under author.   For example, Lasser's annual income tax guides are entered under his name.   Serials issued by corporate bodies are entered under title or the name of the body, depending on the type of publication and the terminology used in the title.   Periodicals, monographic series, or serially published bibliographies, indexes, directories, biographical dictionaries, almanacs or yearbooks issued by corporate bodies are entered under title, with an added entry for the corporate body.   However, when a title includes the name of the issuing body (fully written out or abbreviated), or consists only of a generic term (bulletin, journal, etc.), the main entry is under corporate body. For example, the annual ALA Handbook of Organization is entered under the American Library Association as corporate author, but American Libraries is entered under its title, with an added entry for ALA.   Other types of serials published by corporate bodies, such as proceedings or reports, are always entered under the name of the body.

If there is a change in personal or corporate author, the work is recataloged under the new author with a reference from the former author and title (see cards 87 and 88). If many volumes have been cataloged under the old name, the work may be left under the former author with a reference from the new one.

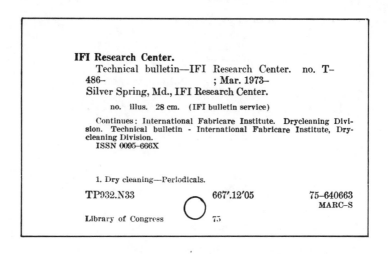

IFI Research Center.
    Technical bulletin—IFI Research Center.    no. T–
486–                    ; Mar. 1973–
    Silver Spring, Md., IFI Research Center.

        no.  illus.  28 cm.   (IFI bulletin service)

        Continues: International Fabricare Institute. Drycleaning Division. Technical bulletin - International Fabricare Institute, Drycleaning Division.
        ISSN 0095–666X

        1. Dry cleaning—Periodicals.

    TP932.N33                    667′.12′05            75–640663
                                                       MARC–S
    Library of Congress              75

Card 87.    New main entry; change in name of author

International Fabricare Institute.  Drycleaning Division.
    Technical  bulletin — International  Fabricare  Institute,
Drycleaning Division.                          –T–485.
    Silver Spring, Md., International Fabricare Institute, Drycleaning Division.  19  –72.

        no.  28 cm.   (IFI bulletin service)

        Continues: National Institute of Drycleaning. Bulletin service. Technical bulletin.
        Continued by: IFI Research Center.  Technical bulletin - IFI Research Center.
        ISSN 0095–6678

        1. Dry cleaning—Periodicals.

    TP932.N33                    667′.12′05            75–640664
                                                       MARC–S
    Library of Congress              75

Card 88.    Old main entry for periodical recataloged in card 87

Note that the printed LC cards leave space open to fill in
the holdings, and that the volume numbers and dates follow
directly after the title.  This form is in accordance with
AACR, but small libraries will find it simpler to use the
"library has" style of entry.

Title.  A short title is preferred in cataloging serials
if this makes possible the continuous treatment as one entity
of a title which has experienced minor changes in wording,
e. g. , The World Almanac rather than The World Almanac &
Book of Facts.  Subtitles are generally omitted unless needed
for identification or clarification.

If a serial undergoes a major change of title during
the course of publication (Vocations for Social Change to
Workforce, for example), it is cataloged with a separate entry for each new title, with a note relating the new title to
the serial it continues or supersedes.  A serial which has
ceased publication may be uniformly entered under a title
other than its latest title, if an earlier title has continued
for a much longer period of time than the later one.

When the title of a serial entered under a corporate
body includes the name of the body, the name is omitted unless it is given in a significantly different form from that in
the heading and its omission would distort the title:

> Title page:
> Annual report of the Librarian of Congress for
> the fiscal year ... Library of Congress ...
> Enter under:
> U.S.  Library of Congress

If a number which is part of the title is treated as a
volume number, it is omitted from the title (e. g. , Report of
the first annual meeting becomes Report of the annual meeting).

Imprint.  Only the place of publication and the name
of the publisher are given.  Changes in the publisher's name
or in the place of publication that do not warrant specific
description are indicated by the abbreviation "etc. "  If the
name of the publisher is essentially the same as the title of
the publication, as is often the case with periodicals, it is
omitted.

Collation.  The collation describes the completed set

for serials that have ceased publication. If the serial is still being published, the collation describes the set as it is at the time of cataloging. Only those types of illustrations that are important to the set as a whole are included.

Frequency notes. Complicated descriptions of frequency belong in the notes, but if the frequency can be given in a single adjective or brief phrase, it is given immediately after the collation, e.g.: annual, monthly (except July and August). When the frequency is obvious from the title, e.g., Library Quarterly, it is not repeated. If there are numerous changes in frequency of publication, this is indicated by a general note, "Frequency varies."

Holdings notes. The statement of the numbers or volumes or years of a serial that a library owns begins with the phrase "Library has" on the line below the frequency note, beginning at the second indention. On the line below, beginning at the first indention, are given the volumes or the years, or both, of the issues in the library in straight columns. They are put on the same line with a dash between the numbers if the volumes are consecutive, giving the latest one in pencil so that it may be changed when the next number comes in. A line is skipped to indicate each gap, not each volume lacking, and statements that need to be changed are written in pencil. Such statements as "Forty-third issue," "Third edition," and "Second annual report," may be written "v. 43, v. 3, v. 2."

Another method is to purchase printed record cards from a library supply house and tie the card or cards to the main entry card. These record cards are ruled in columns or squares and have printed on them "Year," "Volume," or are just blank cards ruled. The library checks or writes in each square the years or volume numbers as they are received.

If the serial is still being published or the library has only part of the set, an open entry (i.e., one with no terminal date) may be used in order to keep changes and modifications to a minimum. Similar entries may be used for frequently re-issued publications, such as directories, guidebooks, manuals, etc., even though they may not be true serials.

An alternative to writing in the latest volume held or leaving the entry open is to write "to date" in pencil after the dash. Libraries which regularly discard periodicals older than a given number of years omit the date and type in "last five years," or whatever the appropriate number is.   A third possibility is to type in:   "For a full record of the library's holdings, ask at the reference desk. "

Supplementary notes.   Notes other than frequency may be given on a separate extension card (as in cards 84 and 86), since "library has" statements may take up more space if there are many gaps in the set.   Later, if the first card should be filled up, a second and, if need be, a third card could be inserted between the first card and the card giving the notes.   The following types of notes are frequently necessary for serials:

Report year:   If the period covered by an annual publication is older than that of the calendar year, the fact is noted.

Report year ends June 30.

Suspension of publication:   If a serial stops publication but intends to resume at a later date, the entry is left open, and a note is used to give the date or volume and number of the last issue.   When publication resumes, the note is expanded to give the inclusive dates of the period of suspension.

Suspended with v. 11
Suspended with Dec. 1942
Suspended 1923-31

Numbering:   Irregularities in the numbering of a serial are described, but not if confined to parts of a volume.

Issues for Feb. -Mar. 1939 have no vol. numbering but constitute v. 1, no. 1-2.

Connection with preceding or subsequent publications:   A serial that is published under a different title or different corporate author but keeps the numbering of its predecessor is held to be a continuation of the original.   If the numbering is changed, the new version is said to "supersede" the old. When a serial is continued, superseded, or absorbed by, or merged with another publication, the appropriate statement is given in a note, as in cards 87, 88, 89 and 90.

Missing issues:   If after issues are discovered to be absent from an otherwise continuous series, noting the missing

```
          Society.  New Brunswick, N.J.,
            Trans-action Periodicals Consortium.

          10 no. a year.
          Library has
          v. 9, no. 4-          Feb. 1972-

          Continues Trans-action
            Bimonthly as of v. 10, no. 2, Jan./
          Feb. 1973
```

Card 89.  Main entry for continuation under new title, but
same numbering; open entry

```
          American Library Association
            ALA bulletin.  v. 1-63; 1905-1969.

          63 v.  11 no. a year.

          Superseded by American libraries.
```

Card 90.  Main entry for serial superseded by new title and
with new numbering; closed entry

issues in a supplementary note saves tampering with the holdings statement.

Special numbers.  Special numbers of serials are cataloged as separate works, with the relationship to regular issues shown, cataloged with analytical entries, or simply noted
informally.  If they are to be shelved with the regular numbers and are not particularly important, no special adjustment in cataloging is needed.

## BOUND WITHS

Two or more works by the same author or works of
different authors are sometimes bound or published together
in one volume.  If the book has a title page for each work
as well as a table of contents, a preface, and separate paging,
each work may be called informally a "bound with."  The book

is cataloged as a separate book, but on the cards for each work there is a note of the other work or works with which it is bound. The true test of such a volume is that it could be cut into two or more works, each of which if bound separately would be a complete volume, not showing in any way that it had ever been bound with another.

A similar sort of work may have one title page which gives all or at least some of the different titles; or it may have a common title for the volume and the individual titles may be given only on half title pages preceding the different sections of the book. The half title is a brief title on a page preceding a title page, or a separate work where there are several in one volume. It does not include the imprint. The title pages for two such volumes follow:

How to Live

By
Arnold Bennett

A Special Edition for the Bookman Subscribers Only,
Containing "How to Live on Twenty-Four Hours a Day,"
"The Human Machine," "Mental Efficiency,"
"Self and Self Management."


A BOOK OF
GREAT AUTOBIOGRAPHY

Christopher Morley
Joseph Conrad
Selma Lagerlöf
Helen Keller
William McFee
W. N. P. Barbellion
Walt Whitman
Etsu Inagaki Sugimoto

The first of these examples, the volume of Bennett's works, includes four of his essays, published separately, brought together in one volume under a common title. The one title page lists all the essays and each of them has a half title, a table of contents, and is paged separately. But all of the copyright dates, in this case a different copyright date for each work, are given on the back of the title page. The second example, A Book of Great Autobiography, also

has only one title page on which is given the common title
for the volume and the list of authors whose works are included in the volume. Each work is separately paged and
preceded by a "Publisher's Note." Some works of these
types have continuous paging throughout the volume.

While examining these title pages and half titles, the
librarian must keep in mind such questions as these: What
is there in these volumes that readers would want? Under
what would they look in the catalog? A reader may be looking for The Human Machine, A Daughter of the Samurai,
Helen Keller's The Story of My Life, something by Walt Whitman. Title analytics would be needed for each of the essays
in the volume by Bennett; and both author and title analytics
for each of the works in A Book of Great Autobiography.
The main entry for the latter work would be under the title
(see card 91).

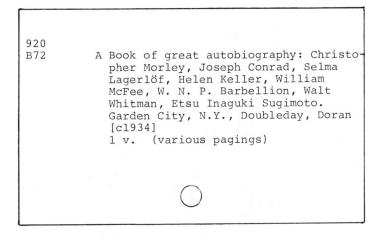

```
920
B72        A Book of great autobiography: Christo-
           pher Morley, Joseph Conrad, Selma
           Lagerlöf, Helen Keller, William
           McFee, W. N. P. Barbellion, Walt
           Whitman, Etsu Inaguki Sugimoto.
           Garden City, N.Y., Doubleday, Doran
           [c1934]
           1 v. (various pagings)
```

Card 91.   Main entry for several works with common title--
           not a bound with

Similar, yet different, is this bound with:

WHEN WORLDS

COLLIDE

By

EDWIN BALMER

and

PHILIP WYLIE

J. B. LIPPINCOTT COMPANY
PHILADELPHIA    NEW YORK

On the back of this title page is given:

Copyright 1932, 1933, by
Edwin Balmer and Philip Wylie

The title page is followed by the Table of Contents, then the text.    Next in this volume is a half title page:  "After Worlds Collide," then the title page:

AFTER WORLDS

COLLIDE

By

EDWIN BALMER

and

PHILIP WYLIE

Authors of "When Worlds Collide"

J. B. LIPPINCOTT COMPANY
PHILADELPHIA    NEW YORK

And on the back of this title page:

Copyright, 1933, 1934, by
EDWIN BALMER and
PHILIP WYLIE

The paging for this book is:  When Worlds Collide, viii, 344 p. ; After Worlds Collide, xiii, 341 p.

These works would be cataloged as any other work except for the notes, each of which refers to the other title. The classification number and the book number, if they are used, would be the same for both since there is only one physical volume on the shelf.

The bound-with note takes the following form:  the

```
        Balmer, Edwin
          When worlds collide, by Edwin
        Balmer and Philip Wylie.  Lippincott
        [c1933]
          344 p.

          Bound with: the authors' After
        worlds collide.
```

Card 92.   Main entry for the first work in a bound with

```
        Balmer, Edwin,
          After worlds collide, by Edwin
        Balmer and Philip Wylie.  Lippincott
        [c1934]
          341 p.

          Bound with: the authors' When
        worlds collide.
          Sequel to When worlds collide.
```

Card 93.   Main entry for a work other than the first in a
           bound with

author's name in catalog entry form, with forenames (if more
than one) represented by initials, brief title.  If the author
is the same then use "the author's (or authors')."  If there
are more than two titles bound together all are cited only in
the entry for the first item in the work.

The added cards are traced on each main entry card as usual. In addition the main card or cards for the other work or works in the volume are traced simply by giving the author headings in full, if the authors differ; where the authors are the same as in the case of Balmer and Wylie, by the first author's surname and the first word of the title bound with it, e. g. , Balmer After. There is only one card for the shelf list as there is only one book on the shelf and one call number. The shelf-list card is made for the first work in the volume, in this case When Worlds Collide.

CHAPTER 10


## AUDIOVISUAL MATERIALS


An increasing variety of audiovisual materials is being more widely used in all types and sizes of libraries, and it is no longer possible to exclude a communications medium from a discussion of cataloging for the small library on the assumption that it is too expensive or exotic to be acquired by any but the largest institutions. Today films and video-tapes are found even in small libraries.

The librarian's approach to the organization and cataloging of audiovisual materials will depend on the community served. The following questions should be asked:

--Who will use the material (staff, students, general public, researchers, etc.)
--What is the function of the material in terms of the goals of the institution (reference, program support, enrichment, teaching aid, etc.)
--What special storage and maintenance problems does a particular medium pose.

A library in an academic institution committed to the multi-media approach to teaching and learning might choose to handle all materials uniformly, shelving them together and interfiling catalog cards so as to bring attention to all print and nonprint items on a given topic. A public library, however, might include cards for nonprint materials in its central catalog but house audiovisual material separately in order to minimize storage space or maximize security. It would follow that the school library with the integrated collection would have to classify all types of materials in the same way as books, but that the public library with a separate audiovisual collection could use two or more different systems. In choosing forms of entry, however, each library would have to use headings and styles of entry for its nonprint materials which are compatible with those for books in order to bring all material on the same subject or by the same person together in the card catalog. On the other hand, a special library of material in a single format, such as a picture collection, or a library devoted to a single field but requiring a mixed media collection, such as a music library, might need to develop special classification and indexing schemes in order to provide a sufficiently detailed breakdown of the collection's contents.

For the general library, professional consensus on the cataloging of audiovisual materials has been reached on most basic points. AECT's Standards for Cataloging Nonprint Materials, 4th edition, [1] is at present the most comprehensive expression of this understanding and the most detailed compendium of specific rules. It is in essential agreement with the revised chapter 12 of AACR, [2] and incorporates the best features of the Canadian Library Association's Nonbook Materials. [3] The key principle is that cataloging should emphasize content, not form. It follows that the code used for books (AACR) should also be applied to nonprint materials. It further follows that subject headings used for print and nonprint materials should be consistent; i.e., if Sears is used for books, it should also be used for audiovisual materials, and media format subdivisions of subject headings should be avoided.

Once these principles are accepted, a library is in a position to interfile cards for all kinds of materials in one central catalog, so that the patron looking for presidential inaugural speeches will discover that he can not only read them in print but can hear a recording of them as well. But how does this patron know that one card refers to a book and the other to a recording? The consensus is that a general "medium designation" should appear on the card for a nonprint item, directly after the title, fully spelled out in singular form, and preferably in brackets. Thus the card might read "Inaugural speeches [Audio-recording]" in the title statement, with the collation clarifying the fact that the item is actually on two cassettes (specific medium designation). If the library user is not interested in a recording, he need read no further. Color coding of catalog cards or the use of symbols in place of fully spelled out media designations are not recommended, because they emphasize form over content and confuse the catalog user. Where coding is necessary to form a call number or for the purpose of automation, the table on pages 192-193 can be applied. These codes should never, however, replace the use of fully written out medium designators.

It is generally agreed that "two or more interdependent media are cataloged by the dominant media, with the less significant media listed in the physical description or in a note, e. g. , a filmstrip and a tape recording which explains the pictures of the filmstrip are cataloged as a filmstrip. ... A package of two or more media, all significant and related but not necessarily interdependent, is cataloged as a kit. "[4]

It is also generally agreed that the description of a nonprint item should tell the potential user enough about the format and content to enable him to decide whether or not he can use it. The collation must include sufficient description to indicate what type of machine is required for playback, projection, etc. Contents notes must be comprehensive enough to minimize the need for auditing or viewing the item in order to determine whether or not it will indeed answer the needs of the patron. Facilities for this may not be readily available, the user may not have the time to do it, or the item may not lend itself to excessive handling.

There remain a number of disagreements to be resolved. One concerns the rules for main entry, with AECT's Standards recommending title main entry in most cases, while Nonbook Materials prefers author main entry where there is a choice. The choice should be governed by the significance of the author versus the title in the identification of the work, and is usually self-evident; in the case of classical music or an original work of art it is the creator of the music or art who is most significant, while a film is always identified by title. A less important disagreement involves terminology, notably the choice of medium designator: audio-, phono-, or sound recording (LC uses phono, AECT audio, and the British prefer sound). On the whole, however, enormous progress toward standardization has been made in the last five years.

Standardization is desirable not merely for the sake of ending the confusion which has plagued bibliographers and catalogers. It encourages the integrated mixed-media central catalogs that are essential if users are to be given full access to a library's total resources, and it clears the way for providing acceptable cooperative cataloging and therefore significant savings in money and time. Using printed cards or participating in a cooperative cataloging service is, of course, the one sure route toward "simple library cataloging," and librarians are urged to take this route whenever it is open. However, in order to choose wisely among the options available and to adapt centralized cataloging to local needs, one must be familiar with the problems posed by some formats as well as with the basic principles which can be applied to all. Inevitably, some cataloging will have to be done locally, especially when materials are created in-house.

Where cataloging of nonprint media must be done at the local level, it is wise to provide the staff with worksheets specifying what information in which order is required for each format. Examples of such worksheets will be found in AV Cataloging and Processing Simplified, 5 which is also very helpful as a guide to processing procedures. Skeleton cards specifying spacing, indention, and punctuation should be given to the typists, so that the preparation of cards for audiovisual material need pose no special problems. An example of such a card (card 94) is given below on page 197.

CLASSIFICATION

On the subject of classification, no standardized solution is likely to be acceptable to all kinds of libraries. There is, however, a general acceptance of the principle of integrated collections for multi-media learning centers. Thus a media center which uses unabridged Dewey and Cutter numbers for books would use these for audiovisual materials also. Whether or not all kinds of materials are actually interfiled on the shelves will depend on the space, type of shelving, and degree of circulation control available in a given situation. Even where books, filmstrips, records, slides, etc. , are scattered in different places, there are advantages to classifying them all in a uniform manner. A new library with adequate space for intershelving may someday replace the old overcrowded one, and meanwhile the mnemonic factor of class numbers is not to be discounted. It saves time in helping the student who needs material on Africa to be able to go directly to the 916's and 960's in the filmstrip cabinet, record bin and film rack as well as in the book stacks. Wherever a computer is available, multimedia subject lists can be more easily produced when all materials have been classified.

For libraries not swayed by the preceding arguments, the decisions on how to organize, whether and how to classify will depend on the type of access given to the user. Is the material to be in locked storage and available only through a staff member, or is it accessible to the patron on a self-

service basis? Where there is no intention of letting the
public browse through a collection, a simple alphabetical (by
main entry) or accession order arrangement can be used, as
long as a good subject index is at hand. Whenever materials
are put out in the open for public browsing, some sort of arrangement by categories will evolve as a result of user preferences, unless the collection is to remain so small that the
patron will not object to searching through every item.

The categories will depend on the medium. For example, records might be grouped as they are in many stores:
opera, folk, spoken, jazz, etc. Slides, however, might be
arranged by artist, country, historical period, etc. These
broad user interest groupings would eventually have to be
broken down more discretely as the collection grew in order
to speed retrieval of specific items.

There is no single, simple solution that will be satisfactory for all types of libraries, nor is it overwhelmingly
important to settle on only one all-purpose arrangement as
long as enough points of access are provided for the user.
If it is necessary to have separate print and nonprint collections with different service points, catalog cards should be
duplicated so that they may be filed at the service point as
well as in the central card catalog.

Some specific organization/classification problems will
be discussed in the sections on individual media in this chapter. For more background on various approaches to handling
different types of media and for sources of cataloging information, see the references at the end of this chapter and Appendix C. Shelf lists for nonprint media are discussed in chapter 11. The Booklist, Media Review Digest, The Elementary
School Library Collection, and Core Media Collection for
Secondary Schools will be found helpful as cataloging aids,
since they suggest DDC numbers and subject headings for
audiovisual materials.

GENERAL RULES

The following general rules are based on AECT's
Standards and on Nonbook Materials, which in turn are based
on the AACR. Amplification, exceptions, and examples will
be given in the sections on individual media. The elements,
arrangement, and style of the catalog card for nonprint material are essentially the same as for printed matter, and it

is assumed that the reader of this chapter is familiar with
the general cataloging principles as discussed in this manual.

Some of the abbreviations used most frequently in addition to those common in both print and nonprint cataloging
are:

| black and white | b&w | opus | op. |
|---|---|---|---|
| color | col. | revolutions per minute | rpm |
| frame/s | fr. | second/s | sec. |
| inch/es per second | ips | side/s | s. |
| millimeter/s | mm | silent | si. |
| minute/s | min. | sound | sd. |

Main entry. Audiovisual material may be entered under title, set title, or creator/author. AACR specifies that
an item should be entered under author where it is clear that
there is a "person or corporate body chiefly responsible for
the creation of the intellectual or artistic content of a work.
Thus composers, artists, photographers, etc. , are the 'authors' of the works they create. "[6] When the item is an exact reproduction of a printed work (e. g. , a picture book reproduced as a film or a filmstrip) or a reproduction of a
painting, it may be entered under the author or painter. However, in most cases, "the extent and nature of the collabora-
tive authorship ... make author entry inappropriate. "[7] Not
only is it impossible to determine authorship for most AV
materials, it is more realistic to enter them under title,
because that is how they are most commonly identified by
producers, reference sources, and users.

Title. If there is an inconsistency between the title
given on the container and that on the material itself, use
the one on the material or closest to the contents. Other
sources of title, should it not appear on the material itself,
are accompanying materials such as manuals, or the container. If the cataloger has to supply a title from an external source, it should be enclosed in brackets. If the title
was previously released under a different title or is known
by a variant title, these titles may be given in a note and
treated as added entries.

Medium designators. The generic term for the type
of material should be given in the singular and in brackets
immediately after the title. The specific designator is given
in the collation. Use the generic media designators and specific designators listed in AECT's Standards (see below) in

| MEDIUM DESIGNATOR | SPECIFIC DESIGNATOR | CODE |
|---|---|---|
| Audiorecording ................................................ | | AA |
| | Cartridge | AR |
| | Cassette | AC |
| | Disc | AD |
| | Reel | AT |
| | Roll | AO |
| Archival/Experimental ..... | Cylinder | AY |
| | Page | AS |
| | Wire | AW |
| | | |
| Chart ....................................................... | | CA |
| | Chart | CH |
| | Flannel board set | CL |
| | Flip chart | CF |
| | Graph | CG |
| | Magnetic board set | CM |
| | Relief chart | CR |
| | Wall chart | CW |
| | | |
| Diorama ................................................... | | OA |
| | Diorama | OD |
| | | |
| Filmstrip ................................................... | | FA |
| | Filmslip | FL |
| | Filmstrip | FS |
| | | |
| Flash card ................................................. | | HA |
| | Card | HC |
| | | |
| Game ...................................................... | | GA |
| | Game | GM |
| | Puzzle | GP |
| | Simulation | GS |
| | | |
| Globe ...................................................... | | QA |
| | Globe | QG |
| | Relief globe | QR |
| | | |
| Kit ........................................................ | | KA |
| | Exhibit | KE |
| | Kit | KT |
| | Laboratory kit | KL |
| | Programed instruction kit | KP |
| | | |
| Machine-readable data file ............................... | | DA |
| Species of file ........... | Data file | DF |
| | Program file | DE |
| Storage medium .......... | Disc | DD |
| | Punched card | DB |
| | Punched paper tape | DP |
| | Tape | DT |

| MEDIUM DESIGNATOR | SPECIFIC DESIGNATOR | CODE |
|---|---|---|
| Map | | LA |
| | Map | LM |
| | Relief map | LR |
| | Wall map | LW |
| Microform | | NA |
| | Aperture card | NC |
| | Card | ND |
| | Cartridge | NE |
| | Cassette | NF |
| | Fiche | NH |
| | Reel | NR |
| | Ultrafiche | NU |
| Model | | EA |
| | Mock-up | EM |
| | Model | EE |
| Motion picture | | MA |
| | Cartridge | MR |
| | Cassette | MC |
| | Loop | ML |
| | Reel | MP |
| Picture | | PA |
| | Art original | PO |
| | Art print | PR |
| | Hologram | PH |
| | Photograph | PP |
| | Picture | PI |
| | Post card | PC |
| | Poster | PT |
| | Stereograph | PG |
| | Study print | PS |
| Realia | | RA |
| | Name of object | RO |
| | Specimen | RS |
| Slide | | SA |
| | Audioslide | SO |
| | Microscope slide | SM |
| | Slide | SL |
| | Stereoscope slide | SS |
| Transparency | | TA |
| | Transparency | TR |
| Videorecording | | VA |
| | Cartridge | VR |
| | Cassette | VC |
| | Disc | VD |
| | Reel | VT |

order to achieve standardized terminology. Even where a separate card catalog is used for one type of medium, the inclusion of medium designator will permit a duplicate card to be filed in the central card catalog.

Several of the media listed by AECT will not be included in this chapter. Machine-readable data files will not be discussed, as few small libraries are likely to have these. Microforms are covered in chapter 7 rather than in this chapter, in accordance with AACR's recommendation that they be treated as print material. While the cataloger will find it easy, using AECT's list, to assign the proper designator to the vast majority of nonprint materials, it should be noted that there is no very satisfactory way to fit toys which are neither games nor models into the scheme. The Standards show sample catalog cards for puppets under realia, but unless the puppets are original handicrafts, that is not a strictly accurate designation. Children's departments with extensive toy lending collections may choose to add a designation for toys, and base their cataloging on the general principles outlined here.

"Authorship" statement. AECT's Standards say that if a nonprint item is entered under the name of the creator, or if primary responsibility for the work can be assigned and is important to the identification of it, an author statement follows the title and medium designation, as in the case of books under AACR's revised chapter 6. In simplified cataloging, this rule can be ignored without any great danger, as long as important credits or the relationship to another work are specified in the notes.

Edition statement. Revised versions of films and other media are not uncommon, and the fact that the item being cataloged is revised, or a third edition, etc., should be indicated.

Imprint. The following data are given in the order listed: producer, production/copyright date, sponsor, distributor or releasing agent, date of release. Place may be omitted in simplified cataloging, unless it is unusual or required to distinguish between two organizations with similar names. Company names may be abbreviated insofar as the abbreviations are familiar. Some libraries may feel that they need not bother with anything but the name of the distributor, and in practice this is generally justified. Use the latest date given on the material itself. If none is given, use accompanying materials, and if necessary try outside sources or estimate the date, as described on page 124. When the copyright/production date and the release date are different, it is important to give both, even in simplified cataloging.

Collation. This will vary with the nature of the medium, but in each instance enough information has to be supplied to permit the potential user to determine whether the item is usable on the equipment at his disposal, will fit the play or show time available, etc. Collation elements suggested for specific media will be discussed under the appropriate section, and the following is simply a list of the most common descriptors required, in the order in which they are cited:

1. Number of pieces and type of medium (specific designator). Where components of a unit are in different formats, each is enumerated and described.

2. Length, such as the running time of a film or the number of filmstrip frames.

3. Sound or silent in the case of films, videorecordings.

4. Color, black and white, tinted, sepia, or a combination.

5. Size. For two-dimensional items, give height x width, and for three-dimensional, height x width x depth; for tape and film, give width; for globes, give the diameter; etc. Metric measurements are recommended by AECT, but for the time being the measurement system most commonly associated with an item is preferable, e.g., mm for film width, inches for tape width.

6. Playback speed and recording mode for audiorecordings.

7. Interdependent accompanying materials, such as a recording intended to be used with a filmstrip, where neither is meaningful without the other.

8. Series title where applicable, following the physical description and enclosed in parentheses.

9. Educational level or special audience for which the item is intended may be stated as the last item in the collation, following the series statement. If preferred, this information can be given as a note or as the last item in the summary. The following terms and abbreviations are standard:

| | | |
|---|---|---|
| Pre-school | (pre-school) | K |
| Primary | (grades K through 3) | P |
| Intermediate | (grades 4 through 6) | I |
| Junior high | (grades 7 and 8) | J |
| Senior high | (grades 9 through 12) | H |
| Adult | (college and adult) | A |

Notes. Any information needed to clarify the description given in the collation, such as the name of a specific machine needed for playback. Other information commonly given in the notes includes:

1. Earlier or varying titles.

2. Accompanying material not included in the collation, such as discussion guides.

3. Relationship to other works, e. g. , a film based on a book.

4. Credits--persons or organizations who participated in the creation or performance of the work, to the extent that they are felt to be of significance to the user.

5. Summary--whenever the title or a listing of contents do not adequately describe an item. This should be brief and objective.

6. Contents, where parts of the unit cataloged have distinctive titles; often, a listing of contents will obviate the need for a summary.

Tracings. For subject entries, use the same list of subject headings which is used for books. Make added entries for personal names when they are important, such as performers or authors, and for original, variant and series titles under which a user might search. Include the medium designator (bracketed) in the tracing after added title entries.

Skeleton card. The model below is adapted from AECT's Standards:

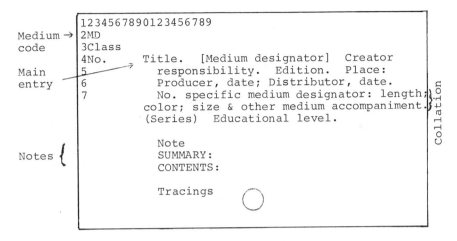

Card 94.   Skeleton card for audiovisual material

In the sections on specific types of media which follow below, some cover every aspect of the catalog entry, while others are confined to those points which pertain to the medium discussed, with the understanding that the reader will refer back to the general rules above.

## AUDIORECORDINGS

An audiorecording is defined by AECT's Standards as "a registration of sound vibrations on a material substance by mechanical or electronic means so that sound may be reproduced." The material may be a disc, a tape, wire, pianoroll, etc.

Main entry.   1) A recording or set of recordings (musical or spoken) containing a single work, several works or excerpts by one composer or author is entered under that composer or author (see cards 95-98).   2) A recording or set containing works by several people which has a collective title is entered under the title (see card 99).   3) A recording or set containing works by several people which does not have a collective title may be entered under the first author/composer of the first work on side one (see cards 100 and 101).   4) A recording or set containing works by several people, with or without a collective title, which are all performed or read by the same person or group may

be entered under the name of the performer(s). The decision
to use performer main entry depends on the cataloger's understanding of the importance of performance versus material
being performed, particularly in terms of user approach.
For example, most libraries would prefer performer main
entry for a collection of arias from various operas by different composers, all sung by Caruso, or for a collection of
songs performed by the Jackson Five.  Where responsibility
for the artistic interpretation is equally shared by two or
more individuals, enter under the first named; by an individual
and a group or groups, enter under the first named individual
or group.  The choice of main entry under author/composer
or performer as against title should be determined by their
importance to the identification of the recording (see card
102).

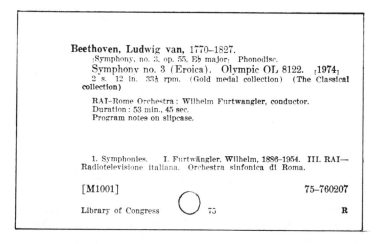

Card 95.    Composer main entry, single work; LC printed
            card

_Title._   Use the title on the label in preference to that
on the container if they vary, unless the container title provides a better identification of the work.   If the recording has
several works without a collective title, list all of them in
the title statement (see card 97); but if there are so many
as to produce an overly lengthy entry, give only the first
title in the title statement and the rest in the contents (for
an alternative method, see page 207.

```
AA
785.1
BEE        Beethoven, Ludwig van
             [Symphony, no. 3, op. 55, E-flat
           major] [Audiorecording]
             Symphony no. 3 (Eroica).  Olympic
           OL 8122 [1974]
             1 disc:  54 min.  mono.


             RAI-Rome Orchestra; Wilhelm Furt-
           wängler, conductor.


             1.  Symphonies   I. Furtwängler,
           Wilhelm        ◯
```

Card 96.   Typed, modified version of card 95

```
           Schubert, Franz Peter
AA           Trio, piano & strings, no.2, op.
785.7        100, E-flat major]  [Audorecording]
SCH        Schubert, Franz Peter, 1797-1828.
             [Trio, piano & strings, no. 1, op. 99, Bb major]  Phonodisc.
             Trio in B-flat, op. 99 (D. 898).   Trio in E-flat, op. 100
             (D. 929).   RCA Red Seal ARL 2-0731.  [1975]
             4 s.  12 in.  33⅓ rpm.  stereophonic.

             Artur Rubinstein, piano ; Henryk Szeryng, violin ; Pierre Fournier,
           violoncello.
             Duration: about 38 min. ; about 40 min., 30 sec.
             Manual sequence.
             Program notes by A. Rich ([2] p.  illus.) laid in container.

             1. Piano trios.    I. Schubert, Franz Peter, 1797-1828.  Trio,
           piano & strings, no. 2, op. 100, Eb major.  Phonodisc.  1975.  II. Ru-
           binstein, Artur, 1886-    III. Szeryng, Henryk.  IV. Fournier,
           Pierre, 1906-

             [M312]            ◯                    75-761161

           Library of Congress       75                     R
```

Card 97.   Composer main entry, two works entered under
           work on first disc--added entry for second work

       Titles of musical compositions often vary in phrasing
and language.  To bring together different recordings of the
same work and to simplify filing and retrieval, it is necessary to use uniform (or conventional) titles.  The rules for

```
AA
FIC
GAI        Gaines, Ernest
             The autobiography of Miss Jane
           Pittman. [Audiorecording]  Caed-
           mon CDL5 2058, 1975.
             2 cassettes:  120 min.

             Includes first nine chapters.
           Read by Claudia McNeil.

             I. McNeil, Claudia  II. Title
```

Card 98.   Author main entry for excerpt from single work

**Jazz in the thirties.** [Phonodisc] Olympic OL 7118. [1974]
2 s. 12 in. 33⅓ rpm. (Gold medal collection)

Title on slipcase: Harlem in the thirties.
Jazz ensembles, featuring Fletcher Henderson, piano.
"Compatible for stereo and 4 channel quadraphonic equipment."
Durations on labels.
Program notes on slipcase.
CONTENTS: You rascal you.—Blue rhythm.—Sugarfoot stomp.—
Low down on the bayou.—Twelfth Street rag.—Milenberg joys.—
After you've gone.—Stardust.—Tiger rag.—Somebody stole my gal.

1. Jazz ensembles.   I. Henderson, Fletcher Hamilton, 1897–1952.
II. Title: Harlem in the thirties.

[M1366]                                              75–761179

Library of Congress          75                            R

Card 99.   Collective title main entry

establishing uniform title given in the AACR aim to bring together and organize a composer's work by musical form, except where a composition is generally referred to by a distinctive title, such as Academic Festival Overture, The Nut-
cracker, Madame Butterfly, etc.  The rules also deal with
the choice of language (Le Sacre du Printemps versus The

```
AA
791.44
JAN        Jane Eyre and This lonely heart; two
              complete radio dramas.  [Audiore-
              cording]  Pelican Records LP 105,
              [1973]
              1 disc, 12 in: 33.3 rpm.  (Original
           radio broadcasts)

              The first based on the novel by
           C. Bronte.
              Starring Bette Davis and Brian
           Aherne in the second.
                            (Continued on next
                               card)
```

Card 100.   Main entry for recording of different works without a collective title

```
           Jane Eyre and This lonely heart...
              [Audiorecording]   (Card 2)

              Originally broadcast March 2, 1941
           and January 14, 1970.

              1. Radio plays  I. Bronte, Charlotte.
           Jane Eyre  II. Davis, Bette  III. Aher-
           ne, Brian  IV. Title:  This lonely
           heart  V. Series
```

Card 101.   Extension for card 103

Rite of Spring, for example), with standardized terms applying to the instrumental and vocal medium of performance,
and with other identifying elements such as keys and opus
numbers.   These rules do not lend themselves to succinct
summary, but it is important for even the smallest library

```
AA
784
GUE        The Guess Who
              Rockin'.  [Audiorecording]   RCA
           Victor LSP 4602, [1972]
              1 disc, 12 in:   33.3 rpm; stereo.

              Words of songs inserted in album.
              CONTENTS:  Heartbroken bopper.--Get
           you ribbons on.--Smoke big factory.--
           Arrivederci girl.--Guns, guns, guns.--
           Running bear.--Back to the city.--Your
           Nashville sneakers.--Herbert's a loser.
           --Hi, Rockers, Sea of love, Heaven
           only moved once yesterday, Don't you
           want me?
```

Card 102.   Main entry under performer

which has a collection of audiorecordings to have a clearly
thought-out and consistent approach to the organization of
what it has.

If the library buys its audiorecordings from a jobber
who can supply catalog card sets with every item, the library simply accepts the decisions made by the jobber's cataloger and adapts its in-house cataloging of recordings acquired through other sources to the jobber's practice.  Similarly, if the library purchases LC cards, or if it participates
in a regional processing system, it must accommodate its
policies accordingly.  When a recording has to be cataloged
at the local level, the cards produced in-house should be
compatible with those obtained from the outside source, and
therefore the same authority file for uniform titles should be
followed at the local level.

When a library chooses to do its own cataloging but
does not subscribe to LC's music and phonorecords catalog,[8]
it needs some other aid in establishing an authority file for
names and uniform titles.  The Schwann Record and Tape
Guide[9] can be used for this purpose, for while its choices
do not always coincide with LC's, Schwann's entries are
familiar to most library record borrowers, and the Guide is
readily available, cheap, and easy to use.  For example, if
you have a recording labeled "Beethoven's Emperor Concerto,"
you will find it in Schwann not under "Emperor" but under

Concerti for piano and orchestra, No. 5 in E flat, Op. 73.
This information should be used to form the uniform title,
arranged in the following order:

| | |
|---|---|
| --form | - concerto |
| --medium of performance | - piano |
| --number | - no. 5 |
| --opus | - op. 73 |
| --key | - E flat |

Only the solo instrument needs to be specified in the case
of a concerto, as the orchestra is understood; similarly, it
is omitted in symphonies, overtures, suites, and other forms
where the medium of performance is implicit in the form.
For the same reason, chorus or solo voices are not specified for cantatas, operas, songs, etc.  Quartets are understood to be for two violins, viola and cello, unless otherwise
indicated, but the instruments for trios, quintets and other
combinations should be spelled out.  When in doubt, consult
a dictionary or encyclopedia of music.  To return to the example above, if the jacket or record label had omitted any
mention of the concerto's number, opus, or key, the information could have been found by looking up Emperor Concerto
in Berkowitz's Popular Titles and Subtitles of Musical Compositions. 10  The catalog entry would look like this:

> Beethoven, Ludwig van
> [Concerto, piano, no. 5, op. 73, E-flat]
> Emperor concerto

Note that the uniform title is bracketed and given on the line
between the composer and the title as it appears on the record album (see cards 95-97).  For composers whose works
are regularly cited by a standard index number, such as
Köchel numbers in the case of Mozart, include the number
(e.g., K. 375) in the uniform title, preceding the key.  LC
cards omit number and opus when an index number is available, but since library users are not consistent in using
these, it is best to provide both approaches.

Another example of how to use Schwann for deriving
a uniform title: if you have a recording labeled Die Zauber-
flöte by Mozart, and need to decide whether to use the German or the English translation, look under both in Schwann
and choose accordingly.  In this case, "Magic flute" would
be your uniform title, which is probably how most library
patrons would search, although AACR prescribes the German

title.  A cross reference will insure that the user can find
the entry regardless of where he looks first.  You may also
want to make a name cross reference if you use Schwann's
entry for Mozart, since it does not give his full name, which
LC gives as Johann Chrysostom Wolfgang Amadeus Mozart.

The following forms of musical compositions generally
require a uniform title:  canons, cantatas, chaconnes, chor-
ales, chorale-preludes, concertos, divertimentos, duets, fan-
tasias, fugues, masses, motets, operas, oratarios, overtures,
passacaglias, quartets, quintets, rondos, scherzos, sonatas,
songs, suites, symphonies, trios, variations.  For complete
or almost complete collections of a composer's works, use
"Works" as the conventional title.  For incomplete collections
of a composer's works, use "Collection," or "Collection,
vocal," "Collection, violin," etc.  One can also add the word
"Selections" to indicate excerpts from an opera or from works
for piano, etc.  For example:

> **Purcell, Henry,** 1658 or 9–1695.
> ₍Works, harpsichord. Selections₎
> Suites and miscellaneous pieces.

The use of Schwann may lead to some discrepancies
with LC usage and AACR's rules for forming uniform titles,
but the most important thing is that you maintain consistency
within your own library catalog, and evolve a system which
is easy to use.

Medium designator.  The word "Audiorecording" in
brackets should follow the title or uniform title, when one is
used.  LC uses the term phonodisc or phonotape, which need
not be changed if a library buys LC cards.  Specific designators are: cartridge, cassette, disc, reel, roll (archival/
experimental, cylinder, page, wire).

Imprint.  This consists of the name of the producer,
followed by the serial identification (label number) and the
date of production/copyright (in the absence of that date, give
the release date).  If the date of performance is different,
it is given in a note.  Pearson suggests that the imprint can
be excluded in cataloging recordings for small library collections, as the publisher and serial number can be readily obtained from trade catalogs and the dates are often unknown
or confused by reissues. [11]

Collation.  This should describe the format sufficiently

to enable the user to know what kind of equipment is needed for playback. The following information is given in the order listed: number of cartridges, cassettes, discs or reels; diameters of discs or reels; playing time, if available; playback speed; recording mode (mono-, stereo-, or quadraphonic). Dimensions of cassettes and cartridges need to be given only when they are other than standard. Reel tape is usually 1/4-inch wide, and only the exceptions need to be noted. Since playback speed for cassettes is a standard 1-7/8 ips, it need not be given (see card 98). For discs, playback speed, size and recording mode might be left out if a library is certain that its collection will never include any other than 12-inch, 33-1/3 rpm discs, and that no one will care whether a record is monaural or quadraphonic. Instead of giving playing time in the collation, a note saying "Durations on label" or "Durations on container," as appropriate, may be given. AACR varies from the above in calling for the number of sides for discs, omitting the recording mode when it is monaural, and relegating duration to the notes.

Notes. Give any important information about the physical format which has not been included in the collation; original or variant titles and relationship to other works; performers and medium of performance; supplementary materials, such as teacher's guide, libretto, song sheets; contents, where not specified or completely given in the title statement. Only the major soloists, the orchestra and conductor need to be given in the performer note. In collections with different performers for the various works, the performer of each can be included in the contents listing (see card 103).

Tracings. Subject entries can be kept to a minimum by eliminating musical form entries if the classification scheme used serves as a substitute and if the audiorecording shelf list and an index to the classification scheme are accessible to the public. For example, if DDC is used, the library patron can readily find all the library's holdings of organ music or English poetry by looking under 786.5 or 821 in the shelf list. If recordings are not classed, the shelf list is out of reach, or the collection needs to be tailored to curriculum-oriented retrieval, it is best to make the necessary form entries, keeping them consistent with the subject headings used for all other materials in the library. Where the general subject heading list is found to be inadequate, Pearson's list, [12] although quite dated now, can serve as a model for additional headings. Care should be used, however, not to destroy the integrity of the general list.

```
AA
784
BLA        Black cat trail.   [Audiorecording]
             Mamlish S3800, [1973]
             1 disc, 12 in:   33.3 rpm; mono.

             Recorded in the late 1940's and
           early 1950's.
             CONTENTS:  Hawaiian boogie (Elmore
           James)--Murmur low (Big Boy Spires)--
           Vacation blues (Johnny Howard)--Bad
           woman blues (Slim Pickens)--Crying
           won't help you (Robert Nighthawk)--

                        ◯ (continued on next
                                 card)
```

Card 103.   Various performers included in contents note

_____

Added entries should be made for works other than
the first one entered, in composer-conventional title order;
performers; title, if distinctive and unique; series, if significant.   Title added entries are not made where a title of
a recording is the same as the performer(s).   Title added
entries are not made for titles of individual songs on a popular recording, of poems or other selections in a collection,
unless a library is unusually well endowed with money, time,
volunteer labor, and catalog card drawer space.

References.   Because so many musical compositions
are known by several titles or titles in different languages,
see references must be made in order to bring listings together under one title.   For example, if you have chosen
"Prélude à l'après-midi d'un faune" as your uniform title for
Debussy's composition, you need to ensure that a borrower
looking for "The afternoon of a faun" will not go away disap-
pointed.   Make the following cards (see opposite).   Doing
this the first time you add a recording of a work with a popular or distinctive title will save making complete title-added
entry cards every time you add a new rendition.

Variations and options.   When audiorecordings are
cataloged in-house, the librarian may choose to prepare a
unit card, duplicate it, and then add the headings.   If, however, each card in a set is typed individually, a variation

Debussy, Claude
   The afternoon of a faun

    see

Debussy, Claude
   Prélude à l'après-midi d'un faune

---

Prélude à l'après-midi d'un faune
Debussy, Claude

Editions of this work will be found
under the composer's name.

---

The afternoon of a faun
Debussy, Claude

   Editions of this work will be found
under

Debussy, Claude
   Prélude à l'après-midi d'un faune

Cards 104, 105, 106.   General reference cards for musical
work known by two titles

on the main entry rules given above should be considered.
For a recording without a collective title containing works
by several composers, separate entries equivalent to main
entries may be made.   These entries are linked by a "with"
note, using the composers' names in inverted order, followed
by the uniform title of each work, as in cards 107-109.
This method results in a less crowded card and more specific
added entries.   It is used regularly by LC on their printed
cards.   The disadvantage is that one ends up with many more
cards to type.   It should also be noted that this approach requires that the classification number be assigned on the basis
of the first item on the recording, or, where no call number
is used (as in an alphabetical arrangement), that the retrieval
words be underlined on each card.

```
AA
785.8
BRA      Brahms, Johannes, 1833–1897.
            [Serenade, orchestra, op. 16, A major]  Phonodisc.
            Serenade in A major, op. 16.  Marlboro Recording So-
         ciety MRS 1.  [ca. 1970]
            1 s.  12 in.  33⅓ rpm.  stereophonic.

            With: Mozart, J. C. W. A.  Sonata, piano, K. 13, F major.
            Marlboro Festival Orchestra; Pablo Casals, conductor.
            Duration: about 32 min.
            Program notes by F. Dorian ([8] p.) inserted in slipcase.


            1. Suites (Orchestra)      I. Casals, Pablo, 1876–1973.   II. Marlboro
         Festival Orchestra.

            [M1003]                                                    75–760909

            Library of Congress            75                             R
```

Card 107.   Works by different composers without collective
            title, entered under two main entries

```
AA
785.8
BRA         Mozart, Wolfgang Amadeus
               [Sonata, piano, K. 13, F major]
            [Audiorecording]
               Sonata in F major, K. 13.  Sonata
            in A major, K. 12.  Marlboro Recording
            Society MRS 1, [1970?]

               1/2 s. of 1 disc, 12 in:  12 & 6 min;
            33.3 rpm. stereo.

               With:  Brahms, J.  Serenade, orches-
            tra, op. 16, A major.
                              (Continued on next
                               card)
```

Card 108.   Other main entry for audiorecording represented
            in part by card 107

────────────────────────────────────────────────────────

        When audiorecordings are not intershelved with other
materials in the library, it is best to have a separate catalog
for the collection nearby.  As suggested at the beginning of
this chapter, the cards should be duplicated in the main cata-

```
AA
785.8
BRA      Mozart, Wolfgang Amadeus
            [Sonata, piano, K. 13, F major]
         [Audiorecording]  (Card 2)

            Pina Carmirelli, violin; Rudolf
         Serkin, piano; David Cole, violin-
         cello.

            1.  Piano music   I. Mozart, Wolfgang
         Amadeus.  Sonata, piano, K. 12, A major.
         II. Serkin, Rudolf
                        ◯
```

Card 109.   Extension for card 108

---

log.  It is possible, however, to be selective in this duplication and still achieve the aim of bringing all forms of materials on a topic to a user's attention.   For example, instead
of copying each set of cards for every recording of a Beethoven work for the central catalog, make one card which refers the patron interested in Beethoven to the audiorecording
catalog.   Selected performers and conductors as well as composers can receive the same treatment, as can broad categories such as folk music.   Spoken recordings require more
specific entries, so that the patron looking for Waiting for
Godot can find entries for the recorded as well as the written version of the play under both title and author.   To keep
track of duplicate or see cards made for the central catalog,
list on the audiorecording shelf list cards which cards have
been duplicated and keep a list of see references made.


CHARTS

     A chart is an opaque sheet, either flat or relief,
which presents information via graphs, pictures, tables, dia-
grams, or outlines.   Flannel or magnetic board sets are also
categorized as charts when the contents for a particular display are stored as an entity.   The boards themselves are
considered equipment, and are not cataloged.   Small or folded
charts are most easily handled by incorporating them into

the vertical file, and need to be marked only with the appropriate subject heading.   Charts or sets too large to fit in
the vertical file, or of special importance to the collection,
or mounted in an unusual way should be cataloged and classified.

Main entry.   Title main entry is preferred, except
when an individual is clearly responsible for the contents
and when the "author's" name appears on the chart and is of
more importance to its identification than the title.

Title.   Take the most appropriate and conspicuous
title appearing on the chart or supply one in brackets if none
is given.   In the case of a set, enter under the set or series
title.

Medium designator.   Use the term "chart" in brackets
after the title, and the specific designators--chart, flannel
board set, flip chart, graph, magnetic board set, relief chart,
or wall chart--in the collation.

Collation.   Number and type of chart, color, size
(height x width), type of mount, or similar physical description, as needed.

Notes.   Amplify the physical description if necessary,
and list accompanying materials such as manuals.   List the
contents for a set, or summarize the contents where it is
not made clear by the title.

Tracings.   Give added entries for photographers,
artists, etc., only if they are well known or especially important to the identification of the chart.


DIORAMA

A diorama is a three-dimensional replica of a scene,
usually in miniature, with modeled figures and a painted
background.

Main entry.   Dioramas are almost always entered under title.

Title.   The title will usually appear on the container
or in accompanying material.   If there is variation, prefer
the latter source.   If a title must be supplied, it is bracketed.

```
CA
613.8    Dial a drug.  [Chart]  By W.R. Spence.
            Spenco, 1970.
            1 wall chart:  col; 36 in. diameter.

            A wheel mounted on a chart permits
         one to dial information about 16
         drugs.



            1.  Drug abuse
                        ◯
```

Card 110.   Main entry for chart; summary to explain purpose

```
CA
634.9       Forest.  [Chart]  Nifty Instructional
               Materials, [197-?]
               6 charts:  col; 24 x 36 in; with
            eyelets for hanging and chart stand.




               1.  Forests and forestry
                        ◯
```

Card 111.   Main entry for chart; collation explains format

Medium designator.   "Diorama" is the designator, given in brackets following the title.   There are no additional specific designators.

Collation.   Where the components of a diorama are too many to be listed succinctly, use the phrase "various

pieces." Give the size of the container if it affects storage
or use.

Notes. Include a summary note which gives enough
description to show the purpose of the diorama. AACR suggests that the physical description be given in a note rather
than in the usual collation position.

```
OA
630
FAR      Farm life.  [Diorama]  Created by
             the third grade, Lincoln School, 1974.
             1 diorama:  30 pieces; col; in box,
         36 x 24 x 12 in.

             Contains figures of animals, people,
         and farm implements; farmyard and
         stable backgrounds.


             1.  Farms
                         ◯
```

Card 112.   Main entry for diorama

FILMSTRIPS

A filmstrip is a strip of film with still pictures and/
or captions meant to be projected in sequence, frame by
frame. Interdependent scripts or audiorecordings accompanying the filmstrip are considered to be a part of the cataloging unit, but if accompanying materials are designed to be
used independently of the filmstrip, treat as a kit. Many
filmstrips are issued and purchased as sets which are clearly meant to be used together, and it is easier and more efficient to catalog these as sets rather than individually. However, where each part of a set is clearly independent and
would require a separate tracing in any case, you may choose
to enter each filmstrip separately, unless the audio accompaniment for several filmstrips is on one disc or tape. When
the filmstrips in a set are apt to be more useful if given different classification numbers, they must of course be cataloged

separately, again provided that audio accompaniment is separate for each filmstrip.

Main entry. Filmstrips are usually entered under
title, either individually or as a set.   When a filmstrip which
is part of a set is cataloged separately but does not have a
distinctive or meaningful title, it is entered under the set
title with the individual filmstrip title as a subtitle (see card
113).   Contrast this with Seeing the New England States (card
116), which must be cataloged as a unit because each filmstrip does not have an audiorecording to itself.

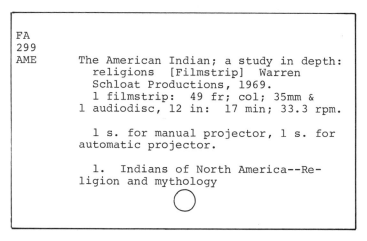

```
FA
299
AME        The American Indian; a study in depth:
               religions  [Filmstrip]  Warren
               Schloat Productions, 1969.
                 1 filmstrip:   49 fr; col; 35mm &
           1 audiodisc, 12 in:   17 min; 33.3 rpm.

               1 s. for manual projector, 1 s. for
           automatic projector.

               1.   Indians of North America--Re-
           ligion and mythology
```

Card 113.   Part of a filmstrip set entered separately, as
           subtitle of set title

When two or more filmstrips without a collective title
are accompanied by a single, interdependent audiorecording,
treat as a unit and enter under the title of the first film-
strip--i.e., the one which matches side one of the recording.   Include the other(s) in the title statement, and make
an added entry for it (see card 117).

When the filmstrip is a reproduction of a work originally produced in another medium, as when the frames of
the filmstrip reproduce the illustrations in a picture book
and the accompanying recording reproduces the text, a library
may choose to enter under author.   For example, the main
entry for card 117 might be under Wildsmith.

```
FA
970.1
AME        The American Indian; a study in depth
              [Filmstrip]  Warren Schloat Pro-
              ductions, 1969.
              6 filmstrips:  col; 35mm & 6 audio-
           discs, 12 in:  33.3 rpm.

              1 s. of each disc for manual pro-
           jector, 1 s. for automatic projector.
              CONTENTS:  Before Columbus. 54 fr,
           19 min.--After Columbus. 40 fr, 14
           min.--Growing up. 47 fr, 15 min.--
                          (Continued on next
                                 card)
```

Card 114.    Entry for set treated as unit

```
           The American Indian   [Filmstrip]
              (Card 2)

                    CONTENTS--Continued
           Religions. 49 fr, 17 min.--Arts and
           culture. 63 fr, 24 min.--The Navajo.
           61 fr, 22 min.


              1. Indians of North America--History
           2. Indians of North America--Social life
           and customs  3. Navajo Indians
```

Card 115.    Extension for card 114

Title.    Use the title given on the title frame of the
filmstrip, not the leader or container, if there are discrepancies.

Medium designator.    "Filmstrip" in brackets follows
the title.    The specific designators are filmstrip and filmslip
(a short, mounted filmstrip).

```
FA
917.4
            Seeing the New England states  [Film-
                strip]  Bill Boal Productions;
                Coronet, 1975.
                4 filmstrips:  col; 35mm & 2 audio-
            discs, 12 in:  33.3 rpm.

            With teacher's guide.
            CONTENTS:  Land and climate. 69 fr.,
            14 min.--Food from land and sea. 65 fr.,
            13 min.--Economy and industry. 53 fr.,
            13 min.--History and people. 67 fr., 16
            min.
                1. New England--Description and
            travel
```

Card 116.   Entry for set which must be treated as one unit--
            audiorecordings accompany two filmstrips each

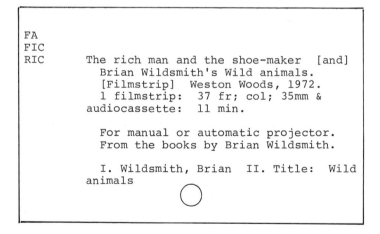

```
FA
FIC
RIC         The rich man and the shoe-maker  [and]
                Brian Wildsmith's Wild animals.
                [Filmstrip]  Weston Woods, 1972.
                1 filmstrip:  37 fr; col; 35mm &
            audiocassette:  11 min.

            For manual or automatic projector.
            From the books by Brian Wildsmith.

            I. Wildsmith, Brian  II. Title:  Wild
            animals
```

Card 117.   Entry for two filmstrips without collective title,
            entered under first title

        Collation.   Give the number of filmstrips, number of
frames of each, color, film width.  If applicable, give the
number and type of sound recordings, duration, size, play-

back speed, recording mode, and/or other accompanying material, such as scripts. The prefix "audio" may be used with specific designators to prevent confusion. The order and form of the collation recommended by AACR Chapter 12 (revised) varies slightly, as shown by the example below:

> 67 fr. : col. ; 35 mm. & disc (33 1/3 rpm.
> mono. 12 inch. 10 min.) and teacher's guide.

Following the Standards, the same information would be arranged as follows:

> 1 filmstrip: 67 fr; col; 35mm & 1 audiodisc, 12 in:
> 10 min; 33.3 rpm; mono.

The teacher's guide would be listed in a note.

Sound synchronization information may be added to the collation by using phrases such as "for manual or automatic projector," "1 s. for manual projector, 1 s. for automatic projector," or "audible and inaudible signals."

When a filmstrip which is part of a set has been entered separately under its own title, it is especially important to give the set title as a series note (see card 118).

```
┌─────────────────────────────────────────────────────┐
│ FA                                                   │
│ 362.2                                                │
│ NAR       Narcotics  [Filmstrip]  Guidance           │
│              Associates, 1970.                       │
│                                                      │
│           1 filmstrip:  101 fr; col; 35mm &          │
│           1 audiocassette; 1 s. for manual pro-      │
│           jector, 1 s. for automatic projector.      │
│           (The Drug information series)              │
│              With teacher's guide.                   │
│                                                      │
│                                                      │
│           1. Narcotic habit  I. Series               │
│                          ◯                           │
│                                                      │
└─────────────────────────────────────────────────────┘
```

Card 118.   Entry under individual title, set title as series
            note

The amount of detail given in the collation can be reduced, depending on the local situation.  For example, if all of a media center's equipment is of the manual type, there is little point in describing an automatic advance feature. However, libraries which serve users who have a variety of machines to choose from will want to include the information. Most borrowers will also want to know how much time is required to use the material.  The number of filmstrip frames is often an indication of the scope and depth of information and should be included when readily available.  Sometimes the frames are numbered, but producers' catalogs and reviews generally give frame numbers and duration.  Citing the number of frames and audio duration for a set can be simplified by giving the range where it is not too varied (e. g. , 52-56 fr. , about 50 fr. , 12-14 min. ), or by including the information in the contents note (see cards 116 and 119).

```
FA
973.7
CIV        The Civil War  [Filmstrip]  American
              Heritage; McGraw-Hill, 1971.
              5 filmstrips:  about 50 fr. each;
           col; 35mm & 5 audiodiscs, 7 in:  7
           min. each s; 33.3 rpm; for manual or
           automatic projector.

              With teacher's guide.
              Narrated by Bruce Catton.
              CONTENTS:  A nation divided.--The
           clash of amateur armies.--The iron vise
           is forged.--Gettysburg.--An ending and
           a beginning.
              1. U.S.-History-Civil War  I. Catton,
           Bruce
```

Card 119.  Number of frames and audio duration summarized in collation

Notes.  Clarify anything important not evident in the collation, such as captions for a silent filmstrip or special equipment needed (for filmstrips in special cartridges, for example).  List accompanying materials, such as guides, not included in the collation.  If a filmstrip is a reproduction of a book, or is correlated with a book which is not stored and cataloged as part of the unit, include that information in the notes. List credits only where they are especially important or likely to be of interest to the borrower. If parts of a filmstrip set cataloged as a unit have distinctive titles, give a contents note. Otherwise write a summary whenever the title is not self-explanatory.

## FLASHCARDS

A flash card is printed with numbers, letters, words or graphics, and is intended for brief display (manual or mechanical) for drill purposes. The cards come in sets and may be coordinated with sound, in which case they may require a special audiocard player. Sets which are not too bulky can be incorporated into the vertical file or picture file. Larger boxed sets can be easily interfiled with books and other media and should be handled in a similar manner.

Main entry. Enter under set title.

Medium designator. "Flash card" is the designator, "card" the specific designator.

Collation. Give the number of cards, color size, and describe any interdependent accompanying material.

```
HA
372.4
PIC        Picto-word cards.  [Flash card]  Pasa-
              dena, CA:  Bilingual Educational
              Services, 1971.
              60 cards:  col; 9 x 11 in.  Primary.

              Cards printed on both sides, drawing
           of object on one side, word on other.
              Intended to build reading-readiness,
           vocabulary.

           1. Reading
```

Card 120. Main entry for set of flash cards; collation amplified by note

Notes. Amplify the physical description as needed, indicating whether cards are printed on both sides, accompanying material such as test sheets or instructions, etc. If the title is not self-explanatory, use a summary note to state the contents and purpose of the set.

```
HA
513
NEW      New math flash cards.  [Flash card]
            Buffalo, NY:  Kenworthy Education
            Service, [196-?]
            4 sets of cards:  390 cards; b&w;
         9 x 3 in; in box.  P-I.

            Presented in horizontal equations.
            CONTENTS:  Addition.--Subtraction.--
         Multiplication.--Division.

            1. Arithmetic--Study and teaching
```

Card 121.  Main entry for flash card sets

GAMES

A game is an activity which tests or teaches skills or concepts by way of competition, simulation, or other prescribed performance governed by specific regulations. For the purpose of cataloging, a game is the package of rules, equipment and/or other materials required for play. Some games, such as those consisting primarily of written material, may be most easily handled by incorporation into the vertical file. Larger boxed games should be processed in the same way as other materials. Games intended for in-library use only, such as chess or checkers sets in a public library's young adult corner, need not be cataloged.

Main entry. While most games are entered under title, simulation games are likely to have a personal author who is clearly responsible for the contents and in those cases author main entry is preferred.

**Medium designator.** Use "game," with the following specific designators: game, puzzle, and simulation.

**Collation.** Enumerate component parts by type, and give color and size if they are significant.

**Notes.** Clarify the physical description as necessary, for example, game board printed on container lid. State the objective of the game where it is not evident from the title. List the minimum and maximum number of players required, and the amount of time it takes to complete the game, if readily available.

```
HA
923
MEE      Meet the presidents.  [Game]  Selchow
            & Righter, 1965.
         1 game:  playing board, 8 markers.

         Object is to move each President
         along a path to the White House.  For
         2, 3, or 5 players, who make moves
         when they answer questions on a spinner
         correctly; 30 to 60 minutes playing time.

         1. U.S.-History   2. Presidents-U.S.
```

Card 122.  Main entry for game

GLOBES

A globe is a sphere which shows a map of the earth (terrestrial), or other planetary body, or of the relative positions of heavenly bodies as seen from the earth (celestial). If a globe has raised surfaces to indicate relative heights of land forms, it is a relief globe. Globes are cataloged like maps, except as indicated below.

**Main entry.** AECT's Standards call for entry under title, which conflicts with AACR, but makes sense for media centers and small libraries.

```
GA
910
EXP        Explorers I.  [Game]  Simile II  [196-?]
           1 game:  map, role cards, manual.

           A role-playing game which teaches
           map skills as well as giving informa-
           tion about the voyages of Columbus,
           Magellan, and other explorers.  For 18
           to 35 players, to be played in 5 to 20
           15-minute periods; grades 4-6.

           1. Explorers  2. Maps  3. America--
           Discovery and exploration
```

Card 123.  Main entry for game

---

Medium designator.  "Globe" is the designator, and
"globe" and "relief globe" are the specific designators.

Collation.  The size is given in terms of the diameter.
When the type of mount or other physical characteristics can

```
QA
551.4
HYD        Hydrographic relief globe.  [Globe]
              Hubbard  [196-]
              1 raised relief globe:  col; 12 x
           12 x 13 in; gyro-disc mounting.

              With study guide.
              Through the ocean surface, represented
           by clear plastic, continental shelf,
           mountain chains, sea mounts, trenches,
           etc., that comprise the ocean floor can
           be seen.

              1. Oceanography
```

Card 124.  Main entry for relief globe

be stated succinctly, they are included in the collation. Otherwise the information is given in a note.

Note. Give the scale, the material of which the globe is made, the type of support, and other physical characteristics (e. g. , wired for internal lighting, designed to be inflated, etc. ) not given in the collation. List any accompanying materials.

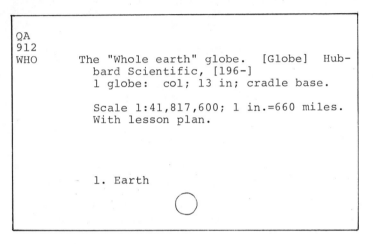

```
QA
912
WHO        The "Whole earth" globe.   [Globe]   Hub-
              bard Scientific, [196-]
           1 globe:   col; 13 in; cradle base.

           Scale 1:41,817,600; 1 in.=660 miles.
           With lesson plan.



           1. Earth
```

Card 125.   Main entry for globe

---

KITS

A kit is a packaged collection of several types of media which are designed to be used together but are not interdependent; that is, each item can be used alone, as opposed to a sound filmstrip set where the pictures would have no meaning without the accompanying recording. In some cases, a kit may be deemed to be of greater potential usefulness when broken down into its components, which are then cataloged separately.

Main entry. Enter under title, unless the kit is more readily identified by author, as is sometimes the case with programmed instruction.

Title. Use the title on the container, as the components are likely to have varying titles.

```
KT
796
WOM        Women who win:  3.  [Kit]  EMC, 1975.
           1 kit:  4 books, 1 teacher's guide
           & 4 audiocassettes:  30 min. each.

           Books by Linda Jacobs.
           The careers and lives of Mary Decker,
           Annemarie Proell, Joan Moore Rice, and
           Rosemary Casals; a reading incentive
           program for grades 4-12; 5th grade
           reading level.

           1. Reading  2. Sports  3. Decker,
           Mary  4. Proell, Annemarie  5. Rice,
           Joan Moore  6. Casals, Rosemary
```

Card 126.  Main entry for kit

```
KT
520
REA        Reading, reporting, researching in
             science; the universe.  [Kit]  BFA,
             1975.
           1 kit:  1 skill book; 8 booklets;
           50 activity cards; 4 filmstrips:  57-
           70 fr; col; & 4 audiodiscs:  13-15 min.

           CONTENTS:  The solar system.--Time.--
           Myths and constellations.--Sky viewers;
           from superstitions to science.

           1. Astronomy  2. Universe
```

Card 127.  Main entry for kit

Medium designator.  Use "kit," with the following
specific designators:  exhibit, kit, laboratory kit, programmed instruction.

Collation.  List the number and types of media com-
prising the kit without giving the full physical description of

each, unless it can be done very briefly in parentheses following each item. Include a description of the container and its size.

Notes. Any supplementary information needed to clarify the description provided by title and collation should be given. A summary pointing out the purpose of the kit may be necessary. The notes for programmed instruction kits should indicate the type of program--linear, branching, or mixed--and the response mode--written or spoken.

MAPS

A map is a flat representation of a terrestrial, planetary of astronomical geographical area; a relief map has raised surfaces to indicate relative heights of land forms. If you wish to avoid confusion between a map that shows elevation pictorially and a map that has raised surfaces, you can use the terms visual relief and raised relief.

Any map that folds is most efficiently handled by incorporating it into the vertical file. Another method of caring for maps is to create a special file just for them, and to arrange them alphabetically by area, thus making it unnecessary to assign any type of call number or to catalog them. The area heading would be written on the folded map, or on a label on the map, in the upper right-hand corner and the maps would be arranged alphabetically. To illustrate, maps may be arranged by: 1) continent, 2) country, 3) state, province, etc. , 4) county, 5) city or town. For instance:

North America.    United States.    North Carolina.
Wake.    Raleigh.

A library might omit from its arrangement for the maps of the area in which it is located:  the name of the continent, even the country; for instance:  N. C. Durham. Durham.

Main entry. If large maps, maps of special importance to the collection, or those mounted on a roller for hanging are to be cataloged, the most vexing problem to be resolved is that of main entry. While AACR specifies entry under "the person or corporate body that is primarily responsible for its informational content," the AECT Standards prefer title entry, as does Nonbook Materials, because "the Anglo-American Cataloging Rules produces too many entries

under publisher, e.g., Rand McNally Co., resulting in cata-
logue drawers full of cards with the same not-too-useful main
entry."13  This is a valid point, but if it is a library's practice to purchase LC cards, there is little to be gained from
doctoring them.  If you do not use LC cards (or other
printed cards which follow AACR), another possible choice
is to enter under geographical area, a practice advocated by
many map librarians.  For small libraries, however, title
main entry is probably the easiest route to take, and the subject headings will provide geographical access in any case.
A set of maps of the same area can be treated as a single
unit.

Title.  Take the most appropriate title given on the
face of the map, preferably from within the border, or supply one in brackets if there is none.  If the mapmaker is of
special significance, follow the title and medium designator
with an author statement.

Medium designator.  Use "map," and map, relief map
and wall map as specific designators.

Collation.  Give the number and type of maps, number of sheets and overlays, size, color, and type of mount,
if significant.  For relief maps, you may want to specify
visual or raised.  If a map is printed on both sides, indicate
this in parentheses.  If a map is printed on several sheets

---

```
LA
551.6
WEA        Weather map.  [Map]  Hubbard Media and
              Materials, [196-?]
              1 wall map:  col; 44 x 50 in; mounted
           with metal rods and hangers.

           With study guide.
           Chalk markable; designed for plotting
           weather.

           1. Weather forecasting
```

Card 128.  Main entry for map

```
LA
917.55
RIC          Richmond street map.  [Map]  [Drawn
                for Atlantic Richfield Co.]  Rand-
                McNally, 1969.
                1 map:  col; 33 x 17 in; fold. to
             9 x 5 in.

                Scale ca. 1:40,000; 1 in. = 0.62 miles
                Continuation of map on verso.
                Title on outside when folded:  Rich-
             mond.
                Index on verso.
                Insets:  Downtown Richmond.--Rich-
             mond, Petersburg and vicinity.

                1. Richmond--Maps
```

Card 129.   Main entry for map

---

which must be joined in order to be complete, count as a
single map, i. e. , map on 4 sheets; but if each sheet has the
characteristics of a complete map, count as 4 maps.  The
size is that of the entire sheet.

Notes.  Give the scale if it can be readily ascertained,
and the prime meridian and type of projection, if unusual.
List in sets and the contents of a set.  Notes also give information as to what data the map shows, e. g. , air routes,
population distribution, etc.  Information of a type not usually found on that kind of map is especially important for notes;
for instance, if a highway map shows points of historic interest, bring it out in a note, as all highway maps do not have
such information.  Notes can, if desired, give the names of
the surveyor, engraver, or cartographer.  They should clarify
the historical period covered, if this is not made explicit in
the title, e. g. , "With international boundaries as of September 1, 1939, the day Germany invaded Poland. "  Accompanying materials such as guides or indexes should also be noted.

MODELS

A model is a three-dimensional replica of an object,
of the same size as the original, or made to scale.  Unas-
sembled kits may also be considered as models.  Museum

replicas of sculpture or other works of art are treated as models, with the addition of information usually given for art reproductions, such as the location of the original (see the section on pictures). A mock-up is a model, usually of a machine device, or process which is meant to be manipulated or operated for training purposes.

Main entry. Title is preferred for main entry, even in the case of museum replicas, as these are seldom exact reproductions.

Title. Usually the title will be found on the container. If the model is not labeled, supply an appropriate title in brackets.

Medium designator. Use "model," and model and mock-up as specific designators.

Collation. Give the number of models and number of separate pieces if necessary; color if significant; size of the model and/or of the container in which it is stored.

Notes. Give the scale, if known. Amplify the physical description as necessary so as to clarify how the model is to be used.

```
EA
551.7
EAR        Earth history.  [Model]  Hubbard,
              1967.
              1 model: 1 rock layer model & 20
           fossils; col; 18 x 24 x 4 in.

              With lesson plan.
              Shows importance of fossils in deter-
           mining age of rocks in which they are
           found.  Represents the geologic column
           for North America, divided into eras,
           periods, and epochs.  Fossils are re-
           movable.

              1. Geology, Stratigraphic  2. Fos-
           sils
```

Card 130.  Main entry for model

```
EA
730.9
MUS        Museo Mexica (Aztec).  [Model]  Bilingu-
              al Educational Services, [19--]
           7 models; in case:  13 x 21 in.

           With teacher's guide.
           Replicas of Aztec art objects from
        the Museo de Antropologia, Mexico City.



           1. Aztecs
```

Card 131.  Main entry for museum replicas

## MOTION PICTURES

A motion picture is a series of still pictures on film
which, when projected, gives the illusion of motion.  An op-
tical or magnetic sound track may appear as a strip down
one side on the film.  Various sizes of film can be used (8,
16, 35, 55 or 70 mm), and the film can be mounted on reels,
in cassettes or cartridges.  A loop film has the start and
end spliced together and is designed to run continuously without rewinding; it is usually mounted in a cartridge.  The
width of the film and the type of mounting determine the kind
of machine needed for projection.

The fragile and costly nature of film requires a minimum of handling and therefore a maximum of description in
the cataloging, especially in terms of contents.  The practice
of using separate printed book catalogs for public library film
collections is almost universal, and will be discussed as an
addendum to this section.  However, the availability of a
separate book catalog for films should not rule out the provision of subject entries for films in the general card catalog in order to alert patrons to the library's film holdings on
a given topic.  School libraries should interfile complete card
sets for films in their general catalog, whether or not they
also choose to print a separate listing of films.

Media centers should use the same classification system as that chosen for other materials, and should consider the possibility of intershelving with other media, especially in the case of loops. Most public libraries keep 16 mm films in locked storage, arranged alphabetically by title or by a code number based on reel size and accession number. They tend to treat 8 mm film more casually, allowing the original illustrated container to take the place of a catalog, since the films are considered to be a browsing collection intended primarily for entertainment.

Main entry. The title is used as main entry, as it is seldom possible to ascribe responsibility to a single person, and as films are known by and listed in producers' catalogs and reference tools by title.

Title. The title frame of the film itself, rather than the container should be the source used. If the film was originally released under a different title, this is given in a note.

Medium designator. Use "Motion picture" with the following specific designators: cartridge, cassette, loop, reel.

Collation. List the number of cartridges, cassettes or reels; running time in minutes; sound or silent; color, black and white, sepia, or a combination; width of the film in millimeters. If the film is super 8 mm, this must be specified.

Notes. Give any additional information needed to establish the kind of projector required, e.g., Kodak cartridge, magnetic sound, etc. List other titles under which the film has been released and state the relationship of the film to other versions, e.g., sound version of originally silent film. Describe accompanying material, such as a discussion guide. If the film is known to be based on a novel or short story, or if it was made to be used with a specific book, cite the author and title. Give credits only to the extent that the potential user would be interested.

Write a brief, objective summary, including enough information to permit the prospective user to judge whether or not the film will meet his needs.

Tracings. Subject headings should be assigned from

```
MA
551.5
AIR        Air is all around us.  [Motion picture]
              Eye Gate House, 1969.
              1 cartridge:  4 min; si; col; super
           8mm.
              (Basic concepts in science, level 1)
              P-I.

              Film guide mounted on container.
              Shows an experiment in which plastic
           bags are waved in the air, closed,
           placed under water, and squeezed so that
           bubbles rise to the surface.

              1. Air
```

Card 132.   Main entry for 8mm film

```
MA
920.72
ACC        Accomplished women.  [Motion picture]
              Produced by Charles Braverman, 1974;
           Films Inc., 1975.
              1 reel:  25 min; sd; col; 16mm.

              Katherine Graham, Dr. Virginia Apgar,
           LaDonna Harris, Shirley Chisholm, Nikki
           Giovanni, and Helen Reddy on the new
           attitude and image women have of them-
           selves.

              1. Women in the U.S.   2. Graham,
           Katherine   3. Apgar, Virginia
           4. Harris, LaDonna   5. Chisholm, Shirley
           6. Giovanni, Nikki   7. Reddy, Helen
```

Card 133.   Main entry for 16mm film showing producer and
            distributor

the same list used for the other materials in the library.
Added entries for sponsors, producers and distributors can
be omitted, but filmmaker and performer entries can often
be very useful.  Make author-title added entries for films
based on or correlated with print material, and enter variant
titles under which the user might search.

```
MA
573.2
LAD      The Ladder of creation. [Motion picture]
            London:  BBC-TV; New York:  Time-Life
            Films, 1973.
            2 reels:  52 min; sd; col; 16mm.
         (The Ascent of man, no. 9)

            CREDITS:  Producer and director, Ad-
         rian Malone; writer and narrator, Jacob
         Bronowski.
            SUMMARY:  Explores the controversy
         around the theory of evolution developed

                        ◯  (Continued on next
                              card)
```

Card 134.  Main entry for two-reel film, part of series

```
MA
573.2
LAD      The Ladder of creation.  [Motion pic-
            ture]  (Card 2)

         simultaneously by Alfred Wallace and
         Charles Darwin.


            1. Evolution  I. Bronowski, Jacob
         II. Series

                        ◯
```

Card 135.  Extension for card 134

Book catalogs.  Where film collections have developed independently, are housed apart from a library's overall collection, or where films are the only holdings (as in a regional film center), the book catalog has proven to be the most efficient means of access for the borrower who comes seek-

ing a film for a particular kind of program, rather than any
kind of material on a topic.

The same information which would be given on a catalog card is included in a book catalog format, with the exception of medium designation and film width (where all are
the same), which are given only once, on the cover or in
the introduction. Descriptions of the films are more likely
to be annotations than summary notes, since they can be
longer and less formal, and because the catalog also serves
as a promotional tool. Tracings take the form of an index
to the catalog, which may include names of filmmakers, performers, etc., in the same alphabetical sequence as subjects
or in a separate "name" index. If the films are housed in a
library and serve only that library's borrowers, the same subject heading list used for other materials in the collection
should be used, and--ideally--subject cards and selected added
entry cards should be filed in the central card catalog.
Where a film collection is a separate, independent entity, or
where it serves several institutions, a list such as Public Library Subject Headings for 16mm Motion Pictures[14] may be
used as a guide for developing a subject heading authority
file.


PICTURES

        A picture is a visual image produced on a flat opaque
surface by painting, drawing, photography, printing, etc.
Study prints (pictures with accompanying text) and art prints,
as well as original works of art are included in this medium
designation.

        Unframed small pictures are most easily handled by
filing them in a vertical file, arranged in alphabetical order
by subject. Unmounted pictures can be placed in folders. If
the same subject heading list as for other materials in the
library is used, a set of guide cards can be filed in the central card catalog to refer users to the picture collection. It
is helpful to incorporate see and see also references directly
into the file itself. An alternative is to use Dane's The Picture Collection as an authority list. [15]

        Boxed sets of study prints which will most likely be
used as a unit can be fully cataloged and shelved with books,
and a cross reference entered in the picture file. Framed
works of art require separate storage and are usually valuable

# SUBJECT INDEX

# FILM ANNOTATIONS

**Only those films added to the collection since publication of the 1970-71 catalog are described here. Descriptions of all other films can be found in the earlier catalog.**

**AI-YE**                                   **Color   24 Min.   1950**

A poetic interpretation of the story of mankind. The material was photographed in Mexico, Cuba and Puerto Rico by Ian Hugo. Osborne Smith improvised the drum and chant accompaniment. (Radim)

**ALGOMA**                                  **Color   14 Min.   1968**

The Algoma district of Ontario is shown as it would be discovered travelling along the Trans-Canada Highway or via the Algoma Central Railway that cuts through valleys and forests. Many kinds of recreation are shown—lakes, beaches, fishing, and the unspoiled beauty of the land. (Canadian Travel Film Library)

**ALPHABET**                                **Color   6 Min.   1969**

The film shows the alphabet in a fast moving, ever-changing series of visual examples, depicting things starting with each letter. There is no narration, but the animation is accompanied by a combo with a lively beat. Conceived and animated by Elliot Noyes Jr. Music by Pierre Brault. (National Film Board)

**AMERICAN TIME CAPSULE**                   **Color   3 Min.   1968**

By means of rapid cuts of paintings, monochrome photographs, still pictures, drawings, news-

These part-pages are reproduced from the Los Angeles Public Library's Film Catalog Supplement, 1970 to 1971.

enough to warrant cataloging. A public library which provides a circulating art collection will find that in addition to
cards in the catalog, borrowers who wish to place reserves
will appreciate a separate list of the holdings, especially if
it is illustrated with photographs of the pictures. Libraries
which are fortunate enough to be able to acquire original art
work as well as reproductions should consult Foster's Prints
in the Public Library. 16

     Main entry. When a picture is an original work of
art or an exact reproduction, enter under the name of the
artist. Sets of study prints and graphic material which is
of value for its informational content rather than its artistic
merits should be entered under title.

     Medium designator. Use "Picture," with the following
specific designators: art original, art print, hologram, photo-
graph, picture, post card, poster, stereograph, study print.

     Collation. Give the number of pictures comprising a
set; color; size, of the image for originals and reproductions,
of the entire item for other pictures; mount or frame, if
applicable.

     Notes. For an art original, indicate the medium (oil,
acrylic, lithograph, etc.) and/or the form (abstract, land-

```
PA
707
REI        Reinhold visuals; aids for art teaching.
           [Picture]  Edited by John Lidstone.
           Reinhold, 1968.
           262 posters:  b&w & col; 18 x 24 in.

           With booklet.
           CONTENTS:  Line.--Mass.--Organization.
           --Surface.--Color.--Movement.--Percep-
           tion.--Space.

           1. Art-Study and teaching
```

Card 136.  Main entry for set of posters

scape, etc. ). For an art reproduction, the location of the original work and other helpful information may be added, such as the medium and actual size. The contents of a set can be listed. Accompanying material such as notes should be indicated.

---

PA
629.4
       Eyewitness to space. [Picture] U.S.
       Government Printing Office, 1969.
       12 art prints: col; 16 x 20 in.
       (NASA picture set no. 3)

       Reproductions of paintings inspired
       by the activities connected with the
       moon launch.

       1. Apollo project   2. Moon--Explo-
       ration   II. Series

---

Card 137.   Main entry for set of art prints

---

REALIA

A real object, or a sample or part of one, and three-dimensional hand-made objects are included in this category. A case could be made for including microscope slides in this category, but AACR makes them an independent category, while AECT lumps them with slides.

Main entry. Enter under title, except for works of art, which are entered under the name of the artist.

Medium designator. Use "Realia," and the name of the object or "specimen" as specific designators.

Imprint. When realia have been collected rather than purchased, the date of collection and place of discovery substitute for the usual imprint.

Collation. Itemize the pieces, the type and size of container, and any other pertinent physical characteristics.

Notes. If the item or its purpose is not adequately described by title and collation, clarify or further describe it.

```
RA
590
ANI      Animal kingdom.  [Realia]  Ward's
            Natural Science Establishment, [19--]
            60 specimens:  mounted in bio-
         plastic mounts.

            With teacher's manual.
            Animals from 11 of the most important
         phyla are represented.

            1. Animals

                        O
```

Card 138.   Main entry for realia

```
RA
593
         Echinoderm morphology collection.
            [Realia]  Hubbard, [196-?]
            7 specimens:  in box 30 x 40 cm. &
         environment chart.

            CONTENTS:  Common starfish.--Aztec
         starfish.--Purple sea urchin.--Giant
         urchin.--Sand dollar.--Brittle star.--
         Urchin mouthparts (Aristotle's lantern).

            1. Marine animals
                        O
```

Card 139.   Main entry for realia, contents listed

SLIDES

Most commonly, a slide is a single frame of 35 mm film in a rigid 2"x2" mount, designed to be projected or examined in a slide viewer. However, any transparent material which can be mounted and projected may be used to create a slide. Special forms are lantern slides, which are larger than normal; stereoscope slides, which are designed to be used in special viewers to give a three-dimensional effect; and audioslides, which have a strip attached to the mount on which sound has been recorded. Microscope slides are also included in this category by AECT's Standards, which may contradict the principle of emphasizing content over form, as most microscope slides are actually specimens, and therefore a kind of realia. A media center with a collection of microscope slides would probably do best to follow AACR's practice of putting them in a separate category by themselves. The collation should say whether the slides are stained, and the notes should indicate the type of stain and specify the kind of microscope to be used, if other than phase or interference.

Slides present few problems as long as they are stored, cataloged and circulated in boxed sets, arranged in trays or magazines ready for projection, or in plastic sleeves. When they are handled as a unit, each requires only one set of catalog cards and can be readily shelved with other media. However, this approach will not serve the user who wishes to retrieve individual slides dispersed among several sets. Since cataloging every slide is expensive, most small libraries will either have to circulate sets only, or forego full cataloging but use a visual display system which allows users to scan the holdings within broad subject areas without actually handling the slides or needing a catalog entry for every single one. The slide sets would be classified using the same system as that chosen for other materials, with the individual slides in the set identified by their number within the set. Thus, if the patron wanted a slide of the Step Pyramid, he would look at the section of the display which houses ancient architecture and scan the slides until he found the appropriate one, number 3 in the set represented by card 140. When the slide is circulated, it is identified as 722A3.

Main entry. If all the slides in a set are reproductions of works by one artist, enter under the name of the artist. Where a set is correlated with a book, enter under author. Otherwise, enter under title.

```
SA
722
ANC      Ancient architecture.  [Slide]  San-
            dak, 1968.
         5 slides:  col; 2 x 2 in.

         CONTENTS:  1.  Temple of Luxor, Egypt.
         --2. Sphinx, Egypt.--3. Step pyramid,
         Egypt.--4. Ancient ruins of Babylon.--
         5.  Persepolis, ruins.

            1.  Architecture, Ancient
```

Card 140.  Main entry for slide set, with contents.

Medium designator.  Use "Slide," with the following specific designators:  audioslide, slide, and stereoscope slide.

Collation.  Give the number of slides in the set, color, size of mount, and type and number of containers.  If the slide is mounted in glass, plastic, or material thicker than the usual cardboard, specify the type of mount in parentheses following the number.  If the slide is made of glass or some material other than film, indicate this in the same way.  The user needs this information because not all projector trays accept the thicker mounts.  If the set comes with an inter-dependent sound recording, give the data on it as discussed in the section on filmstrips.

Notes.  If you circulate slides in projector trays, describe the type of tray and/or projector.  For unusual types of slides, a note about the kind of projector to be used is also needed.  List accompanying materials such as scripts. If the contents of the set are not too extensive, they should be given at least on the main entry card, with a "see main entry card for contents" note on the added entry cards. Where there are too many slides to list each, a partial contents note can be used to indicate the scope of the set.  If you do not list the contents and if the title is not self-explanatory, give a brief description of the nature of the set.

```
SA
731
KIN        Kinetic art.   [Slide]   Educational
             Dimensions, 1974.
             20 slides:   col; 2 x 2 in.

             With teacher's guide.
             Traces the development of kinetic
           art, an innovative, four-dimensional
           art form that expresses itself through
           the use of modern materials and tech-
           niques.

             1. Kinetic art   2. Art, Modern
```

Card 141.   Main entry for slide set

```
SA
597
COM        Common freshwater fishes.   [Slide]
             Society for Visual Education, 1973.
             20 slides:   col; 2 x 2 in; in vinyl
           folder.

             With background notes
             Eight families are represented,
           with information on identification,
           food, and habitats.

             1. Fishes
```

Card 142.   Main entry for slide set; container specified in
            collation

## TRANSPARENCIES

A transparency is an image on transparent material,
usually a sheet of acetate film, designed to be projected by

```
┌─────────────────────────────────────────────────────────┐
│ SA                                                       │
│ 301.32                                                   │
│ SCI      The Science and ethics of population            │
│          control:   an overburdened earth?               │
│          [Slide]  The Center for Humanities,             │
│          1975.                                           │
│          160 slides:   col; 2 x 2 in; in 2               │
│          Kodak carousels & 2 audiocassettes:             │
│          36 min.                                         │
│                                                          │
│          With guide.                                     │
│                                                          │
│          1. Population  2. Birthrate                     │
│                         ◯                                │
│                                                          │
└─────────────────────────────────────────────────────────┘
```

Card 143.   Main entry for sound slide set; projector specified
            in collation

an overhead projector, or viewed over a light box.   It may
be mounted in a cardboard frame, with overlays hinged to
one side of the frame.   Single transparencies or small sets
may be incorporated into the vertical file, while larger boxed
sets may be cataloged and stored as a unit.

```
┌─────────────────────────────────────────────────────────┐
│ TA                                                       │
│ 421                                                      │
│ CON      Consonant blends and digraphs.   [Trans-        │
│          parency]  Hammond, 1969.                        │
│          28 transparencies:   col; 7 1/2 x               │
│          9 1/2 in.                                       │
│                                                          │
│          Use with viewing stage.                         │
│                                                          │
│          1. English language-Pronunciation              │
│                                                          │
│                                                          │
│                         ◯                                │
│                                                          │
└─────────────────────────────────────────────────────────┘
```

Card 144.   Main entry for set of transparencies

```
TA
386
CAN      Canal.  [Transparency]  Milton Bradley,
            1968.
         1 transparency:  col; 7 1/2 x
         9 1/2 in; mobil-graph motion trans-
         parency.

         Use with polatron adapter to secure
         motion.
         Shows the culvert system draining
         the water from one lock to fill anoth-
         er, the gates opening, and the ship
         passing through.

            1. Canals
```

Card 145.  Main entry for motion transparency

```
TA
910
WOR      World distribution.  [Transparency]
            Hammond, 1970.
         8 sets of transparencies:  8 over-
         lays each; col; 9 x 11 in.

         Each set allows examination of tem-
         perature, rainfall, natural vegetation,
         land use, population, transportation,
         climate, resource distribution.
         CONTENTS:  World.--United States.--
         North America.--South America.--Europe.
         --Asia.--Africa.--Australia.

            1. Geography
```

Card 146.  Main entry for set of transparencies with overlays

Main entry.  Enter under title, using the set title for
groups of transparencies designed to be used together.

Medium designator.  "Transparency" is both the medium and specific designator.

Collation. Itemize the transparencies and overlays and give color and size. Describe accompanying audiorecordings as in the section on filmstrips.

Notes. If the contents are too lengthy to list, give a summary so that the purpose of the set is evident.

```
VA
371.7
ABO     About safety, programs 1 and 2.   [Video-
            recording]  Agency for Instructional
            Television, 1973.
            2 cassettes:   12 min. each; sd; col;
        3/4 in. K-P.
        U-matic cassettes.
        Puppets are used in skits to teach
        safety rules.
            CONTENTS:   1.   School bus rules; win-
        ter safety.--2.   Walking to and from
        school.

            1. Safety education   2. Accidents-
        Prevention
```

Card 147.   Main entry for videocassette, with summary and contents

## VIDEORECORDINGS

A videorecording contains video and audio signals on magnetic tape, on disc, or other material, designed to be played back on television equipment. Videotape varies in width and may be on reels or in cartridges or cassettes. As new formats are being developed rapidly, it is essential that the catalog description specify the kind of playback machine required. Public libraries which offer a single type of videorecording may prepare a separate book catalog similar to the film catalog described under the section on motion pictures.

Main entry. Title main entry is preferred, for the same reasons which apply to motion pictures.

Medium designator. Use "Videorecording," with the following specific designators: cartridge, cassette, disc, reel.

Imprint. When there is no indication of a copyright, production or release date, the date of the first broadcast may be used and explained in a note, e.g., "telecast in 1975."

Collation. List the number of reels or discs, etc., and their diameter; duration; sound or silent; color; width of tape; playback speed, if variable; and any other important characteristics which affect playback.

Notes. Specify the machine needed for playback, by make and model number, if necessary. Give the credits if they are likely to be of interest to the patron. Relate to other works and summarize the contents, as for motion pictures.

```
VA
575.01
       The Lysenko affair.  [Videorecording]
       Producer, Peter Jones.  Boston:
       WGBH; Washington, D.C.:  Released by
       The Public Television Library, 1975.
       1 cassette:  60 min; sd; b&w; 3/4 in.
       (PBS Nova)

       U-matic cassette.
       Dramatic reconstruction of the con-
       flict between Lysenko's Soviet form
       of Darwinism and classical genetics.
       Raises the issue of the freedom of
       scientific inquiry.
       1. Genetics
```

Card 148.  Main entry for videocassette

## References

1. Alma M. Tillin and William J. Quinly, Standards for Cataloging Nonprint Materials. 4th ed. (Washington, D.C.: Association for Educational Communications and Technology, 1976).

2. Anglo-American Cataloging Rules, North American Text: Chapter 12 Revised, Audiovisual Media and Special Instructional Materials (Chicago: American Library Association, 1975).

3. Jean R. Weihs and others, Nonbook Materials; the Organization of Integrated Collections. 1st ed. (Ottawa: Canadian Library Association, 1973).

4. Pearce S. Grove, ed., Nonprint Media in Academic Libraries (Chicago: American Library Association, 1975), p. 46.

5. AV Cataloging and Processing Simplified, by Jean Thornton and others (Raleigh, N.C.: Audiovisual Catalogers, Inc., 1973).

6. Anglo-American Cataloging Rules, North American Text (Chicago: American Library Association, 1970), p. 9.

7. Alma M. Tillin, op. cit., p. 5.

8. U.S. Library of Congress, Library of Congress Catalogs; Music: Books on Music and Sound Recordings (Washington, D.C.: Library of Congress, 1953- ).

9. Schwann-1 Record and Tape Guide (Boston: W. Schwann, Inc., monthly). Schwann-2, which lists monaural, spoken, and older popular music, is published semiannually.

10. Freda P. Berkowitz, Popular Titles and Subtitles of Musical Compositions. 2d ed. (Metuchen, N.J.: Scarecrow Press, 1975).

11. Mary D. Pearson, Recordings in the Public Library (Chicago: American Library Association, 1963), p. 66.

12. Ibid., pp. 136-142.

13. Jean R. Weihs, op. cit., p. 97.

14. California Library Association, Audio-Visual Chapter, Subject Headings Committee, Public Library Subject Headings for 16mm Motion Pictures. rev. ed. (Sacramento, Calif.: California Library Association, 1974).

15. William Dane, The Picture Collection: Subject Headings. 6th ed. (Hamden, Conn.: Shoe String Press, 1968).

16. Donald L. Foster, Prints in the Public Library (Metuchen, N. J. : Scarecrow Press, 1973).

CHAPTER 11


THE SHELF LIST


    The shelf list is a record of all the cataloged materials in a library, arranged in the order in which they are shelved. The shelf list is used--

    To take the inventory to see if any materials are missing.
    To show how many copies of a given title the library owns.
    To show what kinds of books or other materials are in a given class as an aid in classifying.
    To show the librarian who is making out orders how much material the library already has in any given class.
    To serve in a limited way as a classed catalog. A classed catalog has its entries arranged by classification numbers rather than alphabetically as in a dictionary catalog, and there is an alphabetical subject index. This classed arrangement brings together all the entries on a given subject.
    To give source, date and cost, if no accession record is kept.
    To serve as a basis for a bibliography or materials list on a specific subject.
    To serve as a record for insurance.

    The shelf list card is a unit card; i.e., it is a duplicate of the main entry card. When printed card sets are purchased, one intended as a shelf list card is always included. If the cards are typed locally, however, notes and contents may be omitted, leaving more space for the shelf list information. If an accession book is used, the accession number is added to this card (see chapter 14 for more on accessioning). The price is useful in public libraries in order to know what to charge a borrower who loses or damages library material. It may be the actual cost or the list price; this is also of value in estimating the collection for insurance

246

purposes. Many libraries also give the source and date of acquisition on the shelf list entry, but this practice may be questioned, as the library would use its current dealer when reordering. An unusual source might be worth noting, and the date may be wanted if it is not intrinsic to the accession number (e.g. 75-0001, which indicates the first acquisition in the year 1975), or if the library does not use accession numbers.

If no accession book is kept, but an accession number is used, this number is added to the shelf list card, as shown in cards 149 and 150, followed by the name of the source, the date received, and cost. Some libraries consider the accession book unnecessary duplication of other records, but like the convenience of having a unique number which stands for each book, audiorecording, etc., in the library.

```
398
        Grimm, Jakob Ludwig Karl
          The juniper tree and other tales
        from Grimm.  Selected by Lore Segal and
        Maurice Sendak; tr. by Lore Segal; with
        four tales tr. by Randall Jarrell.  Ill.
        by Maurice Sendak.  Farrar, Straus, 1973.
          2 v.  332 p.

73-0733 v. 1  B&T.  5-15-73  $6.50
73-0734 v. 2   "             $6.50
73-0921 v. 1  Doe, Mrs. J.  9-5-73  gift
73-0922 v.2    "                    gift

        1. Fairy tales  2. Folklore--Ger-
      many  I. Title
```

Card 149.  Shelf list entry for two-volume work of which the library has two copies, with acquisition data

If an accession number is used, it begins on the second space from the left edge of the card on the second line below the last line of the description--imprint, collation, series note, as the case may be. If there are two or more copies or volumes of a work, the accession numbers are listed on the shelf list cards in numerical order. For multi-

```
AA
822.3
            His infinite variety; a Shakespeare
            sampler. [Audiorecording] Narra-
            ted by Margaret Webster. Miller-
            Brody, 1973.
            4 cassettes:  Approx. 30 min. each.
AC73-0011   v. 1  ESEAII 3-12-73 $6.50
AC73-0012   v. 2     "           $6.50
AC73-0013   v. 3     "           $6.50
AC73-0014   v. 4     "           $6.50

            1. Shakespeare, William  2. English
            drama-History and criticism
            I. Webster, Margaret
```

Card 150.   Shelf list entry for four-volume recording, with
source of purchase funds indicated

volume works, the volume numbers are written opposite their
respective accession numbers.   Thus all copies and volumes
of one work go on the same shelf list card, and there are as
many shelf list cards as there are titles in the library, i. e.,
different works in the library.   If accession numbers are not
used, copy numbers are listed instead.

If it is felt that a record of the source, date, and
cost of an item is needed, the form to be used is shown in
cards 149 and 150.   Abbreviations which will be clear to the
librarian may be used, e. g., B&T for Baker and Taylor.   If
a book is a gift, the name of the donor may be given.   The
number of the month, day, and last two figures of the year
are given, separated by hyphens (the year may be omitted
if it forms a part of the accession number).   The date follows the source, with one space between; then the cost, or
if it is a gift, the word gift.   Note that one ditto mark is
sufficient for both source and date, but that the cost, or the
word gift is repeated for each volume or copy.

Where a record must be kept of disbursement of special funds, such as ESEA II or dedicated trust funds, the
name of the fund should precede the cost entry on the shelf
list card.   An inventory card facilitates accounting for special fund expenditures if an accession book is not kept.

Shelf list cards for nonfiction are arranged exactly
as the books are arranged on the shelves, first numerically
by classification number and then alphabetically by author,
except individual biography, which is arranged alphabetically
by the subject of the biography. Since the figures in all
book numbers are regarded as decimals, B219 would precede
B31, e. g. :

| 973 | 973 | 973 |
|-----|-----|-----|
| B21 | B219 | B31 |

for Bancroft's History of the United States of America and
Bassett's A Short History of the United States, respectively.
If book numbers are not used, the name of the subject of a
biography may be added to the top line of the card just as
it is on the subject card, as an aid in filing the cards by
the subject of the biography.

Shelf list cards for separate collections, such as
adult, young adult, juvenile, reference, audiovisual, etc. ,
are usually filed separately, although a school library which
intershelves different materials may also interfile the shelf
list cards for all types of media. A location symbol such
as J for children's room or R for reference is put at the
head of the call number on all cards. Some libraries have
one shelf list card for all editions of works of fiction in
which case the various editions are shown on the shelf list
card following the copy or accession number and acquisition
data by adding the name of the publisher, edition, and information about the illustrations. The advantages of separate shelf lists are that they can provide a quick overview,
of the juvenile or filmstrip collection, for example, or can
serve as an additional finding aid, as described in the section on audiorecording (chapter 10). When taking an inventory of a particular part of a collection, it is much easier
to work with a shelf list which contains the cards for that
collection only. A disadvantage is that duplicate shelf cards
must be made for titles which are in different collections.
For example, if the library has a third set of The Juniper
Tree (card 149) for reference, another shelf card would be
required for filing in the reference collection shelf list. For
the public card catalog, however, one set of cards suffices,
with each card marked $\frac{R}{398}$ but containing a note: "circulating copy also. "

Where audiovisual materials are not intershelved nor

uniformly classified, the shelf lists for the different media must perforce be separate. If material is arranged and identi-fied by accession number, the shelf list cards are also filed by accession number, so that when filmstrip number 203 is missing, one can go to the shelf list to find its title. If the filmstrips were arranged alphabetically by title, the shelf list would also be in alphabetical order.

Shelf list cards for serials are the same as for other materials, except that the year or volume number appears next to the appropriate accession number or copy number, as in cards 151 and 152.

```
R
310
W92        The World Almanac.  New York, World-
              Telegram.

1102  1950
3106  1956
3612  1958
4523  1959
5502  1960
6512  1964
7000  1966

              ◯
```

Card 151.   Shelf-list entry for a serial

---

For periodicals which are not cataloged, the file of check-in forms for magazines and newspapers can double as a shelf list when all changes in title, frequency, etc. are recorded on the forms.

The shelf list is the most important record in the li-brary. Some libraries microfilm theirs, so that if anything should happen to the public card catalog, it can be recon-structed from the shelf list. In a situation where a library is not yet fully cataloged, the fiction shelf list may serve as an author list and the nonfiction shelf list may serve as a subject catalog (since it brings together all the botanies,

```
R
310
W92        The World almanac.  New York, World-
              Telegram.

Pub.  2-9-50   $1.00   1950
  "   2-15-56  $1.25   1956
  "   2-8-58   $1.25   1958
  "   3-1-59   $1.25   1959
  "   2-16-60  $1.25   1960
  "   2-13-64  $1.50   1964
  "   2-8-66   $1.65   1966
```

Card 152.   Shelf-list entry for a serial (alternative method)

all of the United States histories, etc.) until such time as the library can be completely cataloged.   Before beginning the cataloging of an old library, be sure that there is a correct shelf list to use as a basis for the work.   In a new library, if it is not possible to catalog the new books as rapidly as they are being bought, it is as well to accession (if an accession record is to be made), classify, and shelf-list them at once.   Later, using the shelf list as a check, catalog the different classes.   In a well-organized and well-established library it is best to make the shelf list and catalog cards for each book when it is added to the library.

# CHAPTER 12

## PRINTED CATALOG CARDS AND THE USE
## OF CENTRALIZED SERVICES

No library, however small, should do all of the cataloging locally. It is necessary for the librarian to know where and how to secure printed catalog cards with their suggested classification numbers and added entries. One should also know what is available in the way of centralized processing and cataloging, including that offered by commercial firms. But whether a library does its own cataloging and processing, or utilizes the work of others, the librarian should know how to classify, catalog, and process materials.

Since 1901, printed catalog cards have been available at a reasonable cost. Today there are cataloging centers in state, regional, and county libraries and commercial cataloging companies where libraries can have the bulk of their processing done for them. The individual library must continue to compare classification numbers with its shelf list, so that the classified collection may present a consistent whole over the years, bring material on like subjects together, and keep policies uniform. Likewise, catalog entries must be checked to assure uniform headings for the same person, organization, or subject.

This chapter discusses in some detail the use of Library of Congress printed catalog cards and some of those available from other centralized services. The time that it takes to get these printed cards depends upon the location of the library and whether the cards are available when the order is received. When deciding how much of a time lag is acceptable, the library must take into consideration the amount of time it would take for it to prepare the copy and have the cards typed locally.

### LIBRARY OF CONGRESS CARDS

The Library of Congress prints and sells catalog cards

for books, documents, audiorecordings, filmstrips, maps, slides, etc. In 1966 it began printing annotated catalog cards for children's books. Differences will be found between Library of Congress cards printed at different times as the result of changes in cataloging policies, but since the older cards and the most recently printed ones both describe the material accurately, variations in the details of certain items do not matter. Classification numbers and headings must of course be checked and adjusted in any case.

Card 153 shows the arrangement and punctuation now prescribed by AACR. Note that different sizes and styles of type are used to emphasize or make less conspicuous the different items.

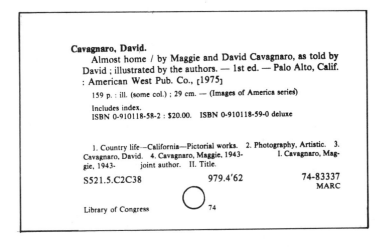

Card 153. Library of Congress printed card

The authorship statement gives the authors in the order in which their names appear on the title page, although the second-named author has been chosen for main entry. Details included in card 153 which are omitted in simplified cataloging are the edition statement (as it is the first), and the ISBN numbers and price. The details about illustrations, the size, and perhaps the series and index notes might also be left out. At the bottom are the tracings for added entries made for the Library of Congress catalog. Below the tracing and to the left of the hole is the LC classification

**Fiesta;** minority television programming ₁by₁ **Wes Marshall**
₁and others₁ Tucson, University of Arizona Press ₁1974₁
xiii, 138 p. illus. 28 cm.
Bibliography : p. 133–135.

1. Mexican Americans and television—Arizona—Tucson. 2. **Fiesta.**
I. Marshall, Wesley P.

PN1992.3.U5F5     384.55       72–79291
ISBN 0–8165–0330–3               **MARC**
Library of Congress     74 ₁4₁

Card 154.    LC card, title main entry

**Greenstein, Julius Sidney,** 1927–    comp.    Contemporary
readings in biology ... ₁1972₁   (Card 2)

CONTENTS—Continued.

evolution. — Dobzhansky, T.   Changing man. — Dunbar, M. J.   The
evolution of stability in marine environments natural selection at
the level of the ecosystem. — Stewart, W. D. P.   Nitrogen-fixing
plants.—Frisch, K. V.   Honeybees : do they use direction and distance
information provided by their dancers?—Arling, G. L. and Harlow,
H. F.   Effects of social deprivation on maternal behavior of rhesus
monkeys.—Kesteven, G. L.   A policy for conservationists.

1. Biology—Addresses, essays, lectures.    I. Title.
₁DNLM : 1. Biology—Collected works.    QH 302 G815c 1972₁

QH311.G768     574'.08       72–6448
ISBN 0–8422–5013–1           **MARC**
Library of Congress     73 ₁4₁

Card 155.    LC extension card, with contents

number.   To the right of the hole is the suggested DDC number, and at the far right is the LC card number, which is to
be used in ordering cards.   MARC beneath that means that
the cataloging information is stored in a machine-readable
format.

**Deegan, Paul J** 1937–
The team manager, by Paul J. Deegan. Illustrated by
Harold Henriksen. Mankato, Minn., Amecus Street; [distributed by Childrens Press, Chicago, 1974, c1975]
39 p. col. illus. 23 cm. (**His** Dan Murphy sports stories, 2)
SUMMARY: Eighth-grader Dan Murphy's basketball team gets a
manager in an unusual way.
ISBN 0–87191–403–4

[1. Basketball—Fiction] I. Henriksen. Harold, illus. II. Title.

PZ7.D359Te [Fic] 74–14515
MARC

Library of Congress 75 A C

Card 156. LC annotated card for juvenile book

Cards 154 through 156 show the LC format for title
main entry, extension cards, and juvenile literature. The
main point to remember about LC cards is that the suggested
headings are based on LC's subject heading list, not Sears,
and that the suggested DDC numbers are derived from the
unabridged edition.

Ordering Library of Congress cards. The librarian
should write to the Cataloging Distribution Service Division[1]
and ask for a copy of instructions for ordering printed cards
and a supply of the forms to be used for each order. Request a supply of order slips for an estimated three-month
period. The directions for making out orders are detailed
and clear and should be followed exactly.

It is possible to order materials and LC cards simultaneously if a multicopy form is used which meets both the
specifications of LC's Card Division and the requirements of
the library's jobber. The copy retained by the library constitutes a record of what materials and cards have been
ordered.

OTHER PRINTED CARDS

Since the lamented demise of The H. W. Wilson Com-

pany cards, there is no comparable source of type-set cards
with Sears headings and abridged DDC numbers. LJ (Library
Journal) cards come the closest, but are available for juvenile titles only; they come in kits which include book cards,
pockets and spine labels (see card 157). This may be acceptable for elementary school libraries and for children's
departments in public libraries.

---

**PLANTS**

580.72  **Podendorf, Illa**
P           The true book of plant experiments; pictures by Bill Armstrong.
          Childrens Press 1960
          48p illus

              The author begins with touch-and-tell experiments to give
          a concept of the parts of plants. Then there are simple experi-
          ments and activities with seeds, green plants, and spore plants.


          1. Botany — Experiments   2. Plants   I. Title


          B 5-306                                                          580.72; 580
          LJ Cards Inc © 1965              ◯                                     p — i

---

Card 157.  LJ card, headed

---

        Libraries which order their books from one of the
large jobbers may find that they can order cards from them
also, or can have the books completely processed by the
jobber. While most companies will not provide cards for
materials which have not been purchased through them, Josten's is one that will. Most of these companies produce
computer-printed cards which are comparable in quality to
locally typed and duplicated cards (see cards 158 through
163). In most cases the library can specify either Sears or
LC subject headings, and unabridged or abridged DDC or LC
classification. Cards may be ordered headed, i. e., with
headings and classification numbers already imprinted, or unheaded, allowing the library to change the headings and classification. Baker and Taylor, Bro-Dart and Josten's base their
cataloging on LC information provided on MARC tapes and
through CIP, using the National Union Catalog for older titles. Some original cataloging is done, and the LC data may

```
        BOTANY, ECONOMIC

581     Milne, Lorus
M          The nature of plants, by Lorus and
        Margery Milne; illus by Norman
        Adams.  Lippincott [c1971]
        206p illus

        Examines the characteristics,
        reproduction, and ecological
        significance of both aquatic
        and land plants




        1 Botany  2 Botany, Economic
        I Jt auth  II T
                      ◯
00004  *D-C        000001      ©THE BAKER & TAYLOR CO.
```

Card 158.  Baker & Taylor card, abridged DDC, Sears

```
            UNDERDEVELOPED AREAS--SOCIAL CONDI-
              TIONS
HC
59.7    Berger, Peter L
.B38864    Pyramids of sacrifice: political
        ethics and social change [by] Peter L.
        Berger. New York, Basic Books [1975,
        c1974]
           xiv, 242 p. 25 cm.

        Includes bibliographical references.


           1.Underdeveloped areas--Economic
        policy. 2.Underdeveloped areas--Social
        conditions. 3.Political ethics. 4.
        Right and left (Political science) I.
        Title.
HC59.7.B38864                309.2'3'091724
ISBN 0-465-06778-6      ◯      74-78304
                     000 306      LC-MARC
                        BRO DART
```

Card 159.  Bro-Dart card, LC classification, headings

be simplified (compare cards 158 and 159), or may be virtually identical, as in cards 163 and 164.  The Josten's card
omits size and ISBN, but adds a full title entry.

For a library which wishes to purchase cards but pre-

```
                 TREES—FICTION

    E        Johnston, Tony
    Jo           Fig tale.  Pictures by Giulio
             Maestro.  Putnam 1974
                32p  illus

                With the anticipation of making souf-
             fles from his very own figs, Gaylord the
             pastry chef buys a fig tree.

                1.Trees—Fiction I.Title
                            ◯
    CATALOG CARD CORP ©
```

Card 160.   Josten's card, "Easy" symbol

```
    811.5409 Boyers, Robert, ed
    B            Contemporary poetry in America; es-
             says and interviews.  Schocken [c1974]
             370p illus

             Based on the spring-summer 1973 issue
             of Salmagundi

             Contains critical reviews of the major
             modern poets by such writers as Howard
             Nemerov, Joyce Carol Oates, and Norman
             Silverstein.  Bibliogs

             1 American poetry--20th century--His-
             tory and criticism  I Salmagundi  II T
                            ◯
    03833           666638      © THE BAKER & TAYLOR CO.   5156
```

Card 161.   Baker & Taylor card, unabridged DDC

fers Sears headings and abridged DDC, one of these services
may be the answer.  The chart on page 261 presents some
of the options and the costs of selected card services for the
sake of comparison, and is not meant to be comprehensive.
A list of companies which supply catalog cards will be found

```
811.5409  Boyers, Robert, ed
B              Contemporary poetry in America; es-
          says and interviews.  Schocken [c1974]
          370p illus

          Based on the spring-summer 1973 issue
          of Salmagundi




          1 American poetry--20th century--His-
          tory and criticism  I Salmagundi  II T
                            O
03833              666638      B   © THE BAKER & TAYLOR CO.  5156
```

Card 162.    Shelf list card from set of which card 161 is the
             main entry card

```
HG
179      Porter, Sylvia Field, 1913-
.P57         Sylvia Porter's Money book : how to
1975     earn it, spend it, save it, invest it,
         borrow it, and use it to better your
         life. 1st ed. Garden City, N.Y. : Dou-
         bleday, 1975.
           1105 p. :

           Includes bibliographical references and
         index.


           1.Finance, Personal. I.Title: Money
         book. II.Title
                            O
          332'.024            HG179.P57 1975
                                    74-11817
```

Card 163.    Josten's card, based on LC data

in Library Journal's "Buyer's Guide," published annually in
the September 1st issue.  Write to each company and request
their specifications, order forms, and latest prices in order
to determine which service most nearly conforms to your library's policies.

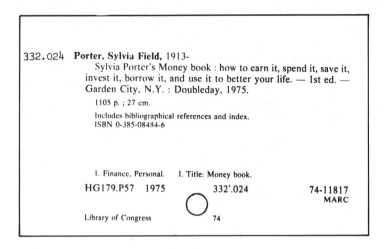

332.024  **Porter, Sylvia Field,** 1913-
　　　　　Sylvia Porter's Money book : how to earn it, spend it, save it,
　　　　　invest it, borrow it, and use it to better your life. — 1st ed. —
　　　　　Garden City, N.Y. : Doubleday, 1975.
　　　　　　1105 p. ; 27 cm.
　　　　　　Includes bibliographical references and index.
　　　　　　ISBN 0-385-08484-6

　　　　　1. Finance, Personal.　I. Title: Money book.
　　　　　HG179.P57　1975　　　　332'.024　　　　74-11817
　　　　　　　　　　　　　　　　　　　　　　　　　　MARC
　　　　　Library of Congress　　　　74

Card 164.　LC card for book represented by card 163.

_Audiovisual materials._　Printed cards for audiovisual
materials are not as readily obtainable as those for books.
LC cards may be purchased for films, filmstrips, audiorecordings, transparencies, slides, and maps, but availability
can be disappointing and long time-lags can occur.　When
ordering from a selection aid which cites LC card numbers,
one can at least be certain that the cards are available.

　　A number of audiovisual producers provide cards with
materials purchased from them, either automatically or on
request.　Examine producers' catalogs as you receive them
and make a note of which ones supply cards.　Bowmar,
Caedmon, The Center for Cassette Studies, Coronet, Filmstrip House, and Weston Woods are among those who will
provide card kits.　The Specialized Service and Supply Company is the largest supplier of catalog card sets for AV producers, but the cards can be ordered only through the distributor from whom the material is bought.　A list of producers who contract with Specialized Service is given below.
Card 165 is a sample of their product.　Baker and Taylor
and Demco are two of the jobbers who distribute audiovisual
materials from many of the major producers and provide
cards--or complete processing--for media bought through
them.

　　_Advantages of using printed catalog cards._　When one
considers the cost of blank cards and the time required to do

Company

| | Baker & Taylor | Bro-Dart | Josten's | LC | LJ (Xerox) |
|---|---|---|---|---|---|
| **Source of Data** | | | | | |
| MARC | X | X | X | | |
| CIP | X | X | X | | |
| Orig. | X | X | X | | X |
| Other | NUC | NUC | NUC | | |
| **Subject Headings** | | | | | |
| LC | X | X | X | X | X |
| Sears | X | X | X | | X |
| **Classification** | | | | | |
| LC | X | X | X | X | |
| DDC | X | X | X | X | |
| Abr. DDC | X | X | X | | X |
| **Book Nos.** | | | | | |
| Cutter | | | | | |
| Author | 1-3 | 1-9 | Abr. 0-3 Unabr. 0-7 | | 1 |
| **Printing** | | | | | |
| Computer | X | X | X | | |
| Type | | | | X | X |
| **Annotations** | | | | | |
| All | X | X | | | X |
| Some | | | Juv. | Juv. | |
| None | X | | | | |
| **Headed** | | | | | |
| Yes | | | | | X |
| No | | | | X | |
| Either | X | X | X | | |
| **Types of Sets** | | | | | |
| Cards only | | | X (& 3 labels) | X | |
| Kits only | X | X | | | X |
| Either | | | | | |
| **Cards/Sets** | 2ME, AEs 1SL | 2ME, AEs 1SL | 1ME, AEs 1SL | 8 | 8 |
| **Cost** | | | | | |
| Cards only | | | | .45 | .44 |
| Cards & kits | .39 | .39 | .30 | | |
| **Availability** | Only for items bought | Only for items bought | For anything on MARC | For anything cataloged | Juvenile only |

## AV PRODUCERS AVAILABLE IN INVENTORY OF
## SPECIALIZED SERVICE AND SUPPLY CO. :

Activity Records
Aims
American Educational Films
Paul S. Amidon & Assoc.
Argus Communications
Associated Film Services-see Aims
Association-Sterling-see Aims
Athletic Institute
Audio Books
AVI-see BFA
Avid Corp.

Barr Films
BFA Educational Media (AVI)
Bowmar
Brunswick Productions

Caedmon Records
CBS (Columbia Records)
Centron Educational Films
Charles Cahill & Assoc. -see Aims
Children's Classics on Tape
Childrens Press
Classroom Materials Co.
Classroom World Prod. Inc.
CMS Records
Columbia Records
Coronet Instructional Films
Creative Education-see Instructional
    Aids
Creative Education Society-see
    Instructional Aids
Creative Visuals
Crestwood House-see Instructional
    Aids
Crowell, Thomas Y. Co.
Current Affairs (Key Prod. )
Curriculum Films (series)

Developmental Learning Materials
DOSIX-see Double Sixteen Co.
Double Sixteen Co.
Doubleday Multimedia

Education Unlimited
Educational Activities
Educational Design, Inc.
Educational Dimensions Corp.
Educational Enrichment Materials-
    see Teaching Resources Films
Educational Filmstrips
Educational Insights
Educational Materials Corp. (EMC)
Educational Projections Corp.
Educational Resources-see Education-
    al Design

EMC-see Educational Materials Corp.
Encyclopaedia Britannica Ed. Corp.
Enrichment Materials

FilmFair Communications
Films for the Humanities, Inc.
Films, Inc.
Filmstrip House, Inc.
Folkway-Scholastic Records
Follett Library Book Co.

Globe Filmstrips
Golden Record
Guidance Associates

Hawkhill Associates, Inc.
Hester and Associates
Hubbard Scientific Co.
Hudson Photographic Ind. , Inc.
Human Relations Media Center

Ideal School Supply Co.
Imperial Films
Imperial Intern'l. Learning Corp.
Insight Media Program
Instructional Aids, Inc.
Instructional Dynamics, Inc.
Instructo Corp.
International Film Bureau

Jackdaws (Viking Press)
Journal Films

Kenalex Corp. (Urban Media)
Kimbo
Klise, Thomas S
Knowledge Aid

Learning Corp. of America
Library Filmstrip Center
Life Educational Productions
Life Filmstrip (Time-Life)
Listener Corp ( Accoustifone)
Listening Library

Marsh Film Enterprises
Mass Communications (MCI)
McGraw-Hill Films (series)
Mealey Productions
Miller-Brody Productions
Milliken Publishing Co.
Modern Learning Aids
Moreland-Latchford-see United Learn-
    ing
Multi-Media Productions

Nystrom, A. J. & Co. (Clearvue)

Pathescope Educational Films
Pathways of Sound

QED Productions

RCA Records
RMI Educational Films

Scholastic
Scott Education
Sing'N'Do (Educational Activities)
Spoken Arts, Inc.
Stallman/Susser
Stanbow, Inc.
Sterling Ed. Films-see Aims
Sunburst Communications
Sussex Tape-see BFA
SVE-Society for Visual Education
   (series)

Taylor Associates
Throne Films
Troll Associates

United Learning
Universal Education and Visual Arts
Urban Media

Viewlex, Inc.
Visual Education Consultants (VEC)
Viking Press (Jackdaws-Grossman)
Visual Publications
Visuals for Teaching
Vocational Films

Ward's Natural Science Establishment
Watts (Franklin Watts)
H. Wilson Corp.
Wollensak (3M)

BOOK PUBLISHERS:

Coward McCann
Doubleday & Co.
Grosset & Dunlap
Harper & Row
Putnam Son's

Morrow
Western Publishing (Golden Press)

Additional producers:

Challenge - see Mealey
Gateway to Learning
Teaching Resources Films
Teaching Technology Corp. - see
   Mealey

IMPORTANT: All requests must be complete with producers name, title, and producers product number.

Producers not appearing on this list are not available. Additional listings will be printed periodically.

February 1, 1976

Filmstrip
553
    Minerals–the crystals that compose rocks.
    Mealey Productions.
    1 sound–filmstrip, 45 fr, col, 1 cassette,
    teacher's guide (Earth science)

    The basic features of minerals, where they are
    found, and their role in industry.
    1 Geology, Economic 2 Mineralogy I Series

    1340–MCTCR

Card 165. Specialized Service and Supply Company card

the cataloging and typing, printed cards are not expensive. One study of preparation and cataloging time concluded that it takes three and three-fourths times as long to catalog, classify and assign subject headings for books if no printed cards are used. [2] Besides, there is no waste of cards or expenditure of time in making and revising typed cards.

The copy for printed catalog cards is prepared by expert catalogers, with all that this implies in regard to author headings, items included on the cards, suggestions as to subject headings, classification numbers, and added entries. LC cards give considerable bibliographic information about the book which may be of great value. Some cards give annotations which are very useful. LC and LJ cards are uniform in blackness, attractive, and very legible, but even the computer-printed cards are acceptable. Using printed cards saves time in preparing the entry, in typing and otherwise reproducing the cards, and in revising type-written cards. One printed card may be compared with the book to see if it matches the particular edition which the library has; then, only the call number and the typewritten headings added to the other cards need to be checked for accuracy. Printed cards are especially useful for books which require several subject cards or numerous added entries. Even when there are not enough cards in a set for analytical entries, the necessary extra cards may be ordered and, by adding call number, headings, and paging, the cards are quickly made into analytical entries.

Typewritten reference cards and short form series
cards have to be made by each library for its own catalog.
If the unit card is used for series entries, printed cards
may be used. The simple form of cataloging for fiction
recommended in this manual makes the process of cataloging
by the library as quick or quicker than ordering printed
cards and adapting them. It is recommended, therefore, that
typewritten cards be used for adult fiction even though printed
cards are ordered for all non-fiction. On the other hand, it
is best to order printed cards for all juvenile books, as subject headings for children's fiction and annotations are very
helpful.

The question of whether to use LC or other printed
cards depends largely on the type of library. The library
for adults and the more scholarly library, as well as most
kinds of special libraries, would do well to use LC cards
with their added bibliographic information. The elementary
school having chiefly books which are reviewed in School Library Journal may find LJ cards most satisfactory. Libraries
which have adult as well as juvenile titles but do not want to
use LC subject headings should consider the commercial companies which offer Sears headings. It is, of course, possible
to use LC cards for adult materials and LJ cards for the
children's collection, ordering LC cards for those juvenile
titles for which LJ cards are not available. A mixture of
LC cards, other printed cards, and typewritten cards in the
same catalog does not reduce the usefulness of the catalog,
as long as consistency is maintained in the use of subject
headings. As a general rule, however, choosing one source
of catalog card supply and sticking with it is more efficient.

Adapting printed cards for use in the catalog. The
librarian compares the cards with the book which they are to
represent in the catalog to see that they agree, and with the
catalog or authority file to see whether or not the form of
heading agrees with what has already been used. If, for example, the printed card has the author's real name on the
first line and it seems better to use the pseudonym, write it
on the line above the real name--beginning at the first in-
dention--followed by a comma, one space and pseud. of.

If the library has entered a few books under another
form of the name, it would be better to change those and
adopt the form used on the printed cards. If, on the other
hand, there are many cards in the catalog under the other
form, it is more expedient to change the printed card and

make a cross reference if one has not already been made.
A line can be drawn through the author heading and the preferred form typed above, beginning with the first indention
as usual.

If the publisher given in the imprint is not the publisher of the edition to be cataloged, or if the date or edition is different, the card must be changed. In the case of
incomplete sets, date and volume should be changed with pencil so that the card may show what the library has and yet
be easily changed when the other volumes are added. Changes
may be made by crossing out or erasing items and typing or
writing in the corrections. As few corrections as possible
should be made, however, so as not to spoil the appearance
and legibility of the cards. It is unnecessary to cross out
any item given on the printed card if it applies to the book
in question.

After the librarian makes the corrections or additions
which may be necessary in order that the printed card may
represent the book accurately, the next step is to add the
call number. The suggested DDC number on the printed card
must be checked with the library's copy of Dewey, as it may
be a number derived from a different edition or may not be
in accordance with the library's policy for that particular
class. For instance, if the number suggested for a biography
is 923 it would not be used by the small school or public library which uses 920 for all collective biography and 92 or
B for all individual biography.

The next step is to examine the tracings. Does the
library need all of the added entries listed? Are the subject
headings the same as those listed in the printed list of subject headings which the library had adopted? Does the amount
of material on the subject make necessary the subdivisions of
the subject given? If a library has only a few books on a
country and is unlikely to ever have many, the name of the
country alone may be sufficient for all of the books about it,
or the general subdivision HISTORY or DESCRIPTION AND
TRAVEL may do rather than the more specific subdivisions
such as CZECHOSLOVAK REPUBLIC. HISTORY, 1938-1945
or IRELAND. DESCRIPTION AND TRAVEL. 19th CENTURY.

If all of the added entries given in the tracing on the
printed card are not used, underscore the number of each
one which is to be used, or cross out the entries not wanted.
If the subject headings given on the card are not compatible

with the printed subject heading list used by the library, use
the heading from the printed list and type it with the tracing
on the front of the card.   If there is insufficient space at
the end of the tracing, type it on the back, and type the word
"over" beside the hole on the front of the card.   Corrections
in the tracing need be made on the main entry and shelf list
cards only.

On unheaded cards which are to be used as added entries the call number is added, any necessary alterations are
made, and the appropriate headings are added.   No change
is made in the tracing on the added entry cards if it is understood that only the main entry card is consulted for tracing.
To make a printed card into an author analytical entry, estimate in advance the number of lines required for the added
heading.   If contents or any other extra information has made
extension cards necessary, use a full set of cards for the
main and all other entries except for title and analytical entries.   For title cards use the first card only, drawing a
line through "Continued on next card. "   For analytical entries,
use the card which contains the part of the contents for which
the entry is made, crossing out "continued" notations as
needed (see card 166).

---

Mansfield, Katherine
    Sun and moon, p. 305-316:
**Jones, Phyllis Maud,** comp.
    English short stories, 1888-1937; selected by Phyllis M.
Jones.   London, Oxford University Press, 1973.

    viii, 403 p.   21 cm.   (Oxford paperbacks)   £0.95    GB 73-06686

    Previous editions have title: Modern English short stories.
    CONTENTS: Hardy, T.  The three strangers. — Harris, F.  The
Holy man.—Jacobs, W. W.  A garden plot.—Wells, H. G.  A slip un-
der the microscope.—Bennett, A.  The lion's share.—Munro, H. H.
The open window.—Munro, H. H.  The music on the hill.—Maugham,
W. S.  The door of opportunity.—Coppard, A. E.  Fifty pounds.—
Forster, E. M.  Other Kingdom.—Wodehouse, P. G.  Lord Emsworth
and the girl friend.—Lawrence, D. H.  The last laugh.—Aumonier, S.
Juxtapositions. — Mansfield, K.  Sun and moon. — Benson, S.  Sub-
marine.—Huxley, A.  The Tillotson banquet.—Beachcroft, T. O.  She

    ~~(Continued on next card)~~

          73-180459

    73 ₁4₁

Card 166.   LC card adapted for analytical entry

---

When cards with headings already printed on them are

used, there is less opportunity for making adjustments.   Unless one can be fairly certain that the choices reflected by
the printed card will be acceptable, it is best to order cards
that do not have subject headings printed at the top of the subject cards nor the classification number in its place in the
upper left-hand corner of the card.

Whether it is the first set of printed cards to be
added to the catalog or the thousandth, any cards added have
to be first checked with the catalog to assure uniformity of
name headings.


CENTRALIZED SERVICES

The service which the Library of Congress, Xerox,
and various jobbers provide for libraries through their sale
of printed catalog cards is centralized cataloging.   The
A. L. A. Glossary of Library Terms[3] defines centralized cataloging as "The preparation of catalog cards by one library
or other agency which distributes them to libraries," and
also as "The preparation in one library or central agency of
catalogs for all the libraries of a system. "   It has long been
the practice of the majority of public library systems and
many of the larger public school systems to have the catalog
department or a central office do the cataloging for the central library and the branches or individual school libraries.

The present trend is towards centralized processing
as well as cataloging and this field is developing very rapidly.
The terms "cataloging," "preparation," and "processing" as
applied in different libraries vary in their inclusiveness.
This variation is reflected in the articles on centralized processing and cataloging.   "Cataloging" as used in this chapter
and in the articles cited includes "classification. "   It is more
often used in connection with books, but many systems include
nonbook materials in their central processing and cataloging
service.   J. W. Henderson[4] states that "processing includes
ordering, cataloging and preparation of library materials,"
adding that the "preparation" which is done by a clerk includes:   stamping the title page with the library's mark of
ownership; putting the accession number in the book; making
the book card, book pocket, holdings record and shelf-list
record for the headquarters library and the shelf-list record
for the individual library.   Centralized processing and cataloging agencies are found at state, regional, county and city
levels.   The participating libraries send their orders to the

central agency and receive the materials ready for the shelves with the catalog and shelf-list cards ready to file.

The American Association of School Librarians, in its Media Programs: District and School, [5] states that: "Processing alternatives include provision of centralized processing at the district level; contracting for processing services that are available from a multidistrict, regional, or state center; use of commercial processing; and combinations of these approaches. Handling of processing at the individual school level is rarely advisable in terms of economy and efficiency."

While some central services customize cataloging and processing to conform with each library's policy, other agencies state frankly that the subscriber must accept their classification, subject headings, cataloging form, processing procedure, and the choice and quality of materials used as determined by the center. The extent of the processing varies; for instance, the North Carolina State Library Processing Center states that stamping the book with the property stamp of the library, assigning an accession or copy number to the book and adding such information to the shelf list is the responsibility of the individual library.

Cost of centralized processing and cataloging. The cost varies with the work to be done and the amount of customizing provided. Several of the large commercial companies offer processing at $.79 per book, which includes a plastic cover for the jacket and book card, pocket and spine label in place, as well as a set of catalog cards. The library would of course have to add its mark of ownership and perform the accessioning.

In comparing the cost of centralized processing and cataloging with the cost of doing the work in the individual library one should include consideration of the space available, any special furniture or equipment required for the work, as well as reference books needed for ordering and cataloging; supplies, e.g., book cards and pockets, date due slips, blank catalog and shelf-list cards; materials for marking books on the spine; and necessary professional and clerical staff. Everett L. Moore[6] points out that certain routines must be performed before and after sending out the order to a cataloging center or commercial firm, and that the cost of this should be added to the costs of the service in making one's decision to use an outside agency. A few examples of work which must be done in the individual library are: filing the catalog and shelf-list cards; checking name and subject headings against the usage of the library; assigning copy numbers.

Catherine MacQuarrie[7] found that among the factors affecting the cost are: size of the library's collection; type of material--e.g., serials, documents, material in foreign languages, and audiovisual materials take more time for the professional side of the work, hence are more expensive to catalog; use of printed cards; having subject entries for fiction; analyzing short story collections; and the use of Cutter numbers. Although her cost figures are now very dated, they still reflect how widely costs may vary.

MacQuarrie states that "In four [public] libraries, all with collections of approximately 100,000 volumes, the range was from 76¢ to $1.00 per title. In college libraries ordering fewer than 3,000 titles per year, the average cost per volume for ordering, cataloging, and preparing, as indicated by the survey, was $3.76." The survey forms were also sent to the school libraries but the librarians, though interested in the results of the survey, were unable to supply the necessary information.

"The exact number and minutes of professional time it takes to catalog a title" seemed important as it is a basic figure not affected by variations in salaries. It was found that in public libraries the "overall average for cataloging a title is 45 minutes, or 10 titles per day." This average included four groups of libraries divided according to their size. In the group including one medium-large and four small public libraries "it takes from 14 to 19 minutes to catalog a title." It was found to be impossible to compute ordering in public libraries on a cost basis as there were too many variations in the libraries studied. The use of plastic jackets seems to be the time-consuming part of the process. These average figures must be used cautiously. They serve as a target to aim towards in setting work standards but cannot be used as a criterion for any particular library since too many variables enter into individual library costs and worktime.

MacQuarrie concludes: "As determined by this cost analysis it is questionable whether, from a strictly dollar and cents viewpoint, it would profit a public library in this area to contract for outside technical processing. The prob-

lems of space, staff, and promptness in cataloging and de-
livery of books to the service outlet might justify having the
work performed on a commercial basis although the resultant
costs might be greater than if the library continued to perform
its own technical work in its entirety. Whether the freeing
of a professional worker for other duties would be sufficiently
worthwhile to outweigh the additional costs is another question.... Libraries that are unable to hire a professional cataloger probably would be better off using an outside agency
than to make do with non-professional catalogers; new libraries that are just organizing their collections and libraries
adding new branches with new collections could benefit from
hiring the work done and freeing the staff for other duties. "

This study of libraries in Southern California shows
clearly that libraries everywhere, small as well as large,
should study closely the services of commercial companies
and of non-profit organizations of libraries in their areas before deciding to do or to continue doing all of their own processing and cataloging with or without printed catalog cards
from other libraries or agencies.

Harry C. Bauer, [8] in his "Three by Five," says: "one
writer wrote the book, one publisher published the book, but
12,000 catalogers cataloged the book. " To quote from Mac-
Quarrie's[9] cost survey again, "... all these libraries in
Southern California hire catalogers, order clerks, and preparation clerks; each catalogs almost identical collections of
new books. "

Advantages and disadvantages of centralized processing
and cataloging. The chief gain is in the time saved by the
local library's professional staff which can be used for more
services to the readers. Many books are purchased by all
the public libraries or all the school libraries in a state and
instead of each school librarian's having to send an order to
one or more jobbers, classify and catalog the same book, the
central agency sends in one order for all of the copies wanted,
decides on the classification, adapts printed catalog cards or
prepares card copy and reproduces it by mechanical means.
There are better discounts when more titles and more copies
are included in one order. Thus there is a saving of expense
as well as of time. A central agency can afford a better reference collection for use in ordering and cataloging books
than an individual library. Better classification and better
cataloging are possible when the work is done by experienced,
able catalogers, not just fitted in with other duties by a gen-

eral librarian. The needed machines, mechanical devices--
too expensive for the individual library--are feasible for the
central agency and on large jobs save time and expense.
Centralization helps to make catalogs uniform, hence lessens
the problems of cataloging when regional libraries are created. The catalogs are kept more up-to-date when the work
is done by a central agency.

The major disadvantage, perhaps, is in adapting centralized processing and cataloging to the needs of the participating libraries. There is, of course, some loss of local
control of subject headings; there are the necessary changes
to be made in the library's classification numbers and in subject and name headings, in order to conform to the central
agency's forms, in the case of libraries which have previously done their own classification and cataloging. Some
writers cite the delay in getting the books to the libraries
as a disadvantage of centralized processing and cataloging;
others cite this as one of the advantages of centralization,
claiming that the books are ready for the shelves sooner.

Two very important considerations, especially in the
case of a commercial centralized processing and cataloging
agency, are: 1) is the agency qualified from the professional
librarian's point of view to perform the services which are
offered? and 2) is the agency likely to continue to offer such
services indefinitely? Undoubtedly failure of an agency,
which would make it necessary for the libraries subscribing
for the service to seek another agency or do their own processing and cataloging, would be very hard on the libraries
dependent on this service.

The uncataloged and unclassified small public or school
library, the one which is only partially classified and cataloged,
or the one with a completely classified and cataloged collection,
whether it be well or poorly done, should most certainly consider having the processing and cataloging done elsewhere.
Your state library agency and larger libraries in your vicinity
can tell you what agencies are available and help you to eval-
uate their services for your library.

The governing board of your library or your principal
would want to know the cost of such services, what work is
included, the extent to which your library would have to conform to all the procedures of the libraries served by the
agency, and the effect of such centralized service on the
length of time before a book would be delivered to your li-

brary. Established libraries will want to check their present processing costs with those of the center. Other questions which would need consideration are: What is the minimum number of books which must be ordered at one time? Will such service be a substitute for a clerical assistant, either part- or full-time? Will it release more of the librarian's time for reader services? When could the necessary funds for initiating this service be made available?

Suppose a small library has a good, accurate catalog; its books are well classified but it is becoming increasingly difficult for the librarian to find time to do this part of the work. The state central library agency offers good centralized processing and cataloging service, but it is not custom cataloging. The library taking advantage of it must accept the agency's classification numbers, subject headings, catalog method and processing. What would be involved in adopting this service? All new shelf-list cards when filed would have to be examined for classification, and in some cases the numbers for the books already in the library would have to be changed to conform with the new numbers--which means changing the numbers on the back of the book, book pocket and card, the shelf-list and catalog cards. But it would be better to adopt the new number for books in that class at once, as in time the majority of the books will have that number. Likewise subject headings and the tracing for them will have to be changed; also some name headings. At first these changes will take additional time and mean additional expense, but very soon there will be little of this work to be done.

## References

1.  Cataloging Distribution Service Division, Library of Congress, Building 159, Navy Yard Annex, Washington, D. C.  20541.

2.  W. B. Hicks & A. M. Lowrey, "Preparation and Cataloging Time in School Libraries," School Library Association of California.  Bulletin 30:7-10 (May, 1959).

3.  A. L. A. Glossary of Library Terms (Chicago, American Library Association, 1943).

4.  J. W. Henderson, "Centralized Processing of Library Materials in West Virginia and Other Matters," Survey. [1959?].

5.  American Association of School Librarians, Media Programs: District and School (Chicago, American Library Association, 1975), p. 49.

6.  Everett L. Moore, "California Junior College Libraries," Library Resources & Technical Services 9:312 (Summer, 1965).

7.  Catherine MacQuarrie, "Cost Survey: Cost of Ordering, Cataloging and Preparations in Southern California Libraries," Library Resources & Technical Services 6: 337-350 (Fall, 1962).

8.  Wilson Library Bulletin 35:393, Jan., 1961.

9.  MacQuarrie, op. cit., p. 343.

# CHAPTER 13

## ARRANGEMENT OF CARDS IN A CATALOG

Next in importance to making the cards for the catalog is their arrangement in the trays of the catalog case.
Unless all cards with the same heading are found together
and all cards are arranged according to some definite plan,
a card catalog is of very little use.   One of the most important mechanical points is to watch that the trays do not
become overcrowded.   A good rule is never to fill a catalog
tray more than two-thirds full; space is needed to shift cards
so that the one being consulted may be handled easily.

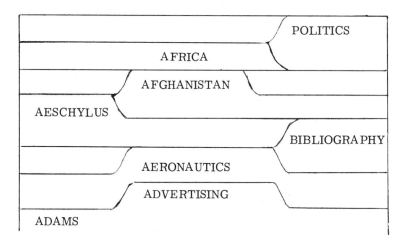

Another important matter is to label the trays so that
the reader can easily locate the tray which contains the author, title, or subject for which he is searching.   Adequate
guide cards, preferably cut in thirds, should indicate the approximate location of the desired card.

A very good method of arranging guide cards in the
catalog is to have the authors' surnames on the left, main

subject headings in the center, and subdivisions of the subject on the right. This plan enables the caption on the guide card to be short and near enough to the top of the card so that it may be read. So far as possible there should be a guide card for every inch of tightly held cards. A very minor point is to have a blank card in the front of each tray so that the first card will not become soiled.

One of the signs telling how to use the catalog, which may be purchased from a library supply house, may be placed in a poster holder on top of the catalog if it is a low cabinet, or hung beside it. Be sure that the printed directions fit the catalog.

Some large libraries file cards in the catalog once a week; small libraries may file more or less often than this. It is not worthwhile to file a few cards if there will be more tomorrow; if it might be a week or more before there are others, those ready may be filed so that the readers may have the use of these new cards.

Before filing cards, they should be sorted into catalog and shelf-list cards, and counted for the library reports.

After this preliminary sorting the cards are arranged for the catalog alphabetically, according to the rules used in this catalog. The next step is to interfile the cards with those already in the catalog trays, leaving the new cards above the rod. Later, go over these new cards, making sure that they are in their right alphabetical place. Next, pull out the rod and allow the cards to drop into place, locking them in with the rod.

Filing should not be continued for a long period. Since filing cards requires close attention, the eye becomes tired and mistakes are likely to occur. If the same person both files and revises, several hours should elapse between the filing and the revising.

There is no dictionary catalog with all cards filed absolutely alphabetically, word by word or letter by letter. In all catalogs there will be at least a few logical exceptions and in certain areas a chronological or numerical arrangement. Before beginning to file in an unfamiliar catalog, observe what alphabetizing code was used. Whatever code has been used, continue to follow it unless it is unsatisfactory, and be sure that the change will be an improvement before deciding to refile an entire catalog.

The rules given below should prove adequate for filing cards in the dictionary catalog of a small library. These rules are based on the ALA filing rules.[1] Many of the illustrations in this chapter are from the same source. If more information on filing catalog cards is desired, it will be found in this filing code.

There are two fundamental methods of filing alphabetically; namely, word by word and letter by letter.

| Word by word filing: | Letter by letter filing: |
| --- | --- |
| Book | Book |
| Book collecting | Bookbinding |
| Book of English essays | Book collecting |
| Book of famous ships | Bookish |
| Book scorpion | Book of English essays |
| Bookbinding | Book of famous ships |
| Bookish | Books |
| Books | Books and reading |
| Books and reading | Book scorpion |
| Books that count | Booksellers and bookselling |
| Booksellers and bookselling | Books that count |

In word by word filing, each word is a unit, and thus Books that count precedes Booksellers and bookselling, since Books precedes Booksellers; while in letter by letter filing no attention is paid to words but each letter is considered. Thus Books that count follows Booksellers because bookst follows bookse. To take another example: Book scorpion precedes Bookbinding in word by word filing as Book precedes Bookb, but in letter by letter filing Bookbinding precedes Book scorpion because bookb precedes books.

## BASIC RULE

Arrange all entries alphabetically according to the order of the English alphabet.

Arrange word by word, alphabetizing letter by letter within the word. Apply the principle of 'nothing before something,' considering the space between words as 'nothing.' When two or more headings begin with the same word, arrange next by the first different word.

Every word in the entry is regarded, including articles,

prepositions and conjunctions, but initial articles are disregarded.

> I met a man
> Image books
> Imaginary conversations
> In an unknown land
> In the days of giants

In a dictionary catalog, interfile all types of entries (author, title, subject, series, etc.) and their related references, in one general alphabet.

## ABBREVIATIONS

Arrange abbreviations as if spelled in full in the language of the entry, except Mrs. and Ms. which are filed as written.

> Dr. Jekyll and Mr. Hyde
> Doctor Luke
> Dr. Norton's wife
> Doctors on horseback
> Documents of American history

> Miss Lulu Bett
> Missis Flinders
> Mister Abbott
> Mr. Emmanuel
> Mistress Margaret
> Mitchell, Margaret
> Mrs. Miniver
> Ms. O'Hara
> Much

> St. Denis, Ruth
> Saint-Exupéry, Antoine de
> Saint Joan
> St. Lawrence River
> Ste Anne des Monts
> Sainte-Beuve, Charles Augustin
> Saintsbury, George Edward Bateman

## AMPERSAND

Arrange the ampersand (&) as 'and,' 'et,' 'und,' etc.,

according to the language in which it is used.

> Aucassin and Nicolete,...
> Aucassin & Nicolette: an old French love story....
> Aucassin et Nicolette,...
> Aucassin und Nicolette;...

## ANALYTICAL ENTRIES

Author: Arrange an author analytic by the title of the analytic. If there are no main entries for the work in the catalog, file an author analytic in its alphabetical place. Arrange analytics made in the form of author-title added entries after main entries for the work, the analytics subarranged by their main entries.

> Huxley, Thomas Henry, 1825-1895.
>> On a piece of chalk, p. 157-187:
> Law, Frederic Houk, 1871-
>> Science in literature ....

> Huxley, Thomas Henry, 1825-1895.
>> Science and education....

Title: Arrange title analytics by the entry for the analytic if different from the main entry for the whole book.

> Peabody, Josephine Preston, 1874-1922.
>> The piper ....

> Peacock pie, v. 2, p. 95-218:
> De la Mare, Walter John, 1873-
>> Collected poems ....

> Peacock pie.
> De la Mare, Walter John, 1873-
>> Peacock pie ....

> Peacocks and pagodas.
> Edmonds, Paul.

Subject: Arrange subject analytics by the entry for the analytic if different from the main entry for the whole book.

> MASARYK, TOMAS GARRIGUE, PRES. CZECHOSLO-

VAK REPUBLIC, 1850-1937.
Masaryk, Jan Garrigue, 1886-1948, p. 337-355:
Ludwig, Emil, 1881-1948, ed.
The torch of freedom, edited by Emil Ludwig and Henry
B. Kranz.

MASARYK, TOMAS GARRIGUE, PRES. CZECHOSLOVAK
REPUBLIC, 1850-1937.
Selver, Paul, 1888-
Masaryk, a biography ....


ARTICLES

Disregard an initial article in all languages and file
by the word following it.   In English the articles are 'A, '
'An, ' and "The. '"

A apple pie
Apache
An April after

Laski, Harold Joseph
The last of the Vikings
LATIN AMERICA

All articles occurring within a title or a heading are
to be regarded, except those that actually are initial articles in an inverted position or at the beginning of a subdivision.

Powder River
Power, Richard Anderson
POWER (MECHANICS)
The power of a lie
Powers, Francis Fountain

STATE, THE
STATE AND CHURCH

AGRICULTURE - U.S.
AGRICULTURE - THE WEST
AGRICULTURE - WYOMING


AUTHOR ENTRY ARRANGEMENT

Works by the author:  Alphabetize the titles according to the basic rules for alphabetical arrangement.

Interfile all main and added entries under the same author heading in one file. Subarrange alphabetically by the titles of the books.

In both main and added entry headings disregard designations that show the relationship of the heading to one particular work, as 'comp.,' 'ed.,' 'ill.,' 'tr.,' 'joint author,' 'editor,' etc.

Pennell, Joseph, 1857-1926
The adventures of an illustrator.

Pennell, Joseph, 1857-1926, illus.
Van Rennselaer, Mariana Griswold
English cathedrals ....

Pennell, Joseph, 1857-1926
Etchers and etching ....

Pennell, Joseph, 1857-1926, joint author
Pennell, Elizabeth Robins
The life of James McNeill Whistler.

Pennell, Joseph, 1857-1926
Our journey to the Hebrides

Arrange different titles that begin with the same words by the title proper, the shorter title before the longer, disregarding any subtitle, alternative title, 'by' phrase, etc. that may follow the shorter title.

Auslander, Joseph
The winged horse; the story of the poets and their poetry.
The winged horse anthology.

At the beginning of a title the author's name, even in the possessive case, should be disregarded if it is simply an author statement transcribed from the work. However, if the name in the possessive case is the author's pseudonym, or if an author's name is an integral part of the title, do not disregard it in filing. Do not disregard a name other than the author's.

Barlow, Peter
An essay on magnetic attraction

[Barlow's] tables of squares, cubes, square roots....
A treatise on the strength of timber....

Shakespeare, William
    Selections from Shakespeare.
    The Shakespeare apocrypha.
    Shakespeare's wit and humor.

<u>Works about the author</u>: Arrange the subject entries for works about the author after all entries for works by the author, in two groups as follows:

1.  Subjects without subdivision, subarranged by their main entries, or if an analytic, by the entry for the analytic.

<u>Exception</u>: An author-title subject entry files in the author file in its alphabetical place by the title in the heading, immediately after the author entries for the same title if there are any.

2.  Subjects with subdivisions, arranged alphabetically by the subdivisions.

Shakespeare, William, 1564-1616
    The winter's tale.

SHAKESPEARE, WILLIAM, 1564-1616
Alexander, Peter
    Shakespeare.

SHAKESPEARE, WILLIAM, 1564-1616
Brandes, Georg Morris Cohen
    William Shakespeare, a critical study.

SHAKESPEARE, WILLIAM, 1564-1616 - BIBLIOG-
    RAPHY
SHAKESPEARE, WILLIAM, 1564-1616 - CHARAC-
    TERS
SHAKESPEARE, WILLIAM, 1564-1616, IN FIC-
    TION, DRAMA, POETRY, ETC.
SHAKESPEARE, WILLIAM, 1564-1616 - NATURAL
    HISTORY

BIBLE

Entries for Bible, the sacred book, follow entries for the single surname Bible.

Arrange Bible entries in straight alphabetical order word by word, disregarding kind of entry, form of heading, and punctuation. Under the same author heading subarrange alphabetically by titles.

Arrange headings which include a date alphabetically up to the date, then arrange the same heading with different dates chronologically by date.

Arrange different kinds of entries under the same heading in groups in the following order:
Author (main and/or added entry), subarranged alphabetically by titles.
Subject, subarranged alphabetically by main entries.

Numbered books of the Bible follow in numerical order the same name used collectively without number.

> Bible, Dana Xenophon
> Bible
> BIBLE. ACTS. see BIBLE. NEW TESTAMENT.
>     ACTS
> BIBLE AND SCIENCE
> BIBLE - ANTIQUITIES
> The Bible in art
> Bible. New Testament.  Corinthians
> Bible. New Testament.  1 Corinthians
> Bible. New Testament.  Matthew
> Bible. Old Testament.  Daniel
> Bible. Old Testament.  Genesis
> BIBLE STORIES


COMPILER  See Author entry arrangement.


COMPOUND PROPER NAMES

Arrange names consisting of two or more separate words, with or without a hyphen, as separate words. Alphabetize with regard to all words in the name, including articles, conjunctions, and prepositions.

> New Jersey
> A new way of life
> New York
> Newark

## COMPOUND SURNAME ENTRIES

Interfile compound surname entries alphabetically with the group of titles, etc. , following entries for the first part of the name alone as a single surname.

> Smith, Woodrow
> Smith College
> Smith Hughes, Jack
> Smith-Masters, Margaret Melville
>
> Saint among the Hurons
> Saint-Gaudens,
> St. Petersburg
> Saint Vincent
> San Antonio
> Sanborn

CONGRESSES  See Numerical and chronological arrangement.

## CORPORATE NAME ENTRIES BEGINNING WITH A SURNAME

Arrange a corporate name consisting of a surname followed by forenames, etc. , in its alphabetical place among the personal names in the surname group.

> Rand, Edward Kennard
> Rand, Winifred
> Rand McNally and Company (McNally is the surname of
> a member of the company)
> Randall, John Herman
> Randall-MacIver, David
>
> Wilson, Forrest
> Wilson (The H. W. ) Company
> Wilson, James Calmar
> Wilson, Margery

Arrange a corporate name consisting of a surname only, followed by a designation, and compound and phrase names in their alphabetical place in the group of titles, etc. , following all surname entries under the same name.

> Prentice, William Reed
> The prentice

Prentice-Hall book about inventions
Prentice-Hall, inc.
Prentice-Hall world atlas

EDITOR   See Author entry arrangement

ELISIONS

Arrange elisions, contractions, as written.   Do not
supply missing letters.   Disregard the apostrophe and treat
as one word any word or contraction of two words that contains an apostrophe, unless the apostrophe is followed by a
space.

Who owns America?
Who reads what?
Who'd shoot a genius?
Who's who in American art?
Whose constitution

FIGURES   See Numerals

FORENAME ENTRIES

Disregard a numeral following a given name except
when necessary to distinguish between given names with the
same designation.   Arrange first alphabetically by the designation, then when there is more than one numeral, numerically by the numeral.

Arrange all given name entries, both single and compound, after the single surname entries of the same name,
interfiling alphabetically in the group of titles, etc., beginning with the same word.   Alphabetize with regard to all
designations and words, articles and prepositions included,
and disregard punctuation.

When an ordinal numeral follows a given name in the
title entry, arrange it as spoken.

Charles, William
Charles Auchester (title)
Charles Edward, the Young Pretender

        CHARLES FAMILY
        Charles III, King of France
        Charles I, King of Great Britain
        Charles II, King of Great Britain
        Charles the Bold,      see Charles, Duke of Burgundy
        Charles II and his court (Charles the second)
        CHARLES W. MORGAN (SHIP)


HYPHENATED WORDS

        Arrange hyphenated words as separate words when the
parts are complete words.

        Happy home.
        Happy-thought hall.
        Happy thoughts.

        In the case of compound words that appear in the cat-
alog written both as two separate words (or hyphenated) and
as a single word, interfile all entries, including corporate
names, under the one-word form.

        Campfire adventure stories
        Camp-fire and cotton-field
        Camp Fire Girls
        The Campfire girls flying around the globe
        CAMPFIRE PROGRAMS
        CAMPING


ILLUSTRATOR   See Author arrangement.


INITIAL ARTICLES   See Articles.


INITIALS

        Arrange initials, single or in combination, as one-let-
ter words, before longer words beginning with the same initial letter, wherever they occur in an entry.   Interfile entries consisting of initials plus words with entries consisting
of initials only.

        Arrange initials standing for names of organizations as
initials, not as abbreviations.

Arrange inverted initials standing for authors' names alphabetically with other initials, disregarding the inversion and the punctuation.

A.
A. A.
AAAA
AAA Foundation for Traffic Safety
AAAS Conference on Science Teaching. . . .
A. , A. J. G.
AAUN news

JOINT AUTHOR  See Author arrangement.

NAMES WITH A PREFIX

A name with a prefix is one that begins with a separately written particle consisting of an article (e. g. , La Crosse), a preposition (e. g. , De Morgan), a combination of a preposition and an article (e. g. , Del Mar, Van der Veer), or a term which originally expressed relationship (e. g. , O'Brien), with or without a space, hyphen, or apostrophe between the prefix and the name.

Arrange proper names with a prefix as one word.

Defoe,
De la Roche,
Delaware
Del Mar, Eugene

El Dorado, Ark.
Eldorado, Neb.

Vanderbilt,
Vanderwalker
Vander Zanden

Arrange names beginning with the prefixes M' and Mc as if written Mac.

McHenry
Machinery
MacHugh
Maclaren, Ian

> MacLaren, J.
> M'Laren, J    Wilson
> MacLaren, James

## NUMERICAL AND CHRONOLOGICAL ARRANGEMENT

A numerical or a chronological arrangement, rather than an alphabetical, should be followed when numbers or dates distinguish between entries, or headings, otherwise identical, with lowest number or earliest date first.

In relation to other entries in the catalog disregard a numeral or date that indicates a sequence.  If the number precedes the item it modifies it must be mentally transposed to follow the item (i.e., file U.S.  Army.  1st Cavalry as U.S.  Army.  Cavalry, 1st).

<u>Titles</u>:  Numerical designations following or at end of titles that are otherwise identical up to that point.

> More, Paul Elmer
>     Shelburne essays.  2nd series.
> More, Paul Elmer
>     Shelburne essays.  Fourth series

<u>Corporate headings</u>:

Dates only:

> Massachusetts.  Constitutional Convention, 1779-1780
> Massachusetts.  Constitutional Convention, 1853

Number only:

> U.S.  Circuit Court (1st Circuit)
> U.S.  Circuit Court (5th Circuit)

Number and date:  Disregard a place name when it follows a number.

> American Peace Congress, 1st, New York, 1907
> American Peace Congress, 3d, Baltimore, 1911
> American Peace Congress, 4th, St. Louis, 1913

Place and date:  If there is no numeral to indicate a sequence, the heading being followed only by a place and date in that order, arrange alphabetically by the place, disregarding the date at the end.

OLYMPIC GAMES
Olympic games, Los Angeles, 1932
Olympic games, Rome, 1960-

For the same heading with and without distinguishing numerals or dates, arrange as follows: 1. No numerals, no subheadings; 2. No numerals, interfiling all corporate and subject subdivisions and longer entries beginning with the same name. 3. With numerals, but no subheadings. 4. With numerals, with all its corporate and subject subdivisions.

Explorer
EXPLORER (ARTIFICIAL SATELLITE)
EXPLORER (BALLOON)
EXPLORER II (BALLOON)
An explorer comes home

Ku Klux Klan in American politics
KU KLUX KLAN (1915-     )

United Nations agreements
UNITED NATIONS - BUILDINGS
United Nations Conference on Trade and Employment. . . .
United Nations.   Economic Affairs Dept.
UNITED NATIONS - YEARBOOKS
United Nations (1942-1945)

When a series of numerals or dates designates parts of a whole and there are also alphabetical extensions of the inclusive heading, arrange the alphabetical group first.

Chiefs of state:  Disregard the name in parentheses that follows the dates.

U.S.   President, 1801-1809   (Jefferson)
U.S.   President, 1953-1961   (Eisenhower)

Constitutions, charters, etc.:

U.S.   CONSTITUTION - AMENDMENTS
U.S.   Constitution.   1st-10th amendments
U.S.   Constitution.   1st amendment
U.S.   CONSTITUTION - SIGNERS

Legislatures:

U.S.   CONGRESS - BIOGRAPHY

>U. S.   Congress.   House.   Committee on. . . .
>U. S.   CONGRESS - RULES AND PRACTICE
>U. S.   Congress.   Senate
>U. S.   63d Congress, 2d session, 1913-1914.   House
>U. S.   86th Congress, 1st session, 1959

Military units:  Military units with distinctive names are arranged alphabetically by their names.   Units beginning with a
number are arranged alphabetically by the word following the
number, then numerically by the number.   Regard the full
name of the unit but disregard subdivisions or modifications
of a unit except in relation to other headings under the unit
with the same number.

>U. S.   Army.   A. E. F. , 1917-1920
>U. S.   Army Air Forces.   8th Air Force
>U. S.   Army Air Forces.   Air Service Command
>U. S.   ARMY - BIOGRAPHY
>U. S.   Army.   1st Cavalry
>U. S.   Army.   II Corps
>U. S.   Army.   Corps of Engineers

## NUMERALS

Arrange numerals in the titles of books, corporate
names, cross references, etc. , as if spelled out in the language of the entry.   Spell numerals and dates as they are
spoken, placing 'and' before the last element in compound
numbers in English, except in a decimal fraction where the
'and' must be omitted.

>EGYPT
>1848:   chapters of German history.
>Ekblaw, Sidney E.
>ELECTRIC BATTERIES

>Nilson, Arthur Reinhold.
>1940:   our finest hour.
>1939:   how the war began.
>99 stanzas European.
>Norcross, Carl.

>On borrowed time.
>ONE-ACT PLAYS
>100, 000, 000 allies--if we choose.
>One hundred non-royalty one-act plays

One man caravan.
1001 mechanical facts made easy.
1000 questions and answers on T. B.
O'Neill, Eugene Gladstone.
OPERA.

Arrange a numeral following a given name in a title as if spelled out in the language of the title, as spoken. In English the numeral is read as an ordinal preceded by 'the. ' See also Forename entries.

The Henry James reader
Henry V, King of England, 1387-1422    (Henry King of England, 5)
Henry VIII, King of England, 1491-1547 (Henry King of England, 8)

Henry VIII                              (Henry the Eighth)
Shakespeare, William

Henry V                                 (Henry the Fifth)
Shakespeare, William

## ORDER OF ENTRIES

When the same word or combination of words, is used as the heading of different kinds of entry, arrange the entries in two main groups: 1) Single surname entries, arranged alphabetically by forenames.   2) All other entries, arranged alphabetically word by word, disregarding kind of entry, form of heading, and punctuation.

Arrange subject entries under a personal or corporate name immediately after the author entries for the same name.

Interfile title added entries and subject entries that are identical and subarrange alphabetically by their main entries.

Love, John L.
LOVE, JOHN L.
Love, William

Love
Bowen, Elizabeth

       LOVE
Magoun, F. Alexander

Love and beauty
LOVE POETRY
LOVE - QUOTATIONS, MAXIMS, ETC.
LOVE (THEOLOGY)
Love your neighbor

## PLACE ARRANGEMENT

Entries beginning with a geographical name follow the same name used as a single surname.

Arrange all entries beginning with the same geographical name in one straight alphabetical file, word by word, disregarding punctuation.

Arrange different kinds of entries under the same geographical name heading in groups as follows:

1) Author (main and/or added entry) without subheading, subarranged by titles.

2) Subject without subdivision, and identical title added entries, interfiled and subarranged alphabetically by their main entries.

3) Heading with corporate and/or subject subdivisions interfiled alphabetically with each other and with titles, etc., disregarding punctuation; each corporate author heading followed by its own subject entries.

Arrange headings for the official governmental divisions of a place (i. e., bureaus, committees, departments, etc.) by the first distinctive word of the subheading.

      U.S.   Dept. of <u>Agriculture</u>
      U.S.   Bureau of <u>Education</u>

Different places, jurisdictions, and governments of the same name are alphabetized by the geographical or parenthetical designations following the names. Arrangement is first by the complete designation, then under each different heading according to the general rules above.

United States
UNITED STATES
U.S.   Adjutant-General's Office
U.S. - ADJUTANT-GENERAL'S OFFICE
U.S.   Agricultural Adjustment Administration
The United States among the nations
United States Steel Corporation
U.S. - TERRITORIAL EXPANSION

New York Academy of Medicine
New York and the Seabury investigation
New York (City) Health Dept.
NEW YORK (CITY) - HEALTH DEPT.
New York (City) Police Dept.
NEW YORK (CITY) - POOR
New York (Colony)
New York (County)   Court House Board
New York (State)
NEW YORK (STATE) - GEOLOGY
New York Edison Company
New York tribune

Lincoln, William Sever
Lincoln and Ann Rutledge
LINCOLN CO. , KY.
Lincoln, Eng.
LINCOLN HIGHWAY
Lincoln, Neb.
Lincoln plays

London, Jack
LONDON - DESCRIPTION
London, Ky.
London, Ont. Council

California as I saw it
California, Mo.
CALIFORNIA, SOUTHERN
California State Chamber of Commerce
California.   University.   Library
California.   University.   School of law
California.   University.   University at Los Angeles

GERMANY - BIBLIOGRAPHY
Germany.   Constitution
Germany (Democratic Republic)
GERMANY (DEMOCRATIC REPUBLIC) - ECONOMIC
   CONDITIONS

GERMANY - DESCRIPTION AND TRAVEL
Germany divided
GERMANY, EASTERN
Germany (Territory under Allied occupation, 1945-
1955)


POSSESSIVE CASE   See Punctuation marks.


PREFIXES   See Names with a prefix.


PUBLISHER   See Corporate name entries.


PUNCTUATION MARKS

Disregard punctuation marks that are part of a title
or corporate name.

Boys' book of photography
Boys' life of Will Rogers
Boys' Odyssey
Boys of 1812
Boys will be boys

Life
Life--a bowl of rice
"Life after death"
Life, its true genesis
Life! physical and spiritual


REFERENCES

A reference or explanatory note precedes all other entries under the same word or words.   In relation to other
entries in the catalog consider only the heading on a reference or explanatory note; disregard the words see and see
also, the heading or headings referred to, and the note.

If a see reference is the same as an actual entry, arrange the see reference first, except that a surname entry
always precedes a reference.

Corea, Lois Fleming
COREA,  see KOREA

File a see also reference before the first entry under the same word or words.

CHILDREN,  see also. ...
CHILDREN
CHILDREN - CARE AND HYGIENE,  see also
CHILDREN - CARE AND HYGIENE
CHILDREN - CARE AND HYGIENE - BIBLIOGRAPHY


SUBJECT ARRANGEMENT

Subject entries follow the same word used as a single
surname.

Arrange entries with the same subject heading alphabetically by their main entries, then by title.  Arrange subject analytics by the entry for the analytic if different from
the main entry for the whole book.

BISON, AMERICAN
Allen, Joel Asaph
The American bisons, living and extinct.

BISON, AMERICAN
Anderson, George S.
Roosevelt, Theodore
American big-game hunting

Arrange a subject, its subdivisions, etc. , in groups
as follows:  1) Subject without subdivision; 2) Period divisions,
arranged chronologically; inclusive periods preceding subordinate periods; 3) Alphabetical extensions of the main subject heading:  form, subject, and geographical subdivisions,
inverted subject headings, subject followed by a parenthetical
term, and phrase subject headings, interfiled word by word
in one alphabet with titles and other headings beginning with
the same word, disregarding punctuation.

MASS (MUSIC)
Mass of the Roman rite
MASS (PHYSICS)
MASS - STUDY AND TEACHING

        U.S.  - HISTORY - REVOLUTION
        U.S.  - HISTORY - 1783-1865
        U.S.  - HISTORY - 1783-1809
        U.S.  - HISTORY - WAR OF 1812
        U.S.  - HISTORY - CIVIL WAR
        U.S.  - HISTORY - BIBLIOGRAPHY
        U.S.  history bonus book
        U.S.  - HISTORY - SOURCES
        U.S.  - IMMIGRATION AND EMIGRATION


## TITLE ENTRY ARRANGEMENT

        Title entries are arranged alphabetically, considering
each word in turn; the initial article is disregarded, but all
other articles and prepositions are to be regarded.

        In an unknown land.
        In and out of the old missions of California.
        In and under Mexico.
        In the Amazon jungle.
        In the days of the giants.
        In the days of the guilds.
        In this our life.
        In tidewater Virginia.

        Why Europe fights.
        Why I believe in religion.
        Why the chimes rang.
        Why the weather.


TRANSLATOR  See Author entry arrangement.


## UMLAUT

        Disregard umlauts and other letter modifications.

        Muellen, Abraham
        Mullen, Allen
        Müllen, Gustav
        Mullen, Pat


UNITED STATES  See Place arrangement; Subject arrangement.

## WORDS SPELLED IN DIFFERENT WAYS

When different entries, including corporate names, begin with or contain the same word spelled in different ways (e.g., Color and Colour) choose one spelling, according to the criteria below, file all entries under that spelling, and refer from the other spellings.

Generally choose the most commonly accepted current usage.

When there is a choice between the American and English spellings, choose the American.

LABOR CONTRACT
Labor in America.
LABOR LAWS AND LEGISLATION
Labour production of the cotton textile industry.
Labor supply.

## WORDS WRITTEN IN DIFFERENT WAYS

Arrange hyphenated words as separate words when the parts are complete words.

An epoch in life insurance
Epoch-making papers in United States history
The epoch of reform

Arrange as two words compound words that are written as two separate words. Arrange as one word compound words that are written as one.

In the case of compound words that appear in the catalog written both as two separate words and as a single word, interfile all entries, including corporate names, under the one-word form.

SEA-POWER
Sea power in the machine age
Seapower in the nuclear age
Sea-power in the Pacific
Search

## Reference

1. <u>A L A Rules for Filing Catalog Cards.</u> Prepared by the A L A Editorial Committee's Subcommittee on the A L A Rules for Filing Catalog Cards, Pauline A. Seely, Chairman and Editor. 2d ed. abr. (Chicago: American Library Association, 1968).

CHAPTER 14


RELATED TOPICS AND
MISCELLANEOUS INFORMATION


For the librarian of the small library who has not yet
found it feasible to participate in a centralized processing
and cataloging center, there are a few closely related matters
about which some information may be helpful. With a staff
of one or possibly two, ordering, accessioning, classifying,
cataloging, and preparing materials for circulation are so
closely associated that they are thought of almost as one process. This chapter contains some practical hints regarding
these processes.


## ACQUISITION

Materials are usually selected by the librarian, but
the order may be sent out by a clerk, principal, superintendent, or purchasing office. When the order and the bill
are received, the bill is checked with the materials to be
sure that the titles and editions received are those which
were ordered. Some libraries write the name of the dealer
from whom a book is purchased, the date it is received, and
the cost in the inner margin of the book on the right-hand
page following the title page, writing it parallel to the sewing
of the book. This information is useful when one is examining a book with reference to having it rebound, or when
checking a book's use over the period in which it has been
available for circulation.


## WEEDING THE COLLECTION

Before beginning to classify and catalog an old library,
weed the collection, removing material that is worn out, out
of date, unsuitable for that particular library, or that has
been superseded by a better title. In doing this it is well
for the inexperienced librarian to seek the guidance of a

trained and experienced librarian, or to check with the best printed selection aids in the field represented in that library. Material that needs mending or rebinding should be put in good physical condition before being cataloged.

## MECHANICAL PROCESSES

After checking the bill for a new book, one should cut the pages when necessary and open the book correctly, i.e., take a few pages at the front and at the back alternately and press them down gently against the covers, until the middle of the book is reached. This makes it easier to open and read the book and minimizes the danger of breaking its back. Audiorecordings should be examined to make sure they are not warped or otherwise damaged; filmstrips should be checked to see that they are in their proper containers, and so forth.

The next step is to put the mark of ownership on the item, either by stamping, embossing, or engraving, or--in the case of books--pasting a book plate inside the front cover. For audiovisual material, it is usually more feasible to attach labels to each item, although an electric stylus can be used to mark directly on surfaces not amenable to stamps or embossers.

## ACCESSIONING

The A.L.A. Glossary of Library Terms[1] defines accession as "To record books and other similar material added to the library in the order of acquisition." The accession number is a serial number given to an item as it is added to the library. The lines in an accession record book are numbered consecutively, beginning with one. A brief description of the item follows, and the number on this line is written in the book or on the media label, on the shelf-list card, circulation card and pocket. Some libraries do not keep an accession book, but do assign accession numbers. They use a numbering machine and number each item as it is added to the library. The source, date of acquisition, and cost are the only information which the accession book gives that the shelf list ordinarily does not, hence these three items may be added to the shelf-list cards instead of keeping an accession book. Even the date may be omitted if a new series of numbers, prefixed by the year, is initiated each January or at the start of the library's fiscal year (e.g.,

75-0001 could be the first book purchased in 1975, while 74-0912 might be the last acquired in 1974, automatically telling the library how many volumes it had purchased in that year).

An accession number is useful in identifying books; e. g. , number 1312 means a particular book, even a certain copy or volume. The accession number shows the number of books which have been added to the library, either within a given period or the total number, keeping in mind that some books have been withdrawn from the library. A count of the shelf-list cards before filing, however, enables the librarian to keep any necessary record of the number of titles or individual items added to the library, without the duplication of records involved in keeping an accession book. These statistics usually appear in the monthly or annual reports. Even if the library has always kept an accession record, it may be discontinued at any given date and the accession numbers on older materials ignored or replaced by copy numbers. The two reasons most commonly given for keeping an accession record book are: 1) that a card, i. e. , a shelf-list card, may be more easily lost than a book; and 2) that if the library received books from different funds, the accession book is a convenient record of this. Most libraries have abandoned the accession book--and many the accession number as well--feeling that copy numbers are sufficient identification. Before abandoning the accession book, however, it is wise to check its possible requirement by law or established policy.

If an accession record is to be used, the following information is entered under the proper column heading: 1) the date of the bill for the item, or, if there is no bill, the date on which it is being accessioned; 2) the author heading as found on the title page; 3) brief title; 4) the publisher in abbreviated form; 5) date of publication, or copyright if there is no publication date; 6) volume number; 7) the name of the dealer through whom the material was purchased; and 8) the cost to the library. These are the essential items for an accession record. Follow the rules for cataloging in giving the title, capitalizing, etc. If the item is a gift, give the donor's name instead of the dealer's, and enter the word "gift" in the cost column. Use ditto marks where information for successive titles is the same. Give the date of accessioning (month, day, and year) on the top line of each page of the accession book. If a page is not filled during one day, give the new date on the line for the first entry for that day.

The accession number is written in each volume or copy on the first right-hand page after the title page, in the center of the lower margin about one inch from the bottom, or as nearly in this place as possible considering the printing on the page. The accession number should also be written on one other page, e.g., the page which is stamped with the name of the library. Audiovisual materials which are accessioned must also be marked with the assigned number in such a way that it will neither damage the item nor be in danger of being obliterated. By means of the accession number one can turn at once to the description of the material in the accession record.

## CATALOGING ROUTINE

The first step in the cataloging process is to order the cards if printed cards are used, a step which should coincide with the ordering of the material itself whenever possible. If printed cards are not used, the first step is to classify and assign subject headings. As soon as the classification number is determined, it should be written in pencil on the page following the title page, about one inch from the top of the page and one inch from the hinge of the book. If the number is too close to the top or the hinge, it may be cut off when the book is rebound. Most nonprint materials can be marked with an engraver or permanent marking pen, although some require labels. All pieces in a set should be marked insofar as possible.

The next step is to decide on the form of the heading for the main entry and for other added entries besides subject entries. Check with the name authority file or the catalog to insure consistency in headings and search aids if the name is new to the catalog and there is no CIP data or printed card. If Cutter numbers or author letters are used, they are assigned as soon as the heading for the main entry is determined. The book number is written below the classification number. If there are printed cards, they are checked with the item to be sure that they match; if there are no printed cards, the cataloger prepares a slip from which the cards will be typed.

The third step is to type the main entry card, including the tracing for the added cards; or to add the headings and call number and make any changes which may be necessary on the printed cards. If there are no printed cards,

the added entry cards and shelf-list card are typed or otherwise reproduced and revised.   Duplicating machines for making the required additional cards from the unit card save
time, but may be expensive for the small library.   If the library cannot afford a duplicating machine for its exclusive
use, possibly it can use one belonging to another department
of the locality or organization which it serves.   When cards
are typed, each card has to be revised for accuracy, but
mechanically reproduced cards are exactly like the master
card or copy.   Consult your state library or state department of education regarding duplicating machines or commercial card reproduction centers which may be able to reproduce your catalog cards correctly, quickly, and less expen-
sively than you could have them typed in your library.   The
small library as well as the large library should constantly
be on the alert for new technological methods.

The circulation card and pocket are made at the same
time as the catalog and shelf-list cards.   The circulation card
should have the call number in the upper left-hand corner;
the accession number, if one is used, in the upper right-hand
corner; the surname of the author or full heading, if a corporate author, on the line below the call number; and the
title below that.   Indent the first letter of the title to the
third space to the right, to make both author and title more
prominent.

When an added copy is acquired by the library, it is
necessary only to remove the shelf-list card from the tray,
add the accession or copy number (and source, date, and
cost of the new copy, if required) and refile the card, since
no change is made on the catalog cards.   On the other hand,
when another volume is added to the library, notation of the
new volume must be added to the catalog cards as well as to
the shelf-list card.   When a new edition is added, it is
necessary to catalog it as a new book, except that as a rule
the same classification number and the same subject headings
will be used.

After each new order is cataloged, or periodically in
a library buying continuously, the catalog and shelf-list cards
should be sorted, the latter counted and totals recorded.
They are then filed above the rod in the public and shelf-list
card catalogs respectively, the filing is revised, the rod
pulled out, and the cards dropped and locked in the trays.

Marking the spines of books.   Call numbers should

appear on the backs of books of nonfiction for greater convenience in locating a given book or returning it to the shelf. If the library participates in the service of a centralized processing center, the books may come with the call numbers already on the spines, or labels may be provided for the library to apply to each book. Otherwise the library should adopt a simple, inexpensive system for marking books on the spine.

The call number should be placed at the same distance from the bottom of all books for the sake of ease in locating books and the appearance of the shelves. A stiff card with this distance marked on it should be used as a guide. One and a half inches from the bottom of the book usually avoids any printing and is a convenient height.

The most efficient method is to type the call numbers for a group of books at one time on sheets of self-adhesive labels, using the largest type face available. The labels are then peeled from the backing sheet and attached to the book jackets at the appropriate height, before the jackets are covered with their clear plastic protective covers. When labels are attached directly to the spine, they should be sprayed with a clear lacquer or covered with strong transparent tape to prolong their life. The process of marking uncovered books by hand is an alternative which may be preferred by some, and may be outlined as follows:

1. Mark the place to be occupied by the call number, noting the exact place where each line begins if the call number consists of two lines.
2. Remove the sizing by painting over the spot with acetone or book lacquer.
3. Write the call number in white ink or with an electric stylus and transfer paper at the place marked. For light colored books use black ink or dark transfer paper.
4. Cover the lettering with a thin coat of book lacquer. Some libraries prefer to cover the entire book with lacquer as it also serves as an insecticide.

Make the figures of the call number vertical and round rather than angular, so that they may be easily read and so that there may be less variation when the lettering is done by different workers.

Typed self-adhesive labels should be used for nonprint

materials whenever possible.    Labels in shapes appropriate for audiodiscs, cassettes, filmstrips, etc. are available from library supply houses.

Preparation process check list:

Clerical assistant:    1.    Check items received with bill.
2.    Write in each book the name of the dealer, date received, and cost. (This step may be omitted. )
3.    Cut pages.
4.    Open correctly.
5.    Stamp with mark of ownership unless book plate is used.
6.    Accession.    (This process may be omitted. )
7.    Order printed cards, if they have not already been ordered.

Librarian:    8.    Classify and assign subject headings, making note of them on a slip.    If printed cards are available, compare suggested classification number and headings with the shelf list and the library's official classification schedule and list of subject headings.
9.    Decide upon the added entries other than subject heading.
10.    Determine heading for author and such added entries as editor, translator, illustrator.    If printed cards are used, compare forms of names with those in the catalog or name authority file.
11.    Note adaptations to be made on printed cards or prepare main entry card copy.

Clerical assistant:    12.    Type cards, label, circulation card and pocket.

Librarian:    13.    Revise typed cards, label, etc.

Clerical assistant:    14.    Paste in pocket, date slip, and book plate, if used.
15.    Attach label or mark spine, cover jacket, insert card in pocket, put out for use.

|                |     |                                              |
|----------------|-----|----------------------------------------------|
|                | 16. | Sort cards and count for statistics.        |
|                | 17. | File cards in shelf-list and catalog trays above rod. |
| Librarian:     | 18. | Revise filing and lock cards in trays.      |

## WITHDRAWALS

When an item is added to the library it is noted in various records; when it is withdrawn or discarded from the library, those records must be changed. When a book wears out and is to be replaced by a new copy, a note is made on the shelf-list card that the particular copy has been withdrawn, and the addition of the new copy is noted. Since the cards in the public catalog do not show how many copies of a given title are in a library, withdrawing a book does not affect the catalog so long as other copies remain. If, however, there is only one copy of the book and it is not to be replaced, the catalog cards must be taken out of the catalog, and the shelf-list card must also be removed from the shelf list, after having the withdrawal note, the abbreviation "W" and the date, written on it; e.g., W 5-17-75. Some libraries give the cause; e.g., W 5-17-75 Worn out. If one wishes to make a study of the number of books being lost by borrowers, worn out, etc., with reference to a possible change in policy, it is worthwhile noting the cause of withdrawal. This note may be made only as long as it is needed to show the chief cause or causes of withdrawals. It is unnecessary to continue this additional information indefinitely. Instead of using "W" one can draw a line through the accession or copy number to show that a book has been withdrawn.

If a volume of a set is being withdrawn, note should be made, usually in pencil, on the catalog card that the particular volume is lacking. If it is to be replaced as soon as it can be secured, this penciled note can be easily erased when the new copy of the missing volume is added to the library.

Occasionally it will happen that the book being withdrawn is the only one entered under that name, under that subject, etc. If that is the case, not only should the catalog cards and the shelf-list card be removed, but the name or subject cross references to and from these headings and the corresponding cards in the name and subject authority files should be withdrawn. If a book is to be replaced as soon as funds are available or if it is lost but there is the possibility of its being found, the cards may be withdrawn from the files, properly labeled, and put aside to be used later.

If there are more copies or volumes in the library, after making the proper withdrawal note on the shelf-list card, refile the card in the shelf list.

If the book withdrawn is the only copy or volume, the shelf-list card for that book, with the withdrawal note on it, may be filed alphabetically by author in a special file called a withdrawal file.   This file can be a great convenience when some question comes up as to what has become of a book, whether or not the library ever had a copy, etc.   The cards do not need to be kept indefinitely, but might well be kept for several years.

A count of books withdrawn should be made, just as the count of books added is made.   The inventory should show the number of books in the library at the beginning of the year for which the report is being made, the number added during that period, the number withdrawn, and the number in the library at the end of the year.

All library marks of ownership should be removed or "Withdrawn by--(name of library)" should be written or stamped in the book before selling it for old paper or giving it away.   Some libraries are governed by definite laws affecting disposal of books.   The first time that a book is withdrawn, the policy should be carefully worked out, note made of the procedure to be followed, and a withdrawal file set up.


WHERE TO CATALOG

The smallest library should have a place in which to catalog, even though it is only a desk or a table in a corner.   Have shelves nearby on which the necessary cataloging tools and aids and the books to be cataloged may be kept.   Label these shelves, so that it will be possible to tell at a glance what stage of preparation the books are in.   Leave any unfinished work clearly marked so that it may be resumed with a minimum loss of time.   A quarter of an hour or half an hour may be used advantageously to mark ten books on the back, to order printed cards, or the like.   The longer periods may be used for determining the form of the author's name, classifying and assigning subject headings, or typing the main cards. The added cards can be typed by any good typist who is given adequate instruction and supervision at first.

## CATALOGING SUPPLIES

A few suggestions as to the supplies which will be found necessary in cataloging a collection as described in this manual may prove useful.

Accession record book. Any of the simplified accession record books which are sold by library supply houses will be found satisfactory. A loose-leaf accession book, which may be used on a typewriter, is preferable. Accession books are listed according to the number of lines they contain. As each volume in the library requires one line, the number of lines desired depends upon the number of volumes on hand and the approximate number that will be added in the next two or three years.

Catalog cards. Cards of the same quality may be used for the shelf list and for the catalog. Medium-weight cards are best as they are strong enough to stand the wear, without taking up unnecessary room or adding unnecessary weight to the card cabinets. The medium weight is similar to that of the printed cards, and for that reason is much more satisfactory if the library uses printed cards in addition to its own. It pays to buy the best catalog cards, and it is important to use only one kind so that all the cards in the catalog will be of the same size and thickness and, therefore, can be handled more quickly in the trays. For fiction, at least three cards for each book, namely, author, title, and shelf list, will be necessary. For nonfiction, if many analytical entries are made, an average of five cards for each book is the minimum number to count on. Catalog cards come in boxes of 500 or 1,000 and cost less if bought in these or larger quantities.

Catalog guide cards. Guide cards should be inserted at intervals of about one inch. Satisfactory plain buff guide cards, punched for a catalog tray rod, cut in thirds or halves (i.e., the tab is one-third or one-half the width of the cards) may be purchased in packages of one hundred, five hundred, or one thousand. These cards are available either plain, with labels for typing headings, or printed with headings suitable for various types of libraries.

Sets of shelf-list guide cards for libraries using the Dewey Decimal Classification may also be purchased.

Miscellaneous supplies. If extension cards for the catalog are to be tied to the first card, use heavy linen thread, which may be purchased at any department store.

The special supplies needed for marking call numbers on the spine of books are an electric pencil or an electric stylus and transfer paper, which may be ordered from a library supplier. Transfer paper comes in white, black or dark blue, white for dark colored books, dark for light colored books. A bottle of acetone is needed to remove the sizing from the back of the book before applying the ink; and a bottle of book lacquer to put over the ink when it is dry. Any good pen point, the type depending upon the choice of the person doing the lettering, is satisfactory. Usually a bowl pointed pen is preferred.

A good steel eraser or a razor blade with a bar top with which to erase words, or more especially letters, is a necessity. A good bar pencil and ink eraser is also very useful. Liquid typewriter eraser and Ko-rec-type should also be on hand.

A typewriter is a necessity in any library for the typing of cards, orders, etc. An electric typewriter which has, in addition to a regular platen, a removable platen with a steel grip for holding cards in position is recommended. If possible, invest in the kind of machine which allows the use of different type sizes by changing the element, for while elite type is best for typing cards, the largest possible type size should be used for typing spine labels.

Card catalog cabinets. Although there are many firms making card catalog cabinets, it pays to get the best. Cabinets come in varying sizes from one to sixty trays, and supplier catalogs give an estimate of the number of cards which the cabinets of different sizes will hold. Knowing the number of books in the library and the approximate number of new books added each year, one can easily determine the size of cabinet needed by counting five cards to a book.

Card catalog cabinets should have standard trays and should be purchased from the same firm so that they will match exactly and so that the trays will be interchangeable when cards are shifted with the expansion of the catalog.

Each tray should have a follower-block to hold the cards erect when the tray is only partially filled, and a rod which runs through the holes in the cards and locks them into the tray. It is also very important to have the cards fit the tray exactly so that they will stand straight, drop in easily, and remain in alignment for the rod. Catalog trays should be only two-thirds full if the cards are to be consulted easily.

If the library can afford it, the sectional cabinet is best, as added units are less expensive than the same number of trays in a separate cabinet and the sections fit together and form one cabinet. If as many as eight or nine trays are needed or will be needed relatively soon, it will pay to buy the sectional cabinet, which may be bought in units of five, ten, or fifteen trays. The same base and top will serve for several units.

## Reference

1. <u>A. L. A. Glossary of Library Terms</u> (Chicago: American Library Association, 1943).

APPENDIX A


ABBREVIATIONS


These abbreviations are used anywhere in the entry
except that words in the title up to the first mark of punctuation are not to be abbreviated. Abbreviations given on the
title page are to be used whether included in this list or not.


| | |
|---|---|
| abridged | abr. |
| analytic, analytics | anal., anals. |
| arranged | arr. |
| association | assoc. |
| augmented | augm. |
| baronet | bart. [1] |
| black and white | b&w |
| book | bk |
| born | b. [1] |
| Brother, Brothers | Bro., Bros. [2] |
| bulletin | bull. |
| centimeter, centimeters | cm. |
| circa | ca. |
| colored, color | col. |
| Company | Co. |
| compiled, compiler[1] | comp. |
| Congress | Cong. |
| copyright | c |
| Corporation | Corp. |
| corrected | corr. |
| County | Co. |
| Department | Dept. |
| died | d. [1] |
| edited, edition, editor, editors | ed., eds. |
| engraved, engraver | engr. |
| enlarged | enl. |
| et alii | et al. |
| et cetera | etc. |
| folded | fold. |
| frame, frames | fr. |

| | |
|---|---|
| Government Printing Office | Govt. Print. Off. |
| His (or Her) Majesty's Stationery Office | H. M. Stationery Off. |
| illustration, illustrations, illustrator, illustrated | ill. |
| inch, inches | in. |
| inch or inches per second | ips |
| incorporated | inc. |
| International Standard Bibliographic Description | ISBD |
| International Standard Book Number | ISBN |
| International Standard Serial number | ISSN |
| introduction, introductory | introd. |
| joint author | jt. auth. |
| Junior | Jr. |
| limited | ltd. [2] |
| millimeter, millimeters | mm |
| minute, minutes | min. |
| number, numbers | no., nos. |
| numbered | numb. |
| opus | op. |
| page, pages | p. |
| part, parts | pt., pts. |
| photograph, photographs | photo., photos. |
| plate, plates | pl. |
| portrait, portraits | port., ports. |
| preface, prefatory | pref. |
| President | Pres. [3] |
| press (in publisher's name) | Pr. |
| printing | print. |
| privately printed | priv. print. |
| pseudonym | pseud. |
| publication, published, publisher, publishers, publishing | pub. |
| revised | rev. |
| revolutions per minute | rpm |
| Saint | St. [4] |
| second (number) | 2d [5] |
| second, seconds (time) | sec. |
| Senior | Sr. |
| series | ser. |
| session | sess. |
| side, sides | s. |
| silent | si. |
| sine loco | s. l. |

| sine nomine | s. n. |
| sound | sd. |
| supplement, supplements, supplemented | suppl. |
| table | tab. |
| Territory | Ter. |
| third | 3d[5] |
| title page | t. p. |
| translated, translation, translator[1] | tr. |
| United States | U. S. |
| university (as publisher) | Univ. |
| unnumbered | unnumb. |
| volume, volumes | v. , vol. ,[6] vols. [6] |

Geographical names. Abbreviations for geographical names in headings are to be decided upon and a list made of those to be used in a given catalog. U. S. for United States is customarily used in all headings, but in titles the usage of the title page is followed. The usual abbreviations for states are used when they follow the name of a city. A library may also compi a list of abbreviations for well-known cities to be used whenever they occur on catalog cards, except as the first word of a heading.

Publishers. Here is a selected list of publishers, with their abbreviations, which can be used without indicating place of publication:

| Abingdon Press | Abingdon |
| American Book Company | Am. Bk. |
| American Library Association | A. L. A. |
| Appleton-Century-Crofts | Appleton |
| A. S. Barnes & Company | Barnes, A. S. |
| Bobbs-Merrill Company, Inc. | Bobbs |
| R. R. Bowker Company | Bowker |
| The British Book Centre, Inc. | British Bk. Centre |
| Coward, McCann & Geoghegan | Coward-McCann |
| Thomas Y. Crowell Company | Crowell |
| Crown Publishers | Crown |
| The John Day Company | Day |
| Dodd, Mead & Company, Inc. | Dodd |
| Doubleday & Company, Inc. | Doubleday |
| E. P. Dutton & Company, Inc. | Dutton |
| Farrar, Straus & Giroux, Inc. | Farrar, Straus |
| Funk & Wagnalls Company, Inc. | Funk |
| Ginn & Co. | Ginn |

| | |
|---|---|
| Grosset & Dunlap, Inc. | Grosset |
| Hammond, Inc. | Hammond |
| Harcourt, Brace, Jovanovich | Harcourt |
| Harper & Row, Publishers | Harper |
| D. C. Heath & Company | Heath |
| Holt, Rinehart, & Winston, Inc. | Holt |
| Houghton Mifflin Company | Houghton |
| Alfred A. Knopf, Inc. | Knopf |
| J. B. Lippincott Company | Lippincott |
| Little, Brown & Company | Little |
| Lothrop, Lee & Shepard Company, Inc. | Lothrop |
| McGraw-Hill Book Company, Inc. | McGraw |
| The Macmillan Publishing Company, Inc. | Macmillan |
| G. & C. Merriam Company | Merriam |
| William Morrow & Company, Inc., Publishers | Morrow |
| Thomas Nelson, Inc. | Nelson |
| W. W. Norton & Company, Inc., Publishers | Norton |
| Prentice-Hall, Inc. | Prentice-Hall |
| G. P. Putnam's Sons, Inc. | Putnam |
| Rand McNally & Company | Rand McNally |
| Random House, Inc. | Random House |
| The Scarecrow Press, Inc. | Scarecrow |
| Scott, Foresman & Company | Scott |
| Charles Scribner's Sons | Scribner |
| Simon and Schuster, Inc., Publishers | Simon & Schuster |
| Superintendent of Documents, Government Printing Office | Supt. of Doc. |
| Van Nostrand Reinhold Company | Van Nostrand |
| The Viking Press, Inc. | Viking |
| Albert Whitman & Company | Whitman, A. |
| John Wiley & Sons, Inc. | Wiley |
| The H. W. Wilson Company | Wilson, H. W. |
| The World Publishing Company | World Pub. |

## References

1.  Used only in headings.

2.  Used only in names of firms and other corporate bodies.

3.  Used only in a personal name heading.

4. Used only when preceding the name, as St. Paul's Cathedral.

5. All other ordinal numbers are abbreviated as usual, e.g., 1st, 4th.

6. Used at the beginning of a statement and before a Roman numeral.

## DEFINITIONS OF TECHNICAL TERMS

The definitions given below are based on the sources listed in "References" at the end of this appendix; in the main, they are drawn from the A. L. A. Glossary and AACR. Definitions of audiovisual materials are incorporated in Chapter 10.

ACCESSION. To record books and other similar material added to a library in the order of acquisition.

ACCESSION NUMBER. The number given to a volume in the order of its acquisition.

ACCESSION RECORD. The business record of books, etc. , added to a library in the order of receipt, giving a condensed description of the book and the essential facts in its library history.

ADAPTATION. A rewritten form of a literary work modified for a purpose or use other than that for which the original work was intended, e. g. , Lamb's Tales from Shakespeare.

ADDED ENTRY. An entry, additional to the main entry, under which a bibliographical entity is represented in a catalog; a secondary entry.

ADDED TITLE PAGE. A title page preceding or following the title page chosen as the basis for the description of the publication. It may be more general, as a series title page, or equally general, as a title page in another language. In the case of a facsimile edition, or a reprint edition with a new title page, a reproduction of the original title page is not treated as an added title page.

ALTERNATIVE TITLE. A second title introduced by "or"

or its equivalent, e. g. , <u>The tempest; or, The enchanted island</u>.

ANALYTICAL ENTRY.   An entry for a work or part of a work that is contained in a collection, series, issue of a serial, or other bibliographical unit for which another, comprehensive entry has been made.   An analytical entry may be under the author, subject or title for a part of a work or of some article contained in a collection (volume of essays, serial, etc. ) including a reference to the publication which contains the article or work entered.

ANONYMOUS.   Of unknown authorship.

ANONYMOUS CLASSIC.   A work of unknown or doubtful authorship, commonly designated by title, which may have appeared in the course of time in many editions, versions, and/or translations.

AREA.   A major section of a catalog entry, e. g. , the imprint area.

AUTHOR ANALYTICAL ENTRY   <u>see</u> ANALYTICAL ENTRY.

AUTHOR ENTRY.   An entry of a work in a catalog under its author's name as heading, whether this be a main or an added heading.   The author heading may consist of a personal or a corporate name or some substitute for it, e. g. , initials, pseudonym, etc.

AUTHOR NUMBER   <u>see</u> BOOK NUMBER.

AUTHOR-TITLE ADDED ENTRY.   An added entry consisting of the author and title of a work.

AUTHORITY LIST OR FILE.   An official list of forms selected as headings in a catalog, giving for author and corporate names and for the forms of entry of anonymous classics the sources used for establishing the forms, together with the variant forms.   If the list is a name list, it is sometimes called Name list and Name file.

BODY OF THE ENTRY.   That portion of a catalog entry that begins with the title and ends with the imprint.

BOOK NUMBER. A combination of letters and figures used to arrange books in the same classification number in alphabetical order.

CALL NUMBER. The combination of a location symbol and/or a media code, the classification number, and the book number (if used) which determines the position of an item on the shelves. See also BOOK NUMBER; LOCATION MARK.

CARD CATALOG. A catalog made on separate cards and kept in trays.

CATALOG. A list of books, maps, etc., arranged according to some definite plan. As distinguished from a bibliography it is a list which records, describes, and indexes the resources of a collection, a library, or a group of libraries. See also DICTIONARY CATALOG.

CATCHWORD TITLE ENTRY see PARTIAL TITLE ENTRY.

CLASSIFICATION. "The putting together of like things." Book classification, as defined by C. A. Cutter, is "the grouping of books written on the same or similar subjects."

COLLATION. That part of the catalog entry which describes the work as a material object, enumerating its volumes, pages ... and the type and character of its illustrations.

COLLECTION. If by one author: Three or more independent works or parts of works published together; if by more than one author: two or more independent works or parts of works published together and not written for the same occasion or for the publication in hand.

COMPILER. One who produces a work by collecting and putting together written or printed matter from the works of various authors. Also, one who chooses and combines into one work selections or quotations from one author. (cf. EDITOR)

COMPOSITE WORK. An original work consisting of separate and distinct parts, by different authors, which constitute together an integral whole.

COMPOUND SURNAME. A surname formed from two or more

proper names, often connected by a hyphen, conjunction, or preposition.

CONTENTS NOTE. A note in a catalog or a bibliography entry that lists the contents of a work.

CONTINUATION. 1. A work issued as a supplement to one previously issued. 2. A part issued in continuance of a book, a serial, or a series. See also PERIODICAL; SERIAL.

CONTINUATION CARD see EXTENSION CARD.

CONVENTIONAL TITLE see UNIFORM TITLE.

COPYRIGHT DATE. The date of copyright as given in the book, as a rule on the back of the title leaf.

CORPORATE BODY. An organization or group of persons that is identified by a name and that acts or may act as an entity. Corporate bodies cover a broad range of categories of which the following are typical: associations, institutions, business firms, non-profit enterprises, governments, specific agencies of government, conferences.

COVER TITLE. The title printed on the original covers of a book or pamphlet, or lettered or stamped on the publisher's binding, as distinguished from the title lettered on the cover of a particular copy by a binder.

CROSS REFERENCE see REFERENCE; "SEE ALSO" REFERENCE; "SEE" REFERENCE.

CUTTER NUMBER see BOOK NUMBER.

DICTIONARY CATALOG. A catalog in which all the entries (author, title, subject, series, etc.) and their related references are arranged together in one general alphabet. The subarrangement frequently varies from the strictly alphabetical.

DISCARD. A book officially withdrawn from a library collection because it is unfit for further use or is no longer needed.

EDITION. 1. All the impressions of a work printed at any

time or times from one setting of type, including those printed from stereotype or electrotype plates from that setting (provided, however, that there is no substantial change in or addition to the text, or no change in make-up, format, or character of the resulting book). A facsimile reproduction constitutes a different edition. 2. One of the successive forms in which a literary text is issued either by the author or by a subsequent editor. 3. One of the various printings of a newspaper for the same day, an issue published less often, as a weekly edition, or a special issue devoted to a particular subject, as an anniversary number. 4. In edition binding, all of the copies of a book or other publication produced and issued in uniform style.

EDITOR. One who prepares for publication a work or collection of works or articles not his own. The editorial labor may be limited to the preparation of the matter for the printer, or it may include supervision of the printing, revision (restitution) or elucidation of the text, and the addition of introduction, notes, and other critical matter. For certain works it may include the technical direction of a staff of persons engaged in writing or compiling the text. (Cf. COMPILER.)

ELEMENT. A sub-section of an area of the catalog entry, e.g., a parallel title.

ENTRY. 1. A record of a bibliographical entity in a catalog or list. 2. A heading under which a record of a bibliographical entity is represented in a catalog or list; also, in the case of a work entered under title, the title. See also HEADING.

ENTRY WORD. The word by which the entry is arranged in the catalog, usually the first word (other than an article) of the heading. (Cf. HEADING.)

EXTENSION CARD. A catalog card that continues an entry from a preceding card. Sometimes known as Continuation card [or Second card].

FACSIMILE EDITION. An edition which not only provides an exact replica of the text of the work reproduced, but which has as its chief purpose to simulate the physical appearance of the original work.

FILING MEDIUM. The word, phrase, name, or symbol on a card or material to be filed that determines its place in a systematic arrangement. Sometimes called Filing term or Filing word.

FILING TITLE see UNIFORM TITLE.

"FIRST" INDENTION. The distance from the left edge of a catalog card at which, according to predetermined rules, the author heading begins; also called Author indention.

FORM DIVISION. A division of a classification schedule or of a subject heading based on form or arrangement of subject matter in books, as for dictionaries or periodicals. The latest editions of the Dewey Decimal Classification call these divisions "Standard subdivisions."

FORM HEADING. A heading used for a form entry in a catalog, e.g., Encyclopedias and dictionaries, Periodicals, Short stories. Sometimes known as Form Subject Heading.

GUIDE. A card having a projecting tab higher than the material with which it is used, inserted in a file to indicate arrangement and aid in locating material in the file. For a card the term Guide card is also used.

HALF TITLE. A brief title without imprint and usually without the author's name, printed on a separate leaf preceding the main title page, the text or introducing the sections of a work.

HANGING INDENTION. A form of indention in cataloging in which the first line begins at author indention, and succeeding lines at title indention.

HEADING. In cataloging the word, name, or phrase at the head of an entry to indicate some special aspect of the book (authorship, subject content, series, title, etc.) and thereby to bring together in the catalog associated and allied material.

HOLDINGS. 1. The books, periodicals, and other material in the possession of a library. 2. Specifically, the volumes or parts of a serial in the possession of a library.

ILLUSTRATION. A pictorial or other representation in or belonging to a book or other publication, as issued; usually designed to elucidate the text. In the narrow sense the term stands for illustrations within the text (i.e., those which form part of the text page).

IMPRINT. The place and date of publication, and the name of the publisher or the printer (or sometimes both); ordinarily printed at the foot of the title page.

IMPRINT DATE. The year of publication or printing as specified on the title page.

INDENTION. The distance from the left edge of a catalog card at which, according to predetermined rules, the various parts of the description and their subsequent lines begin.

INTRODUCTION DATE. The date of a book as given at the beginning or at the end of the introduction.

JOINT AUTHOR. A person who collaborates with one or more associates to produce a work in which the contribution of each is usually not separable from that of the others.

LOCATION MARK. A letter, word, group of words, or some distinguishing character added to catalog records, often in conjunction with the call number, to indicate that a book is shelved in a certain place, as in a special collection. Also called Location symbol. See also CALL NUMBER.

MAIN ENTRY. The complete catalog record of a bibliographical entity, presented in the form by which the entity is to be uniformly identified and cited. The main entry normally includes the tracing of all other headings under which the record is to be represented in the catalog. See also ADDED ENTRY; UNIT CARD.

MONOGRAPH. A work or a collection, regardless of format, that is not a serial.

MONOGRAPHIC SERIES (MONOGRAPH SERIES) see SERIES 1.

NAME AUTHORITY FILE see AUTHORITY LIST OR FILE.

NOTATION. A system of symbols, generally letters and figures, used separately or in combination, to represent the division of a classification scheme.

OPEN ENTRY. A catalog entry which provides for the addition of information concerning a work of which the library does not have a complete set, or about which complete information is lacking.

OTHER TITLE. A title other than the title proper or a parallel title appearing in the publication, e.g., an alternative title, a subtitle.

OTHER TITLE INFORMATION. Phrases, other than titles, a statement of authorship, or an edition statement, appearing on the title page, in the preliminaries, or in the colophon and indicative of the character, contents, etc. of the publication, or the motive for, or occasion of, its publication.

PARALLEL TITLE. The title proper in another language or in another script.

PARTIAL TITLE ENTRY. An added entry made for a secondary part of the title as given on the title page, e.g., a catchword title, subtitle, or alternative title.

PERIODICAL. A serial appearing or intended to appear indefinitely at regular or stated intervals, generally more frequently than annually, each issue of which normally contains separate articles, stories, or other writings. Newspapers disseminating general news, and the proceedings, papers, or other publications of corporate bodies primarily related to their meetings are not included in this term.

PLATE. A leaf containing illustrative matter, with or without text, that does not form a part of the numeration of the pages or leaves of text. It is not an integral part of the gathering. Plates may be distributed throughout the publication or gathered together; they may be numbered or unnumbered. A plate is usually, although not always, made of a different type of paper from that used in the rest of the publication.

PREFACE DATE. The date given at the beginning or end of the preface.

PRELIMINARIES. The half title, the added title page, the verso of the title page, the cover, and the spine.

PSEUDONYM. A name assumed by an author to conceal or obscure his identity.

PUBLISHER. The person, firm, or corporate body undertaking the responsibility for the issue of a book or other printed matter to the public.

REFERENCE. A direction from one heading or entry to another.

SECOND CARD see EXTENSION CARD.

"SECOND" INDENTION. The distance from the left edge of a catalog card at which, according to predetermined rules, the title normally begins; also called Title indention and Paragraph indention.

SECONDARY ENTRY see ADDED ENTRY.

"SEE ALSO" REFERENCE. A direction in a catalog from a term or name under which entries are listed to another term or name under which additional or allied information may be found.

"SEE" REFERENCE. A direction in a catalog from a term or name under which no entries are listed to a term or name under which entries are listed.

SEQUEL. A work, complete in itself, that continues a narrative from an earlier work.

SERIAL. A publication issued in successive parts bearing numerical or chronological designations and intended to be continued indefinitely. Serials include periodicals, newspapers, annuals (reports, yearbooks, etc.), the journals, memoirs, proceedings, transactions, etc. of societies, and numbered monographic series. See also PERIODICAL; SERIES 1.

SERIES. 1. A number of separate works issued in succession and related to one another by the fact that each bears a collective title generally appearing at the head of the title page, on the half title, or on the cover; normally issued by the same publisher in a uniform style, frequently in a numerical sequence. Often termed "monographic series. " 2. Each of two or more volumes of essays, lectures, articles, or other writings, similar in character and issued in sequence, e. g. , Lowell's Among my books, second series. 3. A separately numbered sequence of volumes within a series or serial, e. g. , Notes and queries, 1st series, 2d series, etc.

SERIES ENTRY. In a catalog, an entry, usually brief, of the several works in the library which belong to a series under the name of the series as a heading.

SERIES NOTE. In a catalog or a bibliography, a note stating the name of a series to which a book belongs. The series note ordinarily follows the collation.

SHELF LIST. A record of the materials in a library arranged in the order in which they stand on the shelves.

SPINE. That part of the cover or binding which conceals the sewed or bound edge of a book, usually bearing the title, and frequently the author.

SUBJECT ANALYTICAL ENTRY see ANALYTICAL ENTRY.

SUBJECT AUTHORITY LIST OR FILE. An official list of subject headings used in a given catalog and the references made to them.

SUBJECT HEADING. A word or a group of words indicating a subject under which all material dealing with the same theme is entered in a catalog.

SUBSERIES. A series whose title is indistinctive and is dependent on the title of another series.

SUBTITLE. The explanatory part of the title following the main title; e. g. , The creative adult; self-education in the art of living.

"THIRD" INDENTION. The distance from the left edge of a catalog card at which, according to predetermined rules, certain parts of the description begin or continue; generally as far to the right of the second indention as the second indention is to the right of the first indention.

TITLE. 1. In the broad sense, the name of a work, including any alternative title, subtitle, or other associated descriptive matter preceding the author, edition, or imprint statement on the title page. 2. In the narrow sense, the name of a work, exclusive of any alternative title, subtitle, or other associated descriptive matter on the title page; the title proper. See also ALTERNATIVE TITLE; OTHER TITLE; PARALLEL TITLE; PARTIAL TITLE ENTRY.

TITLE ANALYTICAL ENTRY see ANALYTICAL ENTRY.

TITLE ENTRY. The record of a work in a catalog or a bibliography under the title, generally beginning with the first word not an article. In a card catalog a title entry may be a main entry or an added entry.

TITLE PAGE. A page at the beginning of a publication, bearing its full title and usually, though not necessarily, the author's (editor's, etc.) name and the imprint.

TITLE PROPER see TITLE 2.

TRACING. 1. In the broad sense, any record of entries or references that have been made in connection with the cataloging of a particular work or publication, or with establishing a particular heading. 2. In the narrow sense, the record on the main entry of the additional headings under which the publication is represented in the catalog.

UNIFORM TITLE. The particular title by which a work that has appeared under varying titles is to be identified for cataloging purposes.

UNIT CARD. A basic catalog card, in the form of a main entry, which when duplicated may be used as a unit for all other entries for that work in the catalog by the addition of the appropriate headings.

VERSO. The back, or overleaf of a page, such as a title page.

WITHDRAWAL. The process of removing from library records all entries for a book no longer in the library.

## References

A. L. A. Glossary (Chicago: American Library Association, 1943).

Anglo-American Cataloging Rules, North American Text (Chicago: American Library Association, 1970).

Anglo-American Cataloging Rules, North American Text: Chapter 6, Separately Published Monographs (Chicago: American Library Association, 1974).

Corinne Bacon, Classification. rev. ed. (Chicago: American Library Association, 1925).

C. A. Cutter, Rules for a Dictionary Catalog. 4th ed. rewritten (Washington: Govt. Print. Off., 1904).

## AIDS IN THE CATALOGING
## OF A SMALL LIBRARY

The following list has been selected with reference to the availability of the material and its probable usefulness to the librarian of the small library. General reference tools for the verification of personal, corporate, and geographical names are not included as it is assumed that every library would have these in its collection, or acquire them (Reference Books for Small and Medium-sized Libraries, 2d ed. , American Library Association, 1973, is a good selection aid).


ALA Rules for Filing Catalog Cards. 2d ed. abr. Ed. by Pauline A. Seely. Chicago: American Library Association, 1968.

American Book Publishing Record. New York: R. R. Bowker. Monthly, annual cumulations.

Anglo-American Cataloging Rules, North American Text. Chicago: American Library Association, 1970.

Anglo-American Cataloging Rules, North American Text: Chapter 6, Separately Published Monographs. Chicago: American Library Association, 1974.

Anglo-American Cataloging Rules, North American Text: Chapter 12 Revised, Audiovisual Media and Special Instructional Materials. Chicago: American Library Association, 1975.

Bernhard, Genore H. How to Organize and Operate a Small Library. Fort Atkinson, Wis.: Highsmith, 1975.

The Booklist. Chicago: American Library Association. Semi-monthly, once in August.

Brown, Lucy Gregor. Core Media Collection for Secondary Schools. New York: R. R. Bowker, 1975.

California Library Association. Audio-Visual Chapter. Subject Headings Committee. Public Library Subject Headings for 16mm Motion Pictures. rev. ed. Sacramento, Calif. : California Library Association, 1974.

Cutter, Charles A. Alphabetic Order Table, Altered and Fitted with Three Figures by Kate E. Sanborn. (For sale by The H. R. Huntting Co. , 300 Burnett R. , Chicopee, Mass. 01020. )

Daily, Jay E. Cataloging Phonorecordings; Problems and Possibilities. New York: M. Dekker, 1975.

Dane, William J. The Picture Collection: Subject Headings. 6th ed. Hamden, Conn. : Shoe String Press, 1968.

Dewey, Melvil. Dewey Decimal Classification and Relative Index. 18th ed. Lake Placid Club, N. Y. : Forest Press, 1971. 3 v.

Dewey, Melvil. Abridged Dewey Decimal Classification and Relative Index. 10th ed. Lake Placid Club, N. Y. : Forest Press, 1970.

Harmon, Robert B. Simplified Cataloging Manual for Small Libraries and Private Collections. San Jose, Calif. : Bibliographic Research Library, 1975.

Haykin, David J. Subject Headings: a Practical Guide. Ed. by Lee Ash (reprint of 1951 ed. ) Boston: Gregg Press, 1972.

Hicks, Warren B. and Tillin, Alma M. Developing Multi-Media Libraries. New York: R. R. Bowker, 1970.

Hill, Donna. The Picture File; a Manual and Curriculum-related Subject Heading List. Hamden, Conn. : Shoe String Press, 1975.

Lake Placid Club Education Foundation. Guide to the Use of Dewey Decimal Classification; Based on the Practice of the Decimal Classification Office at the L. C. Lake Placid Club, N. Y. : Forest Press, 1962.

Media Review Digest. Ann Arbor, Mich. : Pierian Press.
 Annual, quarterly supplements.

Miller, Shirley. The Vertical File and Its Satellites; a Handbook of Acquisition, Processing, and Organization.
 Littleton, Colo. : Libraries Unlimited, 1971.

Nickel, Mildred L. Steps to Service; a Handbook of Procedures for the School Library Media Center. Chicago:
 American Library Association, 1975.

Osborn, Andrew D. Serial Publications; Their Place and
 Treatment in Public Libraries. 2d ed. rev. Chicago:
 American Library Association, 1973.

Piercy, Esther J. Commonsense Cataloging; a Manual for
 the Organization of Books and Other Materials in School
 and Small Public Libraries. 2d ed. rev. by Marian
 Sanner. New York: H. W. Wilson, 1974.

Schwann-1 Record and Tape Guide. Boston: W. Schwann.
 Monthly.

Schwann-2 Record and Tape Guide. Boston: W. Schwann.
 Semi-annual.

Sears List of Subject Headings. 10th ed. Ed. by Barbara
 M. Westby. New York: H. W. Wilson, 1972.

Tillin, Alma M. and Quinley, William J. Standards for Cataloging Nonprint Materials. 4th ed. Washington, D. C. :
 Association for Educational Communications and Technology, 1976.

U. S. Library of Congress. Subject Headings for Children's
 Literature. 2d ed. Washington, D. C. : Library of
 Congress, Cataloging Distribution Service Division, 1975.

Van Orden, Phyllis, ed. The Elementary School Library
 Collection--A Guide to Books and Other Media, Phases
 1-2-3. 9th ed. and Supplement. Williamsport, Pa. :
 Bro-Dart, 1974-1975.

Weihs, Jean R. and others. Nonbook Materials; the Organization of Integrated Collections. 1st ed. Ottawa:
 Canadian Library Association, 1973.

Wilson (H. W. ) Company. Children's Catalog. 12th ed. New York: H. W. Wilson, 1971.

Wilson (H. W. ) Company. Junior High School Catalog. 2d ed. New York: H. W. Wilson, 1970.

Wilson (H. W. ) Company. Public Library Catalog. 6th ed. New York: H. W. Wilson, 1973.

Wilson (H. W. ) Company. Senior High School Library Catalog. 10th ed. New York: H. W. Wilson, 1972.

The Readers' Guide to Periodical Literature and periodical indexes in particular fields, e. g. , the Education Index, Applied Science and Technology Index, are useful in establishing name headings and suggesting subject headings for new subjects. The Special Libraries Association (235 Park Avenue South, New York, N. Y. 10003) maintains a file of special classification schemes. Lists of special subject headings for special subjects will be found in books, periodicals, and as printed, photo-offset, etc. , lists issued by governmental and other organizations.

INDEX